The True History of
Chocolate

Sophie D. Coe   Michael D. Coe

The True History of
Chocolate

with 97 illustrations, 13 in colour

Thames and Hudson

This book is dedicated to
Alan Davidson

Excerpts on pp. 233–34 from *Sade: A Biography* by Maurice Lever. Translation copyright © 1993
by Arthur Goldhammer. Reprinted by permission of Farrar, Straus, & Giroux, Inc.
Excerpt on p. 235 from *The Dharma Bums* by Jack Kerouac, published by The Viking Press,
New York, 1958; and by Andre Deutsch Limited, London, 1959. Reprinted by permission of
Sterling Lord Literistic, Inc. Copyright © 1986 by Stella Kerouac and Jan Kerouac.

British Library Cataloguing-in-Publication Data
A catalogue record for this book is available from the British Library

ISBN 0-500-01693-3 ✓

Printed and bound in Slovenia by Mladinska Knjiga

❧ CONTENTS ❧

Preface

ॐ

My late wife Sophie Dobzhansky Coe had been thinking about writing a history of chocolate for a long time, as an outcome of her general interest in the food and drink of the pre-Spanish peoples of the New World. Readers of her *America's First Cuisines* (University of Texas Press, 1994) will have seen that an important place was given to chocolate in its three chapters on the Aztecs. However, she had been concentrating on chocolate and cacao (the plant from which chocolate is derived) as far back as 1988, when she gave a paper on "The Maya Chocolate Pot and Its Descendants" at the Oxford Symposium on Food and Cookery; she returned to the same forum again in 1992, when she spoke on chocolate flavorings in Mesoamerica.

The present book had taken shape in her mind in the previous year, by which time she had blocked out its eight chapters, which would take chocolate from its earliest pre-Columbian roots (now becoming better known through archaeology and its sister science, linguistics), up to modern times. Sophie was a stickler about "going to the sources," and she spent many hundreds of hours in the libraries of America and Europe, tracking down all possible references to chocolate—and vast amounts of time in my own Mesoamerican library. Her idea of heaven was working in an ancient library like her beloved Biblioteca Angelica in Rome, turning the pages of 400-year-old books in the search for chocolate data.

Sophie had a genuinely scientific background: she was the daughter of the noted Russian-American geneticist Theodosius Dobzhansky, and she had a doctorate in anthropology. Thus, she brought scientific rigor to her scholarship, and insisted that nothing be presented as fact that could not be backed up by solid data. The idea that food writing and food history could be scholarly was reinforced by the high standards set by the Oxford symposia, and by the culinary books authored by their guiding light, Alan Davidson, whom Sophie greatly admired.

I should say here that Sophie was also a great cook, at home not just in the Russian cuisine learned in her mother's kitchen, but in many other culinary traditions. Over the years she had amassed a remarkable cookbook library, now deposited with the Schlesinger Library at Radcliffe College in Cambridge, Massachusetts. When Sophie wrote about the food of other peoples, even people as exotic as the Aztecs, she wrote about something she usually knew at first hand and loved.

By the winter of 1993–94, she was slowed down in her research and writing by a painful disease which was misunderstood by her doctors. What this was became all too clear the following March, when incurable cancer was diagnosed, and she was told that she had only a few months to live. With great courage, she tried to continue with the book, and even dictated to me some of the third chapter, but she had been able to write only preliminary versions of the first two chapters. She soon realized that she would never be able to complete her history. I promised her that I would do so, with the proviso that she would remain the senior author, since the book would be almost completely based on *her* research, not mine; and the idea and plan of the book were hers in the first place.

After Sophie's death that May, I began work, faced with the not small task of organizing the thousands of pages of notes that she had left, and familiarizing myself with their contents. This took over six months, by the end of which I felt confident that I could put together the kind of chocolate history that she had envisioned. The major part of the writing took place at my farm in the Berkshire Hills of Massachusetts and in Rome. During my Rome stay, I was kindly assisted in many ways by my cousin Count Ernesto Vitetti, and by the library staff of the British School in that city.

I am deeply grateful for the forbearance and understanding of the staff at Thames and Hudson for seeing me—and the book—through a difficult period. A number of colleagues have provided me with critical information, as well as illustrations; I especially thank Alicia Ríos, Nicholas Hellmuth, Chantal Coady, Justin Kerr, David Stuart, Miguel León-Portilla, Stephen Houston, David Bolles, Denis Tedlock, and John Justeson. Alan Davidson has been a true friend, from the very inception of the book, and Sophie and I were in complete agreement that we would dedicate it to him.

Finally, lest it be thought that it was some kind of burden or sacrifice for me to finish Sophie's book, I want to state here that it was a true pleasure. When I was growing up on Long Island's North Shore, there was an inscription over the local high school that read "Who dares to teach should never cease to learn." I have learned much from Sophie, even posthumously, while writing this history. Although I could never hope to duplicate the wry and ironic humor that enlivens her previous book, I hope that something of her wit and scholarship can be found in this one.

Neptune, god of the sea, receiving chocolate from a personified America; this allegorical frontispiece to Cardinal Brancaccio's 1664 treatise on chocolate illustrates its transfer from the New World to Europe.

Introduction

ઠ

"Oh, Pangloss!" cried Candide, "what a strange genealogy! Is not the Devil the original stock of it [syphilis]?"

"Not at all," replied this great man, "it was a thing unavoidable, a necessary ingredient in the best of worlds; for if Columbus had not in an island of America caught this disease, which contaminates the source of life, frequently even hinders generation, and which is evidently opposed to the great end of nature, we should have neither chocolate nor cochineal."

Voltaire, *Candide*

All our ancient history, as one of our wits remarked, is no more than accepted fiction.

Voltaire, *Jeannot et Colin*

Voltaire should have known better. There is not a shred of evidence that Columbus ever contracted syphilis in the New World (though some of his crew may have), nor did he know anything about chocolate (as we shall see), let alone cochineal, a fine red dye derived from the bodies of Mexican scale insects. The reply of the ever-optimistic Pangloss to Candide's question is just one of the countless examples of "accepted fiction" replacing fact in the history of food and cooking. Europeans did eventually learn of these two valuable substances, but this had nothing to do with the great navigator's alleged social disease.

The title of this book about chocolate is adapted from *The True History of the Conquest of Mexico*, penned (or dictated) by the conquistador Bernal Díaz del Castillo, completed in 1572 in Guatemala's capital. Old, poor, and nearly blind, this doughty warrior merely wished to get the facts about the fall of the Aztec straight for once. Unlike others who had written about the feats of Cortés and his men, sometimes in sycophantic terms, Bernal Díaz had actually been there, had known all the main participants— including the Aztec emperor himself—and had no special axe to grind. His only goal was to tell as true a story as possible, free from what he called "lofty rhetoric." He proved to the world that a "true history" could be far more engrossing and enlightening than "accepted fiction."

The history of food (and drink) has only become a respectable scholarly subject in recent decades, at least in the Western world. In North America and Great Britain, we have long suffered from puritanical prohibitions against the discussion of food while at table—and elsewhere, for that matter. Although food, sex, and mortality are the three great givens of human existence, earlier generations of academics generally avoided these topics as not quite respectable. As a consequence, culinary history was long left by default to amateur enthusiasts of one or another food, drink, or cuisine. This is especially the case with chocolate (and the cacao from which it is manufactured), a substance whose origins lie in the difficult and sometimes cloudy area of New World prehistory and ethnohistory. The result is that much food writing about chocolate's past falls into the category of Voltaire's "accepted fiction." We are often reminded of that parlor game where the players sit in a circle, each whispering a story, which they have heard from a neighbor on one side, to their neighbor on the other; the story, of course, becomes increasingly less faithful to the original as it goes around the circle. In this book we have tried to break free of the circle by going back to the original sources.

When we modern Westerners think of chocolate, we think of it in its solid, sweetened form, and this is reflected in the undue emphasis which much food writing gives to solid chocolate. Yet during nine tenths of its long history, chocolate was drunk, not eaten. In our "true history," we have tried to restore the balance by giving more attention to chocolate as a valued beverage. And since most books and articles on the subject devote only a few lines or pages, at the most, to the pre-Conquest era, we have devoted two chapters to this area of study—after all, only about one fifth of chocolate's existence postdates the fall of the Aztec capital in 1521.

The dark brown, pleasantly bitter, chemically complex substance we know of as chocolate bears little resemblance to the pulp-surrounded seeds of the cocoa plant from which it is produced. One would never suspect that one could be derived from the other. To properly understand the origin of the cacao tree (*Theobroma cacao*), and the steps involved in turning its seeds or beans into chocolate, we examine its economic botany and chocolate's chemistry and properties in Chapter One; yet we are fully aware that some of the answers to the continuing puzzle of cacao's origin and domestication may well lie in the future, based on DNA research which is now only in its early stages.

The ultimate origin of processed chocolate, though, seems to lie with the Olmec of the lowland forests of southern Mexico, some three millennia in the past, as shall be seen in Chapter Two. We then turn our attention to the rulers and royal courts of the brilliant cities of the Classic Maya, and present exciting new data on Maya chocolate-drinking based on the recent decipherment of hieroglyphic texts. Chapter Three will survey the incredibly rich documentary evidence on the use and importance of cacao as both drink and coinage among the Aztecs, and the ritual significance of the beverage as a symbol of human blood.

With the cataclysmic destruction of the Aztecs' mile-high capital in 1521, and the downfall of their empire, we enter an era in which chocolate-taking was transformed and creolized by the Spanish conquerors, and even new terminology invented, including the very word *chocolate* itself. Chapters Four and Five will show how the transformed, renamed, and taste-altered drink was brought to Europe, where it was considered a medicine to be taken according to the ancient Hippocratic-Galenic theory of the time. It also had to fit in with rules about fasting prevalent in Catholic countries.

The word "baroque" has come to mean ornateness and complexity employed for dramatic, artistic effects, and certainly in Baroque Europe there was a tremendous elaboration in the preparation of drunk chocolate, and even the inclusion of chocolate in dishes produced for noble and ecclesiastical tables. In Chapter Five, we shall see the deep involvement of the Jesuits and the Catholic Church in all this, and examine daring Italian experiments with the substance, in a way pushing chocolate to its culinary limits.

In Chapter Six we shall tell of the producers who were responsible for the cacao and chocolate that reached the palaces, noble courts, and chocolate houses of Europe. This part of our history concerns colonialism, the transport and exploitation of black slave labor, and Spanish state monopolies, as well as the gradual slipping away of Spanish power as England, Holland, and France gained control of the seas. Eventually, major cacao production was to be transferred from Spain's tropical American possessions to Africa and beyond, to colonies controlled by Spain's deadly rivals.

Following the culinary excesses of the Baroque Age, chocolate preparation during Europe's Age of Reason seems almost tame, but chocolate-drinking continued to be associated with aristocracy, royalty, and the Church—except in England and other Protestant countries, where chocolate (and coffee) houses sprang up as meeting places and eventually clubs for nascent political parties. We shall see in Chapter Seven that when the Revolution brought down the Catholic and royal establishment in France, coffee and tea—the favored hot drinks of the *philosophes* and salons of the Enlightenment—replaced drunk chocolate. Yet the Age of Reason ends with the strange and unreasonable figure of the marquis de Sade, a staunch 'chocoholic' in spite of his wildly anti-establishment prose and actions.

Our history thus far will center on chocolate as a beverage of the elite, whether of brown-skinned Aztec nobles or pale-skinned Jesuit clerics. Chapter Eight will deal with chocolate's modern history, beginning with the industrialization at the beginning of the 19th century, and the subsequent invention of solid chocolate for eating, not as something to be mixed with water and imbibed. Chocolate soon became a snack for the masses, typified by the ubiquitous chocolate bar, a transformation overseen by the great, innovating manufacturers of England, Switzerland, and other European countries. But true mass production techniques were perfected in the United States by Milton Hershey, with his own factory town and Disney-like theme park based on chocolate. Yet as production, mass-marketing, and consumption skyrocketed, the culinary quality of the product plummeted. Nevertheless, we shall end our "true history" on an optimistic note: the debasement of chocolate has led to its own reaction, with the emergence in the late 20th century of elite, premier chocolate for connoisseurs with long pockets—but to be eaten, of course, not sipped, as chocolate had been for most of the thousands of years since that unknown Mexican Indian first turned cocoa beans into "the food of the gods."

Cacao tree in a somewhat schematic early 18th-century engraving from a travel book by
the Dominican priest Jean-Baptiste Labat.

CHAPTER ONE

ॐ

The Tree of
the Food of the Gods

This history begins with a tree, a spindly understory tree, content to grow in the shade of buttress-rooted giants. How the seeds of this tree acquired immense importance socially, religiously, medically, economically, and of course gastronomically, on both sides of the Atlantic will be the substance of the story. In the New World that gave it birth, this seed was so valuable as a foodstuff, as currency, and as a religious symbol that the literature about it is unrivalled in quantity and diversity by writings about any other American plant which made the journey to the Old World.

Our story opens in Mexico and Central America, thousands of years before the Spanish Conquest. The narrative is based on European sources, especially for the later European use of the seed; but the less well-known yet equally extensive documentation from the New World should provide a counterbalance.

The European invaders had to name the plants, all new to them, that they had "discovered," and then struggle to fit them into schemes of classification and into the health theory of the time, all laid down by long-dead classical authors who had been totally unaware of the New World's existence. In their turn, the native peoples of the new lands had to cope with the renaming and re-interpretation of their familiar staples, acquaintances of millennial standing, which were being forced on them by the Europeans.

The face-off between the two worlds is nicely illustrated by the scientific name of our tree: *Theobroma cacao*, given to it in 1753 by

Carl von Linné, the 18th-century Swedish scientist whose cognomen is usually written in its Latinized form as Linnaeus. The binomial system by which we now classify all living things was invented by him, to replace the clumsy descriptive Latin sentences used by his predecessors. The first part of this particular binomial, the name of the genus to which cacao (the "chocolate tree") belongs, is from the Greek and means "food of the gods." It is not clear exactly whose gods Linnaeus had in mind, although he himself is known to have been fond of chocolate. The New World name *cacao*—which, as we shall see, provides a clue for the unravelling of chocolate's earliest history—he found barbaric, and thus put it in second place as the specific name.

The binomial that Linnaeus bestowed on our tree, expressive as it is of the complexities of the encounter between the Old World and the New, has not been changed in the two and a half centuries since it was first imposed; but formal, scientific binomials are rarely used in everyday discourse. It has become a convention in American English, although one that is not consistently observed, that the plant and all its products before processing are referred to as "cacao." After processing, the seeds, whether they are in liquid or solid form, become "chocolate." "Cocoa," which in British English is often used to refer to what Americans call "cacao" and "chocolate," in American English refers only to the defatted powder invented by the Dutchman Coenraad Van Houten in 1828, and it will be so used in this book. But just to confuse matters, the New York Commodities Market prefers to call the unprocessed seeds "cocoa"!

The great Swedish naturalist Linnaeus (1707–78) gave the scientific name Theobroma cacao *to the chocolate tree.*

Simple, reduplicated syllables are frequent among common names for plants, and have led the unwary to find cacao where it did not and does not exist. We must be careful not to confuse *Theobroma cacao* with the coconut palm, *Cocos nucifera*, and its products; these often go under the name "coco" in tropical America. If we are successful in avoiding this obstacle, there is another—also a New World plant and also sometimes used to produce a drink—to stumble over. This is the coca bush, *Erythroxylum coca*, the leaves of which were chewed by the Incas of Peru and their predecessors. Many a reader has come across the word "coca" in accounts of Peru, and has been deceived by it into enrolling the Incas into the ranks of pre-Columbian chocolate drinkers. Today a refreshing tea made from the leaves is administered to tourists suffering from altitude sickness in the Andean highlands; but an infinitely greater quantity of the coca leaf goes to the illicit industry that provides cocaine for the international market. Even this does not exhaust the list of soundalikes. A starchy root eaten in the Caribbean is colloquially called "coco"; scientifically, it is one of the species of the genus *Colocasia*. There are other plants with similar common names, such as the "coco-bean" (a variety of the common bean, *Phaseolus vulgaris*), but enough has been said to make clear that a reference to "cocoa," or something that sounds vaguely similar, is not necessarily proof of the presence of *Theobroma cacao*.

For a tree that bears seeds of such importance, cacao is singularly difficult to grow.[1] With a very few exceptions, it refuses to bear fruit outside a band of 20 degrees north and 20 degrees south of the Equator. Nor is it happy within this band of the tropics if the altitude is so high as to result in temperatures that fall below 60°F or 16°C. If the climate is one with a pronounced dry season, irrigation is a necessity, for cacao demands year-round moisture; if it does not get it, it sheds its otherwise evergreen leaves in a protest that is described as looking like autumn in New England. Poor growing conditions make it even more susceptible than it normally is to the multitude of diseases which attack it, including pod rots, wilts, and fungus-produced, extraneous growths called "witches' brooms." Squirrels, monkeys, and rats steal the pods to enjoy the pleasant-tasting white pulp which envelops the seeds that they contain, but they avoid the bitter-tasting seeds themselves (although they may disseminate them).

When these seeds are planted in soil that suits their requirements, they sprout within a few days; the young trees will bear fruit by their third or fourth year. However, most propagation in today's cacao plantations is carried out by means of cuttings or the transplantation of carefully raised seedlings. The maximum length of time that a seed can retain its viability, its capacity to sprout, is three months—and that assumes the use of the most modern technology available. Exposure to low temperature or low humidity promptly kills the seed. These details of the inner workings of the seed have a direct bearing on theories of the origin and pre-Columbian migration of the cacao plant, and should be enough to convince anyone that protracted journeys in the distant past were out of the question.

Sixteenth-century European writers, eager to make this tree accessible to their Old World readers (an eagerness that was doubled by the fact that among the Aztecs cacao beans were used as money as well as foodstuffs), said that it was about the size of a heart cherry tree or an orange tree, with leaves that were similar to those of the latter, but a bit broader and longer. The manner of the tree's flowering, however, was not at all familiar. Unlike European fruit trees, it did not flower from spurs

Cacao tree, from the 16th-century herbal of Francisco Hernández, royal physician to Philip II of Spain.

along the branches, or from the branch tips. The cacao tree, in a fashion favored by other tropical fruit trees, flowers from small cushions on its trunk and on the larger branches, a pattern technically known as "cauliflory." It is amusing to see European illustrators vainly trying to cope with this alien (to them) way of flowering: those who never saw the actual tree usually moved the cacao pods out to the smaller branches, obviously thinking that the native watercolorists whose work they were engraving had been mistaken in their observations.

Cauliflory is clearly a response to the ecological niche in which the cacao plant flourishes: the damp, shaded understory. The small, five-petalled flowers are pollinated exclusively by midges, which thrive in this environment. Ever since cacao was first domesticated, growers have maintained this shade by interplanting taller trees of other species in their plantations, in the belief that the young cacao trees need protection from the sun. Yet these same growers are puzzled by the fact that even in (or especially in) the most modern plantations, among the many hundreds of flowers produced by a single cacao tree annually, only 1 to 3 percent actually bear fruit. This is biological inefficiency taken to an extreme. Experiments and observation carried out in Costa Rica by the American entomologist Allen Young[2] have shown wherein the real problem lies. Under the somewhat aseptic regimen prevalent in large-scale plantations, midges do poorly. In the usually well-tended groves, the litter and mess natural to the rainforest floor—leaf trash, dead animals, and rotten cacao pods—are absent. Yet this produces the perfect, moist, untidy environment which is the ideal breeding ground for the pollinating midges. Unbeknownst to the commercial planters, the trees which they have planted to shade the cacao are not there to protect *T. cacao* from the sun, but to maintain midge populations, if only poorly. Pre-Columbian peoples probably had a higher rate of return, since they harvested cacao in modest, garden-style plantings near forest streams, not in huge, neatly-manicured plantations.

A *cacao tree in Comalcalco, Tabasco, Mexico. The pods grow directly from the trunk.*

Once pollinated, each flower results in a large pod containing 30 to 40 almond-shaped seeds or "beans" surrounded by sweet, juicy pulp. The plant itself has no mechanism by which the pods can open and the seeds disperse; this must be done by humans in stands of domesticated cacao or by monkeys in stands of wild or feral cacao. The monkeys cannot be seeking the beans, which are made bitter by alkaloids, but the delicious pulp, which is probably what attracted humans to *T. cacao* in the first place.

The pods take some four to five months to reach full size, and then another month to ripen completely. Even though flowers are being fertilized and pods are ripening throughout the year, there are usually two major harvests, as the pods will keep on the trunk of the tree for several weeks, and as harvested pods for another week. However, modern techniques now allow for continuous harvests. Harvesting must be done with care, so as not to damage the cushions, which continually produce flowers, and therefore fruit.

Cacao pods cut open to reveal the deliciously sweet pulp which surrounds the seeds. Top and right are fermented and dried seeds.

Once the pods are opened, and the beans and their surrounding pulp extracted, there are four principal steps which must be taken to produce the cacao "nibs" (kernels) which are to be ground into chocolate.[3] These are: (1) fermentation, (2) drying, (3) roasting (or toasting), and (4) winnowing. No matter what the level of technology, this sequence has been in force for at least three millennia, and still is followed in the modern world.

The length of the fermentation undergone by seeds and pulp varies somewhat: originally, beans of the *criollo* variety were given one to three days, and *forastero* beans three to five, but nowadays they both seem to get five to six days. During the first day, all sorts of chemical and biological processes are taking place; the adhering pulp becomes liquid, and drains away as the temperature rises steadily. But most importantly, the seeds briefly germinate, soon to be killed by high temperatures and increased acidity; this has to take place, as ungerminated beans do not give a chocolate flavor to the finished product. By the third day, the mass of beans, which

23

must be turned from time to time, stays between 45°C (113°F) and 50°C (122°F); it must remain at this higher temperature for several days after germination, for again if it does not, the "chocolate" will not taste like chocolate. Among other things, the fermentation process lowers the astringency of the beans, which is probably what made them unattractive to marauding animals.

Fermentation completed, the beans are dried, traditionally on mats or trays left in the sun; this takes one to two weeks, depending on the weather. During the drying process, the beans lose more than half their weight, although the enzymatic action initiated by the fermentation goes on. Roasting, which lasts from 70 to 115 minutes, involves temperatures of 99°–104°C (210°–219°F) for chocolate and 116°–121°C (240°–250°F) for cocoa powder,

Workers on a cacao plantation extracting the pulp-surrounded seeds from the pods in preparation for fermentation.

and is absolutely necessary for the development of flavor and aroma; through this step, due to chemical changes and further loss of moisture, the nib becomes a richer brown in color, more friable, and even less astringent.

The final step is winnowing, in which the thin and useless shell is peeled off or otherwise removed. The resulting nibs can then be ground into something we would recognize as the subject of this book; this substance is known in the trade as "cacao liquor."

Cacao, like any other long-cultivated plant, has many varieties, and their distribution, as well as that of the wild plant (if it still exists), affords us insights into the origin of the plant, its domestication, and its subsequent relationship with human beings.

In his 1964 revision of the genus *Theobroma*, the botanist José Cuatrecasas[4] defines 22 species, grouped into six sections. He suggests that the genus (but not specifically *Theobroma cacao*) evolved on the eastern slopes of the South American Andes, long before human beings ventured into the New World from Siberia. Only two of the 22 are of any interest to us: *T. cacao* and *T. bicolor*. The other 20 grow in the Amazon basin; along the Pacific coast from Ecuador north to Colombia, Panama, Costa Rica, Nicaragua, El Salvador, Guatemala, and Mexico; and on the northern, that is to say Caribbean, coast of South America.

The less well-known cultivated species, *Theobroma bicolor*, while not a source of cacao, is grown as a kitchen garden crop from southern Mexico south to tropical Bolivia and Brazil. In Mexico, it produces something called *pataxte*, used either as a drink on its own, or to dilute the more expensive cacao. Cuatrecasas never saw a specimen that he considered wild, and makes no guesses as to its place of origin.

The problem of how to identify a tree as "wild" rather than as a feral "escape" is crucial here, and is ultimately a matter of the botanist's good judgment. Cultivated or domesticated trees usually bear larger crops of larger fruit, if that is what they are being culti-vated for. But a domesticated tree can outlast any house, especially one in the tropics, and that tree, or its descendants, growing under difficult conditions, can produce fewer and poorer fruit and in consequence pose a riddle for the investigator, who must guess at the history of the plant, and base his or her hypothesis on this guess.

The identification of the place of origin of the other, far more important, cultivated species of *Theobroma*, *T. cacao*, is obscured by this question of whether or not "wild" plants of the species have been found in Mesoamerica (the high culture area that in pre-Conquest times included the southern part of Mexico, Belize, Guatemala, and portions of El Salvador and Honduras). Those who do *not* accept the existence of wild *T. cacao* in Mesoamerica claim that it was either domesticated in South America and then taken to Mesoamerica, or first taken in wild form to Mesoamerica and then domesticated. Both these hypotheses seem equally implausible, given the brief span of the seed's capacity to germi-nate, and the fragility of seedlings. Parenthetically, when *T. cacao* was disseminated throughout the Caribbean and south to Ecuador by the Spaniards, it was carried in the form of cuttings and possi-bly seedlings in relatively fast, sail-driven ships. The fact that no pre-Columbian inhabitant of South America used *T. cacao* for anything beyond manufacturing a wine from the white pulp surrounding the seeds, and using that same pulp as a nibble, would seem a convincing argument against a South American origin and subsequent transportation to Mesoamerica.

Those who *do* accept the existence of wild Mesoamerican *T. cacao* argue that it was domesticated right there where it was later to be so extensively grown, used, and appreciated. Both Cuatrecasas and a more recent investigator, the Mexican botanist Arturo Gómez-Pompa, assure us that they have found wild *T. cacao* populations in the Lacandón rainforest of the state of Chiapas, in southeastern Mexico, and in the neighboring

Usumacinta River drainage which divides Mexico and Guatemala. Not only do they consider these populations genuinely wild (and not feral), but they also find them highly variable, which is usually taken as a diagnostic sign of an area where domestication might have taken place.

Cuatrecasas suggests an early, wide distribution of wild *Theobroma cacao* on the American continent, ranging from the Mesoamerican focus already described to the other area where today widely scattered specimens of *T. cacao* are to be found, the northern and western portions of the Amazon basin. At some time in the past, the trees in the intermediate area died out (remember that the cacao tree is subject to a host of diseases); and by the time that human beings became interested in the tree, the two isolated populations were on their way to evolving into two different species. The Mesoamerican trees were distinguished by long, pointed, warty, soft, and deeply ridged pods which contained seeds with white cotyledons; while the South American ones had hard, round, melon-like pods, and the seeds had purplish cotyledons. These two varieties are known as the *criollo* and *forastero* varieties respectively. They retain their capacity to interbreed and give fertile hybrids, which they will not do with any other species of *Theobroma*.[5]

To jump ahead of our story for a moment, *criollo* and *forastero*, and their hybrids, provide the raw materials for the modern chocolate industry. *Criollo* is produced by a tree that

19th-century engraving showing the warty ridges of a cacao pod.

is exceedingly finicky, produces fewer pods with fewer seeds in each pod, and is more susceptible to more diseases. Then why does anyone grow it? It is grown because this, the cacao that may have been the prerogative of the rulers and warriors of ancient Mesoamerica, and that then went on to seduce the elite of 17th- and 18th-century Europe, possesses flavor and aroma that are absent from the seeds of the hardier and more productive *forastero* (which does not grow in Mesoamerica, anyway). Needless to say, for economic reasons modern cacao planters and processors prefer *forastero*, which today provides more than 80 percent of the world's cacao crop.

Hybridizers are now making an effort to combine the desirable vigor of the *forastero* plant with the superior quality of the *criollo* bean. The first such hybrids were produced in the 18th century on the island of Trinidad when a "blast," explained by some as a hurricane and by others (more convincingly) as a plant disease, killed many of the *criollo* trees that had been planted there. They were replaced by *forastero* trees grown from South American seed, and cross-pollination between the surviving *criollo* trees gave rise to a new hybrid strain, the *trinitario*. Contemporary breeders are laboring to improve these early efforts, but it remains to be seen how much commercial advantage they are willing to sacrifice for superior flavor.

A Chemical Kaleidoscope

What does the cacao bean contain? Over half the weight of the cured, dried nib (as the shelled and degermed bean is called) is made up of fat, although the exact proportion fluctuates according to the variety of cacao and the growing conditions. The fat that is obtained from the nibs by means of the mechanical process invented by Van Houten in the last century is called "cacao butter" or "cocoa butter"; the cacao solids that are left are "cocoa."

Cacao butter is a valuable commodity because, in addition to its role in the production of high-grade chocolate, it has many uses in cosmetics and pharmaceuticals. It possesses the useful qualities of melting at very slightly below the temperature of the human body, and of going rancid very slowly.

The culinary destination of this cacao butter depends on the good, or not so good, intentions of the manufacturer. If the goal is the making of fine chocolate, it will be added to other superior-grade chocolate being processed, to further enhance its deliciousness; sometimes double the amount is added in the interests of smoothness (but true connoisseurs are more concerned with the percentage of cacao solids). If the intentions are not so benevolent, what up-scale *chocolatiers* refer to as "junk chocolate" will be manufactured, with only 15 percent of the product consisting of cacao solids (really fine chocolate has up to 70 percent), the remainder being sugar, milk solids, and cheaper solid vegetable fat; the valuable cacao butter is taken out and sold elsewhere. Cookbooks of the 18th and 19th century are always warning us about the adulteration of chocolate, with everything from brick dust to red lead being added to replace the cacao solids, and the cacao butter being substituted by cheaper oil of sweet almonds, lard, or marrow. Let us hope that at any rate brick dust and red lead no longer lurk in our chocolate.

So-called "white chocolate" is made out of cacao butter only, but in the United States it must be called "white confectionery coating," since it contains no cacao solids and therefore does not fit the legal requirement for "chocolate." It has the disadvantages of a relatively short shelf-life and a tendency to pick up foreign flavors.

Besides fat, each cacao bean contains less than 10 percent by weight of protein and starch.

It is the remaining portion of the bean, which contains hundreds of identified compounds, that provokes the most varied response to chocolate, so much so that at times one would not know that two authors are writing about the same subject. When they announce that "chocolate contains thus and so," we often have no idea whether they are measuring the contents of raw cacao beans, a processed bean or one particular variety, a low-grade candy bar, or a piece of premium couverture (chocolate confections with a high content of cacao butter in the coating). In fact, the literature about the actual composition of cacao reminds us of nothing so much as the tale of the blind men describing the elephant.

Psychologists tend to dismiss the possibility that any one of the myriad chemical compounds that constitute chocolate, or any combination of them, could have a physical effect on the consumer. Instead, they point to learned factors, how for many of us, sweets in general and chocolate in particular have been used as rewards from earliest childhood: "Eat your vegetables, dear, there's chocolate cake for dessert." Women have the added inducement of being the usual recipients of chocolate as gifts—"sweets to the sweet." The psychologists, however, have to admit that a natural preference for sweetness is not acquired but built in: even new-borns suck faster on sweetened liquids. The essays usually close with a paragraph bemoaning the paucity of our knowledge of all the compounds in question and the way that they might affect human beings, in other words an escape clause in case something to the contrary turns up.

The views of the medical profession on chocolate vary wildly. Some doctors claim it to be an anti-depressant, interacting with female hormones in a way that produces incredible premenstrual cravings for chocolate. Others can find no such effect. The most extensive medical study of chocolate is by a French doctor, Hervé Robert, who published a book in 1990 called *Les vertus thérapeutiques du chocolat*. He disproves, to his own satisfaction, any possibility that chocolate could cause such unpleasant ailments as migraine, acne, obesity, and tooth decay. Quite the reverse: he finds that the caffeine, theobromine, serotonin, and phenylethylamine that chocolate contains make it a tonic, and an anti-depressive and anti-stress agent, enhancing pleasurable activities, including making love. Serotonin is a mood-lifting hormone produced naturally by the brain; phenylethylamine is similar to other mood-changing brain chemicals. Future research may show whether there is any truth in the claims that chocolate has an aphrodisiac effect. Its reputation as an aphrodisiac goes back as far as the European conquest of Mexico, but the reader should stop to consider if there has ever been a consumable substance that has not had this reputation at some time in some place.

Two of the substances mentioned by Dr. Robert, comprising 1 to 2 percent by weight of the cacao, are known to have physiological effects on humans, although perhaps not precisely the ones he mentions. These are the alkaloids (or, more technically, methylxanthines) caffeine and theobromine. What are alkaloids? They are plant products, complex organic compounds that occur in perhaps 10 percent of the world's plants, although exactly what evolutionary benefits the plants get from them is not clear. Alkaloids form salts when treated with acids, and they have physiological consequences on the animals that ingest them. Human animals pursue at least some of them with a passion. This book could be read as illustrating one such pursuit—one that began with the New World domestication of cacao, its promotion to a position near the center of the Aztec state ideology, and then, when the Aztec state was demolished by the Spanish conquerors, continued with the conquest of Spain and other European countries by cacao. It may come as news to many that chocolate, tea, and coffee only became widely available to the European public by the middle of the 17th century, and that chocolate was the first drink to introduce Europe to the pleasures of alkaloid consumption.

The two alkaloids that chocolate brought to the Old World sippers, therefore, were theobromine, and the more familiar caffeine. Theobromine is sparsely distributed in the plant world, occurring in only 19 species, most of them in the Sterculiaceae and Rubiaceae families. It is found, along with caffeine, in the kola nut of Africa, which bestowed its name, as well as its alkaloids, on one particular soft drink, and then, by extension, to a whole class of them. Eight species of the genus *Theobroma* contain theobromine, as do: *Camellia sinensis* (which gives us tea); six species of the genus *Coffea* (including the one that yields coffee); and *Ilex paraguariensis*, the source of *yerba maté*, another New World addition to the alkaloid drink inventory, a South American tea which should be drunk from a silver-mounted gourd through a silver strainer-straw.

What exactly does theobromine do to one? Like all alkaloids, it is a stimulant to the central nervous system, albeit a mild one. Its specific talent is to dilate the blood vessels, and in the past the medical profession has used it for that purpose. It is also a diuretic, that is, it stimulates the flow of urine. But as a whole it is much less pharmacologically active than caffeine, and pharmacists have dismissed it from their armory.

Before we go into the details about caffeine, we should consider the fact that the studies showing the toxic effects of caffeine are made with the pure compound, a substance most of us will never see. While scientifically this makes sense, as they occur in chocolate, tea, and coffee the alkaloids are subject to so many variables that it would be impossible to isolate their effects. If the drink in question is coffee, the actual amount of caffeine fluctuates according to the individual green coffee bean, the method of roasting, the fashion of preparation, and the personal idiosyncrasies of the consumer as to strength, cup size, and frequency of ingestion. Not only does the caffeine's strength vary according to all these factors, but so do the concentrations of all the hundreds of other substances, which may or may not affect the caffeine when they interact with it.

Defining all the variables in the natural product is only half the problem. The individual consumer is also a bundle of permutating factors. Unless you are one of a pair of identical (monozygotic) twins, you are genetically unique. Nobody, past or future, will be genetically identical to you, and this uniqueness extends to the way caffeine and other alkaloids affect you. On top of this individual range of tolerance, there is the factor of an individual's culture: if your particular culture thinks a nice cup of cocoa will comfort you and calm you down, it might just have such an outcome, which it might not have on someone who was brought up to believe chocolate to be a stimulant. Those who are used to thinking of it as a stimulant or soporific tend to get accustomed to the desired effect, and develop greater or lesser degrees of tolerance. The statements of the health authorities, which terrify us about yet another item of everyday use, deserve to be considered with all this information in mind.

In its pure form, the effects of caffeine are said to be caused by stimulation of the central nervous and cardiovascular systems, and include nervousness, anxiety, insomnia, and even worse conditions ranging from confusion to heart attacks. On the other hand, caffeine is also credited with lessening fatigue, enhancing the intellectual faculties, stimulating gastric secretions (which is why it is contra-indicated for ulcer patients), and promoting urination.

Although there are no firm scientific data on the subject available for theobromine, caffeine is definitely addictive, if by that adjective we mean a substance the denial of which will produce withdrawal symptoms. In this case the symptom is severe headache.[6] In fact, on a scale of addictiveness recently drawn up by the U.S. National Institutes of Health, on which heroin stands at the high end and marijuana at the low, caffeine is about in the middle. But before we stand awestruck at the powerful workings of this substance, we should examine how much of it there is in the average cup of cocoa. The answer is, not much. If a cup of percolated or dripped coffee contains from 50 to 175 milligrams of caffeine, and a cup of brewed tea of the same size from 25 to 100 milligrams, then a cozy cup of cocoa provides somewhere between

25 milligrams of caffeine and none at all. Typically for investigations of this nature, nowhere is it stated what sort of cocoa it is. A commercial packet of cocoa-mix with massive quantities of milk powder and sugar, and the barest minimum of chocolate, gives measurements remote from a "grown-up" chocolate—the kind one might be offered at a *cioccolateria* on the Piazza Navona in Rome, for example. The best that we can do with all these pharmacological data, or what passes for them, is to keep them in mind when we read of pre-Columbian chocolate, the chemistry of which we know even less of, if that is possible; and especially should we remember them when we read of the supposed effects of chocolate on its first European drinkers.

These explorations of the contents of chocolate are best summed up with phrases involving the word "unknown." A better way to trace the importance and influence of cacao—source of the world's first stimulating drink—is to go back and follow its history among the very people who discovered and domesticated it, long before Europeans began debating the healthfulness of alkaloid-containing hot drinks, and seeking their biblical and Classical precedents.

*

The Birth of Cacao;
Olmec-Maya Genesis

Many writers of popular works on chocolate indulge in fantasy when treating cacao's New World origins, but the facts as revealed by modern archaeology and ethnohistory are far more interesting than these flights of imagination. Most authors, however, know that the first European encounter with cacao took place when Columbus, on his fourth and final voyage, came across a great Maya trading canoe with cacao beans amongst its cargo (in fact, a very high-priced, modern chocolate product has been named from Guanaja, the place where this happened). There is also a general awareness that chocolate was in use among the Aztecs of Mexico, both as drink and as currency. But instead of delving into the richly detailed, original sources on the Aztecs and their remarkable culture, many writers have substituted speculation for research, in the mistaken belief that not very much is known of these distant people of Mexico beyond their predilection for the extraction of human hearts.

We now realize that the Spanish invaders derived their earliest real knowledge of cacao, and the very word "cacao," not from the Aztecs but from the Maya of the Yucatán Peninsula and neighboring Central America. Even further, exciting research carried out in the past decade has shown that these same Maya, a thousand years before the Spaniards landed on their shores, were writing this same word on magnificent pottery vessels used in the preparation of chocolate for their rulers and nobility. Indeed, it is this selfsame word "cacao" (relegated to second place in his binomial system by Linnaeus) that provides the clue leading us back still further into the mists of New World prehistory—to the people who may well have been the first domesticators and users of cacao.

The Olmec

We must now journey back more than three millennia to the first civilization of the Americas, to the Olmec. Their strange, complex culture arose in the humid lowlands of the Mexican Gulf Coast (in the south part of Veracruz and in the neighboring state of Tabasco) about 1500 BC. Almost certainly the precocity of Olmec civilization was a response to the immense fertility of the natural levee lands which border the sluggish rivers meandering through this landscape of tropical forests and grassy savannahs. The Olmec were prodigious constructors of massive ceremonial centers made up of earth-and-clay mounds and pyramids; scattered throughout these centers, archaeologists have found awesome figures of their gods and their rulers, carved from hard basalt laboriously brought in from great distances. Most famous of Olmec productions are the Colossal Heads—multi-ton stone portraits of their kings—and the exquisitely carved blue-green jades which they buried as offerings to the gods or reverently laid in the tombs of their elite.

The Olmec dwindled around 400 BC, leaving us no writings that we are able to decode—there are a few hieroglyphs on some of their latest monuments, but these are indecipherable. It is a sad fact that we really have no idea of what they called themselves, the designation "Olmec" being a name more properly applied to the late, historically documented people of the area. Because of the dearth of written records, archaeologists have been loath to make even an educated guess as to what language or languages they might have spoken. However, in recent years, linguists have made significant advances in solving this particular puzzle.

A colossal stone head of the Olmec civilization (1500–400 BC). It was probably the Olmec who first made chocolate from cacao.

Their data point to an ancestral form of the Mixe-Zoquean family of languages, some of which are still spoken by thousands of peasant farmers dwelling in and near the lands covered by Olmec remains, such as the Popoluca; during the Yale excavations at the Olmec site of San Lorenzo, a Popoluca shaman used to appear at Saturday night parties. Mixe-Zoquean loan words of considerable cultural significance are found in other Mesoamerican languages, such as the terms for paper and copal incense, and it is now generally thought that these were borrowed from the highly-civilized, Mixe-Zoquean-speaking Olmec during the apogee of their influence over less advanced cultures.

Some of these lexical borrowings concern food plants and their processing. They include the word for "nixtamalization" of maize; this tenpenny word is worth a digression, for upon nixtamalization depended all Mesoamerican civilization. Even before the Olmec, small villages had existed over much of southern Mexico and Central America from the beginning of the second millennium BC. The basic Mesoamerican plants had been domesticated even earlier, so that (among other plants) maize, beans, squashes of several kinds, chilli peppers, and avocados had long been in the diet. Yet domesticated maize, while known since about 5000 BC, was not a starring player on the culinary stage until some time during the second millennium, when the discovery of nixtamalization, most probably by the Olmec, turned it into a true staff of life, the central focus of their religion, and the source of four fifths of the nourishment for the native peoples of Mesoamerica. Maize had now become the carbohydrate staple, the "bread" (in its broadest and most holy sense).

What is "nixtamalization"? Like all great discoveries, it seems ludicrously simple in retrospect. In pre-Olmec times, the hard grains of ripe maize had merely been boiled into softness, or else laboriously pounded or ground into powder on simple milling stones. Instead, it was now cooked with white lime, wood ashes, or even burnt snail shells, and left to cool overnight. The following morning, the Olmec housewife, or her counterpart in other cultures, would wash off the transparent hulls of the grains, the pericarp; the result of the cooking was to make the maize far easier to grind to a smooth dough (*nixtamalli* in the Nahuatl language of the Aztec; *masa*, to use the Spanish term).

To be sure, the convenience of the housewife was a worthy goal, but what the women who made this discovery could not have known, and what until recently modern scholars were not aware of, is that this treatment also dramatically enhances the nutritional value of maize for human consumption.[1] The bad reputation that maize has in some circles is due to the fact that, when Europeans introduced it into the Old World, they thought that they could leave nixtamalization behind, since their powerful mills could handle dried maize kernels without softening. But discarding nixtamalization meant discarding its amino-acid-enhancing properties (an action of the alkali on the protein content), and as a result Europeans suffered from various deficiency diseases like pellagra. A diet of nixtamalized maize can provide sufficient protein for all but the most protein-demanding members of the population (nursing mothers and infants). Thus, the jolt necessary to put Mesoamericans on the road to civilization, and therefore to the leisure in which to enjoy luxuries like chocolate, may have been delivered by the discovery of this process. The old line that "a civilized man cannot live without cooks" should perhaps be amended to "civilization cannot begin without cooks."

It so happens that "cacao" is another one of those loan words from the Mixe-Zoquean family. Originally pronounced *kakawa*, it has been reconstructed by linguists as a vocabulary item in proto-Mixe-Zoquean by about 1000 BC, at the very height of Olmec civilization at such sites as San Lorenzo.[2] It is a shame that the environment favored by *Theobroma cacao* and the Olmec alike— the humid tropical forest—is about the most unsuitable imaginable for archaeological preservation, so that unless a great Olmec stone monument turns up with an indisputable depiction of a cacao tree or pod, we are left with historical linguistics rather than archaeology as our only source of data. But the data are there: it now seems almost certain that it was the Olmec who first domesticated this plant.

From Izapan Civilization to the Classic Maya

The justly renowned civilization of the Classic Maya postdated the Olmec by many centuries, and flourished from about AD 250 until 900, when the catastrophic "Classic Maya Collapse" took place. The ancestors of the Classic Maya entered the Petén low-lands of northern Guatemala around 1000 BC as fairly primitive farmers (as compared to the contemporary Olmec on the Gulf Coast plain). Before that, they lived, as many million Maya yet do, in the cool highlands of Guatemala and the Mexican state of Chiapas, where cacao could only have been known as an exotic import, if at all. If they did use the wild cacao that they found growing in the lowlands when they arrived, they must have had some other name for it, since it was not until some time between 400 BC and AD 100 that they received the word "cacao" (by now pronounced the way we do today, to rhyme with "cow") from Mixe-Zoquean speakers; "cacao" meant then, as it still does, domesticated *Theobroma cacao*, and not any wild form or other species of *Theobroma*.[3]

The Mixe-Zoqueans who apparently donated the word, and probably the substance as well, to the Maya were the bearers of the Olmec-derived culture called "Izapan" by archaeologists; this was a Late Pre-Classic civilization characterized by earth-mound ceremonial centers like those of the older Olmec, and a strongly narrative relief style in stone sculpture. The type site, Izapa, lies on the Pacific coastal plain of Chiapas, in the very midst of what was to become the rich, cacao-producing province of Soconusco, the diamond in the crown of the Aztec empire. The Izapan culture itself was spread southeast along the Pacific littoral and piedmont of Guatemala, and north across the Isthmus of Tehuantepec to the Gulf Coast plain—just those areas once dominated by the Olmec. These two slices of land were, in fact, ideal for the cultivation of cacao. Quite probably it was the Izapans who first planted cacao in Soconusco; in Spanish Colonial times, we never hear of it grow-ing wild there, although other *Theobroma* species do.

Important narrative episodes in the *Popol Vuh* or "Book of Counsel" can be traced back as far as the Izapans of the Late Pre-Classic, specifically to carved stone stelae at Izapa itself. The great epic of the *Popol Vuh* was the sacred book of the Quiché Maya of the Guatemalan highlands, and was written down not long after the Conquest, using the Spanish alphabet; Maya specialists believe that it was transcribed from a now-lost hieroglyphic original.[4] A work of great poetic beauty, it opens majestically with the creation of the cosmos, and ends with the conquest and the imposition of Spanish rule. But it is the mystic doings of several sets of divine twins that concern us here, for it is their story, wonderfully recounted in the *Popol Vuh*, that is reflected on the Izapan carvings.

To tell it briefly, the first set of twins, sons of the old couple who have created the universe, meet their untimely end in Xibalbá, the Maya underworld, where they are beheaded by the sinister lords of that dread place. The severed head of one of this unlucky pair (now known to be the Maize God) is hung up in a tree—said to be a calabash tree in the story, but pictured as a cacao tree on a Classic Maya vase. One day this disembodied head magically impregnates the daughter of a Xibalban ruler as she holds up her hand to it. Expelled in disgrace to the earth's surface, she eventually gives birth to the second divine pair, the Hero Twins Hunahpú and Xbalanqué. Following a series of exploits reminiscent of the Labors of Hercules, the Hero Twins go on to defeat Xibalbá and its ghastly denizens, a true Harrowing of Hell. Their final task is to resurrect their slain father, the Maize God. This having been accomplished, they rise to the sky in glory as the sun and the moon. The story, then, basically deals in symbolic form with the burial (that is, the planting of the seed), growth, and fruition of maize, the Maya—and Mesoamerican—staff of life.

Cacao appears several times in the *Popol Vuh* as it has come down to us, but as part of the market basket, so to

In this detail from a Classic Maya vase, the head of the Maize God is suspended in a cacao tree.

speak, not the revered substance that it was to become. In a later part of the epic, when the gods were creating humans in their final form (their earlier attempts had met with failure), the foods which were to form their bodies had to be sought out, and these the gods found in the Mountain of Sustenance:

> And so they were happy over the provisions of the good mountain, filled with sweet things, thick with yellow corn, white corn, and thick with pataxte [*Theobroma bicolor*] and cacao, countless zapotes, anonas, jacotes, nances, matasanos, sweets—the rich foods filling up the citadel named Broken Place, Bitter Water Place. All the edible fruits were there: small staples, great staples, small plants, great plants.[4]

The Aztecs had a very similar myth—that the domestic plants which were to sustain human life had been hidden in a mountain, and had to be brought to the earth's surface by divine intervention (in the Aztec case, the great god Quetzalcoatl instructed the ants to bring out maize seed). This was truly the "Big Rock Candy Mountain" of the ancient New World!

The ambiguity about the role of cacao in the *Popol Vuh* is heightened when we read in one post-Conquest source[5] that a certain Hunahpú (the name of one of the Hero Twins, it will be remembered) invented the processing of cacao. While this claim is mentioned in other sources, it appears nowhere in the *Popol Vuh*, but then we know that we do not have the complete version of the epic, at least as it was known to the Classic Maya. Just to confuse things, it seems that the Hero Twins' names were later adopted as personal names by some native political leaders, just as "Hercules" and "Hector" appear in Renaissance and modern Europe. The "Hunahpú" mentioned in our principal source was supposedly an early Quiché Maya lord in the Guatemalan highlands; what such an individual was doing instructing lowlanders on the use of a plant which would already have been long familiar to them is hard to imagine. Perhaps some special technological wrinkle was ascribed to him, and his fame survived into Colonial times in this form.

Lords of the Forest: The Classic Maya

While the Izapans were developing major elements of lowland Mesoamerican culture such as hieroglyphic writing, the calendar, monumental carving, an elite mythological cycle centering upon the Hero Twins, and the elaboration of cacao as an elite drink, the Maya cultural giant was stirring in the forests of northern Guatemala and southern Yucatán. By about AD 250, the lowland Maya had entered their Classic phase. Dozens of Maya cities with towering temple-pyramids of stucco-covered masonry had sprung up, some of them capitals of aggressive states bent on conquering their neighbors and sacrificing rival kings and princes. Until their downfall in the 9th century, these capitals and their courts saw an effervescence of art and architecture that recalls in its vigor and brilliance the city-states of ancient Greece and Renaissance Italy. Magnificent temples and palaces, stone relief carvings, wall paintings, lovely jades, and above all delicately painted and carved ceramic vessels testify to the artistic as well as material wealth of this Golden Age—and all this in spite of almost constant internecine warfare between the city-states.

In the pre-Conquest New World, hieroglyphic writing was known only in Mesoamerica, and it reached its highest elaboration among the Maya. We now know, thanks to recent epigraphic research, that they could write everything that was in their language, in a system that has proved to be partly phonetic-syllabic (with signs standing for complete syllables) and partly semantic (with signs standing for units of meaning). We shall see that among the things that they wrote about was cacao. The ancient Maya were truly "people of the book," but sadly, since these were written on perishable bark paper, only four have survived to this day; and all four belong not to the Classic but the Post-Classic period—the period preceding the Spanish Conquest. There must have been thousands of such books, whole libraries of them, in the royal courts of the Classic cities, but all disappeared with the Classic Maya Collapse of the 9th century, or in the bonfires of the Spanish Inquisition.

The most beautiful of these surviving folding-screen books is the Dresden Codex, very late pre-Conquest in date, but with Classic-style calligraphy and with much astronomical and other material passed down through the centuries from the Classic period. Thanks to the remarkable breakthrough made in the 1950s by the Russian epigrapher Yuri V. Knorosov (who "cracked" the phonetic part of the script), we can now read most of these texts.[6] In several sections of the Dresden which deal with ritual activities tied in to their sacred 260-day cycle, seated gods can be seen holding cacao pods, or dishes heaped with cacao beans. We know that this is cacao, since the text written above each deity states that what is held in the hand is "his cacao [*u kakaw*]." And on a Dresden page dealing with the New Year ceremonies so important in Post-Classic Yucatán, the Opossum God travels a sacred road to the edge of the town carrying the Rain God on his back, while the associated text tells us that "cacao is his food [*kakaw u hanal*]."

Opossum God carrying the Rain God during the New Year rites, in the Dresden Codex. The text specifies that cacao is to be offered.

Cacao also appears in the far less artistic Madrid Codex. In one scene, an unidentified young god squats while grasping limbs from a cacao tree (the quetzal bird flying above holds a cacao pod in its beak); in the associated text, the usual *kakaw* phonetic compound is found. The final reference to cacao in the Madrid depicts four gods piercing their own ears with obsidian lancets, and scattering showers of precious blood over cacao pods. This is especially interest-

Maya Gods shedding blood over cacao, from the Madrid Codex. According to the hieroglyphic text, specific numbers of incense lumps and cacao beans are to be offered.

ing, since our ethnohistoric sources tell us that there were strong symbolic associations between chocolate and human blood among both the late Post-Classic Maya and the Aztecs.[7] Another section of the Madrid is of interest to us, since it concerns the rituals for the long-distance merchants and their god (or gods). The reader will later learn that one of the most important articles of merchandise carried by the traders was cacao, although specific trade goods are not mentioned in the codex. If the Maya ever wrote down inventories, accounts, or even recipes, as other early civilizations did, they did it in a form—bark-paper books—which could not survive the sort of climate that cacao demands.

To return to the Classic era, the only written evidence for the Classic Maya use of cacao survives on the elegantly painted or carved vessels that accompanied the elite in their tombs and graves. We have no knowledge of how the ordinary Maya took their cacao, if indeed they could afford to take it at all. Whether the peasant who actually grew the cacao trees could come back

A rare image of the Cacao God of the Classic Maya, carved on a bowl in the Dumbarton Oaks Collection, Washington, D.C. His name appears in the vertical panel, but it cannot yet be read.

A Maya king is seated within his palace, on an 8th-century vase from northern Guatemala. The figures holding torches suggest that this is a night scene. Below the throne is a cylindrical vase for the chocolate drink, and a bowl with an obsidian mirror.

from his plantations, after building walls to mark them off, irrigating them, and fighting off squirrels, rats, and monkeys, to a delicious, frothy bowl of chocolate must remain unknown.

The life, and even the death, of the Maya elite class was luxurious indeed. Burial ceremonies were of the greatest magnificence, and the honored dead were lavishly accompanied by special offerings to sustain them in the afterlife. Clad in specially prepared robes and jaguar pelts, and adorned with collars and bracelets of apple-green jade, the corpse was laid to rest on a bed or litter, amid sacred smoke from copal incense and music from conch-shell and wooden trumpets, rattles, and beaten turtle carapaces. Near the body were placed pottery dishes, bowls, and cylindrical vases which we now realize held the food and drink that the ruler or noble (or his wife) was to enjoy in the abode of the dead. This is known to us because significant portions of the hieroglyphic texts which appear on these vessels can now at last be read, or at least understood. It used to be thought—or at least it was by the late Sir Eric Thompson, the most influential Mayanist of the 20th century—that the ceramic texts were meaningless: that they were little more than decoration, put there by basically illiterate

46

peasant Maya artists. In recent decades, this has been shown to be thoroughly wrong on two counts: (1) the texts are definitely meaningful, as we shall see; (2) the artist-scribes who wrote the texts on them belonged to the highest stratum of Maya society, and were the same as those who wrote and painted the books.[8]

The most common text on these vases is what has been called the Primary Standard Sequence, or PSS for short, a formulaic sequence or pattern of signs in an order that never changes fundamentally (although scribes could use substitutes for individual glyphs within it). When the younger generation of epigraphers began to study the PSS, some of its secrets were revealed. It was found to open with a phrase dedicating the vessel (either to its patron, or to the gods). Next, there follow one or more glyphs which describe the vessel's shape (plate, tripod dish, or deep bowl or vase). Having done this, the artist-scribe then states whether the surface is painted or carved, and even occasionally signs his

a   b   c   d

Primary Standard Sequence (PSS) from a Classic Maya vase (top): a, b, dedicatory glyphs; c, 'vase for drinking'; d, cacao glyph.

Comparison of Classic and Post-Classic Maya cacao glyphs: on Classic ceramics (left); in the Dresden Codex (right).

name. Then comes what epigrapher Barbara McLeod has nicknamed "the recipe"[9]—the actual contents of the vessel. We shall return to this in a moment. The PSS text closes with a personal name followed by a series of noble titles; these apparently identify the patron who commissioned the object, presumably for his or her future interment.

Now let us look at "the recipe." When the vessel is not a shallow bowl or dish (these almost certainly held tamales or other solid maize food), that is, when it is a cylindrical vase or deep, rounded bowl, "recipe" glyphs appear in the PSS. The first "recipe" to be deciphered was the hieroglyph for "cacao," an achievement of the brilliant epigrapher David Stuart, who has been studying Maya writing since the tender age of eight.[10] Stuart saw that this consisted of a drawing of a fish, preceded by a comb-like sign that has been established as the syllabic glyph *ka*, and followed by the sign for final *-w*. The evidence indicated that "Fish" is merely a substitute for the "comb" *ka* glyph (the comb is really a fish fin), so that he read the entire compound as *ka-ka-w*, that is, "cacao." Parenthetically, it was this decipherment that later led to the identification of cacao in the Post-Classic codices. Since the glyph compound is ubiquitous in PSS texts on cylindrical vases, we can assume that these were all used in the production and consumption of chocolate in Maya palaces. We shall see exactly *how* they were used in due course.

One of the more spectacular Classic Maya tombs yet uncovered by archaeologists was found in 1984 at Río Azul, a medium-sized Maya city in the northeastern corner of the Petén region of Guatemala. This tomb proved to be full of the paraphernalia of chocolate consumption. How do we know this? At some time during the last half of the 5th century AD, the corpse of a middle-aged ruler had been laid to rest in this tomb, on a wooden litter covered with a kapok (ceiba-cotton) mattress. Next to the litter the funeral specialists had placed 14 pottery vessels, including six cylindrical vases with lids and tripod feet; some of these vases had rings around their interiors, showing that they had once contained some dark liquid. There was a single example of an extremely rare form, a stirrup-handled pot with a screw-on lid. This strange object had been surfaced with stucco and brilliantly painted with six large hieroglyphs, including two which read "cacao." The entire text, according to David Stuart and Stephen

Houston (another of the younger epigraphers), can be translated as, "A drinking
vessel for *witik* cacao, for *kox* cacao."[11]
We are not sure what *witik* and *kox* refer
to, but they may well be flavorings
for chocolate.

So far, this is all in the realm of hiero-
glyphics. But when a selection of these Río
Azul vessels was sent to the laboratories
of the Hershey Company in Hershey,
Pennsylvania, it was found that the
screw-top jar had contained both caffeine
and theobromine, two of the cylindrical
vases had definite traces of theobromine,
one had possible traces of theobromine, and
the last had no traces of either alkaloid.
The laboratory interpreted these results as
showing that the screw-top vessel had
certainly had chocolate in it, the others
with traces may have contained it, and the
last certainly did not. It sounds as if the
Hershey chemists adhere to the theory
that there was only one chocolate drink
possible among these ancient Maya; it is

*Stuccoed and painted pottery jar on its
own potstand, from a tomb at Río Azul,
Guatemala. Early Classic Maya,
c.AD 500. This vessel once held the
chocolate drink; the cacao glyph
appears on the lock-top lid.*

just as possible that the dead lord began his voyage through the
underworld with sustaining portions of several different chocolate
drinks by his side.

Tall, pottery cylinders of various diameters were thus used as
chocolate containers, but they were also employed in its preparation. Evidence for this is to be found on a breathtakingly beautiful
vase which was probably made in the 8th century AD in the
Nakbé area of the north-central Petén, and which is now among
the treasures of the Princeton Art Museum. Two scenes are
depicted here: on the left, two sinister, masked individuals are in

A woman pours chocolate from one vessel to another in this palace scene from the Princeton Vase, Late Classic Maya (c.AD 750). This is the earliest depiction of the froth-producing process.

the process of decapitating a third, perhaps the father of the Hero Twins, and on the right there is an Underworld palace. The two scenes are tied together by the palace lady farthest to the left, who taps the foot of her nearest companion to draw her attention to the sacrifice. But it is not these ladies that interest us, nor even the Merchant God (God L, to Maya specialists) seated on his throne, nor even the little rabbit-scribe below the throne busily writing a book. It is the lady standing to the right who concerns us, carefully pouring a dark substance from a small cylindrical jar into a larger one. This is the first known picture of a chocolate drink being made, and it illustrates the process of pouring the potion from one vessel into another to raise the foam, which was considered the most desirable part of the drink by the Aztecs, and almost certainly by the Classic Maya. And by the later Maya too, for in very early Colonial dictionaries of the Maya language spoken in Yucatan, there are entries for *yom cacao*, meaning "chocolate foam"; *takan kel*, "to roast the cacao very well in order to make a lot of foam on the chocolate"; and *t'oh haa*, *haa* being a word for chocolate as well as water, *t'oh* meaning to pour from one vessel into another from a height—just what our Classic lady is doing! We still add foam to our chocolate, but ours tends to be extraneous: substances like whipped cream or marshmallows—rather than emanating from the chocolate itself.

Here we shall warn against the simplistic notion that there was one sole chocolate drink made by the Maya or Aztecs. They were every bit as capable of applying individual taste and invention to the raw materials at hand as the most "creative" of modern chefs. Pre-Conquest chocolate was not a single concoction to be drunk; it was a vast and complex array of drinks, gruels, porridges, powders, and probably solid substances, to all of which could be added a wide variety of flavorings, as will be seen in Chapter Three.

Some of these flavorings appear in Classic Maya writings. We have already mentioned two (known only by name) on the Río Azul screw-top jar. Stephen Houston has identified the phrase *ik-al kakaw*, "chilli cacao," on a royal lintel spanning a doorway in the great Maya city of Piedras Negras, on the banks of the Usumacinta River in northwestern Guatemala.[12] On the eve of the Spanish Conquest, chilli pepper was very popular as a chocolate flavoring among the Aztecs, as well it should have been, since it imparts a very pleasurable "burn" to the drink. Both Houston and David Stuart are fairly certain that in a few PSS texts, there are references to a chocolate flavoring called there *itsim-te*. This must have come from the small tree still called by that name, and known scientifically as *Clerodendrum ligustrinum*; parts of this plant were used by the Colonial period Maya of Yucatán to give a good taste and odor to gruels and sweet potato stews, according to the dictionaries. Finally, the cacao glyph on Classic ceramics is often preceded by a modifier read phonetically as *yutal*; this probably meant something like "fruity," but whether this was a flavor or perhaps a special variety of cacao remains a mystery. There is still much to be learned about these PSS texts.

The only other containers named hieroglyphically in Classic Maya tombs are hemispherical clay bowls, a form apparently favored by the Maya for drinks that they wished to keep cool. Although we do not know at what temperature the Classic elite preferred their chocolate, given their culinary sophistication it is very likely that some drinks were cold, some were hot, and some were in between (the late pre-Conquest and Colonial Yucatec Maya favored hot chocolate, it seems). The drinks that was usually kept in such bowls was, according to the PSS texts on them, *sak-ha* or *ul*, sacred white potions made of maize, which are still in ritual use among the Maya of Yucatán. *Sak-ha*, literally "white water," is made from ground mature maize that has not been nixtamalized, while *ul* is made from young maize. These should probably be called "gruels" in English, but both the term and the substance are obsolete in our culinary culture. Such starchy drinks were, however, very common on both sides of the Atlantic at the time of the Conquest; the invading Europeans recognized the Maya examples as kin to their own, and speedily adopted them, especially in the sickroom. For the Maya, these gruels were a handy, quick way of ingesting the calories necessary for the day, without the expenditure of firewood and labor needed to convert nixtamalized maize into a solid breadstuff. Like chocolate, among the late Maya there was no single, standard recipe for such gruels, and often they were stepped up with chilli peppers, herbs, sweetenings, cacao, and combinations of the foregoing.

All of this literary (and chemical) evidence for the Classic Maya use of cacao comes from the Petén of northern Guatemala, where cacao was seldom raised, if at all. A likely source of this cacao was the Pacific coastal plain of Guatemala and Chiapas, certainly a classic cacao-growing region well into late Colonial times. In the first centuries of our era, a great platform had been constructed at the site of Balberta, located on the plain about 45 miles (74 km) southwest of modern Guatemala City. A few centuries later, during the Early Classic period, the people of Balberta were building houses atop this platform, whatever its primary function had been. A small structure among the houses was found to have four large urns, one buried at each of its four corners—a good Mesoamerican custom since the four directions were basic to the way that they structured the universe.

In one of these urns, the archaeologists discovered a cache of what seemed to be perfectly preserved cacao beans; this was rather an astonishing piece of luck, considering the damp and torrid nature of the Pacific plain. Believing them to be petrified, the excavators sent them off to a Guatemalan expert, who identified them as belonging to the *criollo* variety. The surprising nature of this find emerged when the beans were sent to the United States, where a paleo-ethnobotanist discovered that they were not real cacao beans at all, but ingenious copies, each one lovingly made out of local clay—and with all due regard for the individual variation which occurs between natural examples of the seeds of *T. cacao*, var. *criollo*![13]

The meaning of this time-consuming deception we can never know. Were they providing the divinities with a symbolic representation of cacao that could never rot or decay? Or was it worth somebody's while to replace an expensive offering with little molded bits of clay? We have convincing testimony from the Spanish chroniclers that Mesoamericans were expert counterfeiters of these beans, so this explanation might be the right one.

There is other debris near these buildings that also provides hints about the history of cacao. There is much obsidian (volcanic glass), which does not occur naturally anywhere near Balberta, although there are sources in highland Guatemala. For a society that lacked metal, obsidian was a useful substitute, as it could be made into knives and blades that were as sharp as any razor. The obsidian found in the offering of pseudo-cacao, however, is not the black or grey kind from Guatemalan sources, but the unmistakable, transparent green obsidian originating in mines near Pachuca, many hundreds of miles away in the Mexican *altiplano*. Not only is the raw material Mexican, but some of the projectile points from Balberta appear to have been made in Teotihuacan, the New World's greatest pre-Columbian city, which dominated the Valley of Mexico and in fact much of Mesoamerica during the Early Classic period (until about AD 600). Obviously there was extensive trade going on between Teotihuacan and the Pacific

A young blowgunner, probably one of the Hero Twins, hunts quetzal birds in a cacao tree,
on a carved vase fragment from Teotihuacan, central Mexico. Early Classic, c. 500 AD.

coast of Guatemala, but we are frustrated because we only know
what was sent from Mexico to Guatemala, and not what went in
the other direction. Whatever it was, it was perishable, and the
temptation is to assert that it was cacao, which the data show was
available and important at Balberta.

The same evidence for intensive trade with Teotihuacan has
turned up in other Pacific coast sites, often in the form of
Teotihuacan ceramics. Some of the hundreds of hourglass-shaped
pottery censers with lids discovered by looters near the town of
Escuintla are covered with effigy cacao pods, seemingly of the
criollo variety; these censers are in the purest Teotihuacan style,
though they may have been manufactured locally.[14] Probably due
to poor conditions of preservation, no traces of cacao have been
found at Teotihuacan itself, but one carved vase fragment from
the city shows a blowgunner—perhaps one of the Hero Twins—
shooting birds perched in a cacao tree.

Twilight of the Classic Maya

The elaborate edifice of Classic Maya life began to crumble shortly after AD 800. By the end of the 9th century, all political, social, and ceremonial activities had ceased in city-state after city-state, and millions of Maya deserted the Petén, trekking north to Yucatán and south into the highlands, abandoning their brilliant cities to the encroaching forest. The Classic Maya Collapse, as this disaster is called, was triggered by overpopulation and severe environmental degradation, factors which caused a ripple effect across the southern lowlands. Yet the Collapse did not occur everywhere, and several regions had a cultural flowering during what is known as the Terminal Classic. One of these was the area of the Puuc hills in northwestern Yucatán, with the rise to power of such great cities as Uxmal and Kabah. Chichén Itzá, in central Yucatán, also participated in this cultural renaissance.

A key area for understanding what went on in the Terminal Classic, and for the story of cacao, is the Chontalpa zone of eastern Tabasco, a land of tangled, sluggish rivers, swamps, and alluvial plains. This was the homeland of the Chontal Maya, also known as the Putún, who grew rich on their astonishingly productive cacao plantations and their far-flung trading operations. By the time of the Conquest, and probably much earlier, the Putún controlled a coastal, canoe-borne trade network that extended north from the Chontalpa, around the Yucatán Peninsula, and down as far as the commercial centers of Nito and Naco near the Gulf of Honduras; the commodity (and money) that fueled this trading machine was cacao.[15]

As the pre-eminent middlemen of Mesoamerica (Eric Thompson once called them the "Phoenicians of the New World"), the adaptable Putún acquired many traits from their Nahuatl-speaking trading partners from the emporia of central Mexico, including even Nahuatlized personal names. During the final twilight of the Maya cities, people in very Mexican-looking trappings began to be depicted on the late stelae, especially at the riverine metropolis of Seibal, on the Río de la Pasión in the southwestern Petén; these are thought by many archaeologists to have been Putún invaders from downriver, moving into the political vacuum left by the Collapse to take over old Maya trade routes. A similarly hybrid Maya-Mexican culture began to be the norm in Yucatán, especially at the city of Chichén Itzá.

But most importantly for our story, evidence for Putún commercial and military activities comes from a site called Cacaxtla, in the highland Mexican state of Tlaxcala, not far to the southeast of the volcanos that form the eastern rim of the Valley of Mexico. On a hill which both commands the Puebla plain and controls the mountain routes to the lucrative markets of the Valley, we find brilliantly colored murals in a distinctively Maya-Mexican style—in fact, strikingly reminiscent of the Putún Maya reliefs of Seibal. At Cacaxtla we see the old, aquiline-nosed god of the Maya merchants and cacao-growers, Ek Chuah (or God L); with his traveling staff in hand, he stands resting before a cacao tree, his huge backpack propped up behind him. In other episodes depicted in the Cacaxtla mural program, a mighty battle is being fought in gory detail, and Putún heroes (or perhaps gods) dance in Maya-Mexican costume, carrying Maya royal paraphernalia.[16]

How should we interpret Cacaxtla? The Terminal Classic was a true "time of troubles," when kingdoms were crumbling and many peoples—especially the Putún—were on the move. The evidence seems fairly clear: at some time early in the 9th century, an aggressive, commercially-minded group of Putún Maya had fought its way from the Chontalpa up into the Mexican *altiplano*, and established a mercantile kingdom strategically located on what had once been a major Teotihuacan trade route; there they stayed until, as our historical sources tell us, they were defeated by the Toltecs (of whom more later). We have no idea what goods might have traveled from the highlands down to the Chontalpa and beyond, but certainly these foreigners must have monopolized

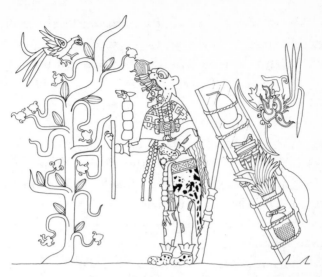

The Maya Merchant God (Ek Chuah) approaches a fantastic cacao tree, on a 9th-century mural at Cacaxtla in central Mexico. A quetzal bird alights on the tree; at the right is the god's back pack and his hat.

the trade in cacao which passed from the rich plantations of their native soil up to the Mexican highlanders on their chilly and cacao-less plateau; with their cacao, they must have brought in tropical products like chocolate seasonings and exotic bird feathers from the lowland rain forests.

The Maya on the Eve of the Conquest

By the 10th century AD, a new people had appeared on the Mesoamerican stage: the Toltecs. Later Aztec accounts describe them as a race of supermen, supremely capable and superbly skilled in the arts, and say that it was they who had passed on high civilization to the Aztecs who eventually replaced them as the dominant power in central Mexico. Not only did the Toltecs vanquish the Putún Maya (whom they called the "Olmeca," just to confuse us!) as the rulers of the Cacaxtla region, but they seem to have journeyed across the Gulf of Mexico to take over all of the Yucatán Peninsula, which they governed from their eastern capital, Chichén Itzá. Much of Mesoamerica fell under the *pax tolteca*, ushering in the Post-Classic period, which ended with the Spanish invasion.

Towards the middle of the 12th century, Toltec hegemony waned, and their western capital, Tula (or Tollan) in the Mexican state of Hidalgo, fell into ruins. Ethnohistoric documents claim that this particular collapse was the result of internal dissension and revolt. The Maya area, particularly the lowlands of Yucatán, fell once more into the traditional Maya political pattern of small, balkanized polities, in an almost perpetual state of war with each other over land and tribute. In the Guatemalan highlands, powerful rival kingdoms, all claiming legitimacy from a fictional origin in faraway Tula, came into mutual conflict, particularly the Quiché and Cakchiquel states.

The real prize for these contending nations was either control over the richest cacao-producing lands, or the establishment of beneficial trading relationships with those who controlled them. The major cacao territories were the Putún-dominated Chontalpa of Tabasco; and the Pacific coastal plain of Chiapas and Guatemala, especially the well watered Boca Costa—the piedmont zone at the foot of the volcanic highlands. The most famous part of this Pacific territory was Xoconochco (a Nahuatl word corrupted by the Spaniards to Soconusco); this was later to be a prime target for Aztec military and commercial imperialism, since its cacao was of the highest quality (it had a reputation as the best in the world up until the 19th century). In pre-Conquest times, there were constant battles to control the cacao-growing areas of the Boca Costa, and these were the main military objective of the most famous Quiché Maya king, Quicab. Not only did highland Maya towns maintain enclaves in these areas, but the conquered native peoples paid heavy tribute in cacao to their new overlords.

Returning to the Maya lowlands, the Chontalpa was renowned for its production of cacao well into the Colonial era, and even today it is the only part of Mesoamerica with commercially significant plantations. As one Colonial source of 1639 tells us, "the business of this country is cacao." Forty years earlier, in a letter sent by Bishop Juan Izquierdo to Philip II, we find this description:

> One hundred leagues from this city is a province called Chontalpa, which is very rich in a fruit named cacao, which is very valuable in this country of New Spain. And all the Indians in this province are always occupied in expanding their cacao properties and are rich in goods and wealth, so that they are openhanded with their gifts to the ministers [the missionaries] who have them in their charge.[17]

The Aztecs called one Chontal Maya-speaking territory, located in the eastern part of the Chontalpa, "Acallan," or "Land of Canoes." Acallan's lands produced no less than four cacao crops a year, the principal one being from April through July. Its capital, Itzamkanac, was divided into four quarters, like many Mesoamerican towns and cities; the god of one of these quarters was Ek Chuah (already familiar to us as the patron deity of cacao and the merchants). By the late Post-Classic, "commerce" was virtually synonymous with the cacao trade.

As for the possibilities of raising cacao trees in Yucatán, there are major natural obstacles. Firstly, its rainfall is relatively scanty, and gets progressively more so as one moves to the northwestern part of the peninsula. Secondly, being a limestone karst plain, there are virually no rivers, and the rich alluvial soils favorable to cacao growth are absent. Only in the lands bordering Chetumal Bay in the southeast, and along the Belize River, were commercially viable cacao plantations possible. Yet cacao had so much religious and social prestige among the Yucatec Maya that they found a means to grow it anyway. This was through the exploitation of humid, soil-filled sinkholes, known locally as *cenotes* (corrupted from the Maya *dzonot*). Our important early Spanish sources on 16th-century Yucatán, such as Fray Antonio de Ciudad Real and the famous (and infamous) Bishop Landa, mention these mini-plantations, Landa even describing them as "sacred groves." They seem to have been the private property of wealthy lineages, but they could never have produced very much cacao—in fact, Ciudad Real assures us that they give "very little fruit."

Recently, Arturo Gómez-Pompa and his colleagues[18] have found cacao trees, along with other useful species, growing in just such sinkholes near the town of Valladolid, Yucatán, in which the damp micro-environment and rich soils provide an ideal setting for this plant in the otherwise dry peninsula. They call attention to a painted capstone from the Temple of the Owls in Chichén Itzá, perhaps of the 10th century AD; this depicts the Maya god Kauil, the lord of sustenance and of royal descent, standing on the jaws of a serpent which emerges from the floor of a *cenote*, while cacao pods dangle from the sinkhole's roof—surely a reference to this highly specialized form of silviculture.

In contrast to the really serious cacao cultivation in Soconusco and the Chontalpa, these Yucatán sinkhole gardens were little more than the pastime of rich hobbyists—rather like the penthouse greenhouses of wealthy Manhattanites, with their tropical orchids and designer tomatoes. It goes without saying that the bulk of the cacao consumed in Yucatán came in by way of trade: Yucatán imported—largely from the Chontalpa—cacao, obsidian, copper, gold, and feathers, and exported salt, fine cotton cloth, and slaves (mostly war captives).

Many books on chocolate mention the use of cacao beans as money or small currency among the Aztecs, yet they usually fail to mention that this custom was found throughout the Maya area; in fact, it was pan-Mesoamerican. Presumably its origins are to be sought in far earlier periods, but archaeology is mute upon the subject (although the Balberta "counterfeit" beans might be significant testimony). Writing in the early 17th century, the chronicler Francisco de Cárdenas[19] tells us that in the Chontalpa, cacao beans were employed as ready cash and to buy the small items used in housekeeping. And we know from documents that in Colonial (and probably pre-Conquest) times, Maya laborers, especially long-distance porters, were paid with this currency, as they were in Aztec Mexico.

The most vivid account of cacao's value as cash is from the pen of the early 16th-century chronicler Francisco Oviedo y Valdés, writing about the Nicarao of Nicaragua,[20] a people beyond the usual boundaries given to Mesoamerica, but quite Mesoamerican nevertheless. Among the Nicarao, a rabbit was worth about ten of these "almonds," eight chicosapote fruits (from the tree which gives us chewing gum) were worth four "almonds," a slave about a hundred of them, and the services of a prostitute, eight to ten "according to how they agree." No doubt similar values prevailed among the Maya.

Bishop Landa has quite a bit to say about the uses and preparation of cacao in late pre-Conquest Yucatán:

> They make of ground maize and cacao a kind of foaming drink which is very savory, and with which they celebrate their feasts. And they get from the cacao a grease which resembles butter, and from this and maize they make another beverage which is very savory and highly thought of . . . .[21] They also parch the maize and grind it, and mix it with water, thus making a very refreshing drink, throwing in it a little Indian pepper [probably allspice, *Pimenta officinalis*] or cacao.[22]

Landa's modern editor, Professor A.M. Tozzer, identified the latter drink as the pan-Mesoamerican beverage known today as *pinole*.

Chocolate drinks played a very important role in Maya rituals and banquets. Similar to the custom among the contemporary Aztecs of the Mexican *altiplano*, the Yucatán Maya merchants and nobles grown rich through commerce were obliged to throw large parties resembling the native North American potlatch, with lavish hospitality and the usual mandatory reciprocity:

> And often they spend on one banquet what they have earned by trading and bargaining many days. And they have two ways of celebrating these feasts: the first, which is that of the nobles and of the principal people, obliges each one of the invited guests to give another similar feast. And to each guest they give a roasted fowl, bread and drinks of cacao in abundance.[23]

The friars, including Landa, were astounded that the pagan Maya had a baptismal rite for boys and girls—might the Gospel have been preached in this barbarous land at some earlier age? The ritual was in the charge of a gorgeously arrayed priest. The children were gathered together inside a cord held by four elderly men representing the Chacs (rain gods), each standing in a corner of the room. Then the noble who was giving the ceremony took a bone and wet it in a vessel filled with water made of "certain flowers and of cacao pounded and dissolved in virgin water, which they call that brought from the hollows of the trees or of the rocks in the forest"; with this liquid he anointed the children on their foreheads, faces, and in the spaces between the fingers and toes, in complete silence.

Even though the sinkhole gardens of the peninsula were of little economic significance, home-grown Yucatán cacao commanded enough respect to have its own special ritual, as described by Landa:

> In the month of Muan, those who owned cacao plantations celebrated a festival to the gods Ek Chuah, Chac and Hobnil, who were their mediators. To solemnize it they went to some plantation belonging to one of their number, where they sacrificed a dog, spotted with the color of cacao, and they burned their incense to their idols and offered them iguanas of a blue color, and certain

feathers of a bird, and other kinds of game, and they gave to each of the officials a spike of the fruit of the cacao [presumably a cacao pod].[24]

Ethnohistoric accounts point to the widespread, perhaps even pan-Maya, use of chocolate in betrothal and marriage ceremonies, particularly among the wealthy. In this respect, chocolate drinks occupied the same niche as expensive French champagne does in our own culture. We are told that when a Quiché Maya king was looking for a wife, his messenger was given a vessel of red drink (whatever that might have been) and a vessel of beaten chocolate. And in the Quiché kingdom there were three lineage lords whose function was to give wedding banquets. As the Quiché specialist Dennis Tedlock notes,[25] one of the things that people did at such festivities was to *chokola'j*, "drink chocolate together"; this is a possible source for the Spanish (and English) word *chocolate* (see Chapter Four). The cacao beans themselves could sometimes have a similar significance, as can be seen in an early Colonial report on the "wild" (that is still unconquered) Chol Maya of the Chiapas forests, cited by Eric Thompson:

> The form of the marriage is: the bride gives the bridegroom a small stool painted in colors, and also gives him five grains of cacao, and says to him "These I give thee as a sign that I accept thee as my husband." And he also gives her some new skirts and another five grains of cacao, saying the same thing.[26]

Cacao Preparation among the Late Maya

Colonial sources and modern ethnographic accounts show that the Maya had—and still have—many ways of making food and drink from *Theobroma cacao*, something that we have already suggested from our examination of the hieroglyphic texts which embellish Classic vases. In the 17th-century Spanish-Maya dictionary now in Vienna's National Library,[27] ordinary chocolate is called *chacau haa*, "hot water" (or "hot chocolate," for *haa* can also mean "chocolate"). Another drink which is made from cacao, maize, and sapote seeds is given the name *tzune*; perhaps this was reserved for special occasions. More commonly drunk was a gruel called *saca* (basically the same term that appears on Classic bowls), prepared from cooked maize, water, and cacao. As we have mentioned before, for "ordinary" chocolate–which from its name was certainly drunk hot—there are entries for the froth, and for the act of beating it to produce this effect.

Two chocolate flavorings are mentioned in these early Yucatec Maya dictionaries: one is vanilla, and the other is the "ear flower." We shall be discussing these fully in the next chapter, for we have much more information on how the Aztecs "stepped up" their cacao with seasonings than we have for the Maya.

Once the lords of a vast domain in eastern Chiapas, the Lacandón Maya today number only a few hundred, surviving in a pitiful remnant of what was in the past one of the New World's greatest rain forests. Nonetheless, in spite of every kind of pressure from modern-day Mexico, the Lacandón retain many cultural traditions, including culinary ones, that must hark back to Classic times. These people grow their own cacao, and prepare two kinds of drinks from it, one for ordinary consumption, and the other to be offered to their gods.

The sacred Lacandón chocolate drink is comparable to the secular, in that the highly treasured froth is produced with a foaming agent, but there are differences.[28]

LACANDÓN SECULAR CHOCOLATE DRINK

The fermented and dried beans are first toasted on a griddle, and the outer membrane removed. Then a section of vine called suqir is cut out; this is to act as a foaming agent. The tougher portion is ground, following which the fiber and liquid are put in a gourd strainer and lowered into a pot of water, while stirring, and the remaining fiber is discarded. Next, the housewife grinds the tender part of the suqir vine together with the cacao beans and toasted corn; the mixture is stirred into the prepared water, and the concoction whipped with a wooden beater without heating or cooking. The resulting foam is spooned off, placed on top of maize gruel, and gobbled up. When all the foam is gone, the remaining chocolate liquid is drunk, "but the foam is the most desirable part."

LACANDÓN SACRED CHOCOLATE DRINK

The ritual sponsor's wife roasts the cacao beans, then grinds them with a stone mano and metate, not the iron hand-mills used in ordinary household kitchens (in fact, she does this in a special cooking hut next to the "god house" where the clay effigy "god pots" are kept). While grinding, she mixes in a grass called aak', which makes the cacao liquid foam as she beats it with a wooden stick. Water is then stirred into the mixture, the liquid strained, and finally poured into bowls containing either balché (a ritual mead flavored with a certain tree root) or sak ha (our already familiar corn gruel). This is then "fed" to the "god pots."

Among the contemporary highland Maya of Guatemala, there are a myriad ways of making cacao into a beverage, many of them using substances introduced by the Spaniards, such as cane sugar, rice, cinnamon, and black pepper (in place of the honey, maize, allspice, and chillis of the indigenous kitchen). One of the most common drinks, widespread in the northern highlands of Guatemala, is called by the Spanish term *batido* (this would be translated as "frappe" in American soda fountains.[29]

BATIDO

The cacao beans are ground, the resulting powder placed in a bowl to which tepid water is added, and a paste produced by beating with the hand. To this paste are added one or more of a variety of spices, the native ones being vanilla, achiote (Bixa orellana, ground and added

to impart a brick-red color), "ear flower" (Cymbopetalum penduli-
florum), and ground sapote kernels. To prepare the batido for drinking,
a teaspoonful of the paste is added to a gourdful of hot water. Since
cacao is very expensive, and Guatemalan Indians are very poor, there is
often very little cacao in the batido, and lots of black pepper.

But even our information on the different forms that cacao can
take among the modern Maya almost certainly does not cover all
the ways in which *Theobroma cacao* was exploited in earliest times.
For instance, although there is still controversy on the subject
among hieroglyph specialists, some of the Classic Maya pottery
texts suggest that the *fresh* beans and/or their pulp were exploited
in some way. Along these same lines, the 17th-century chronicler
Antonio Fuentes y Guzmán, writing about the Pacific slopes of
Guatemala, has this to say: "But returning to record the virtues of
cacao, one should know that as soon as it leaves the pod, it exudes
a most excellent and very fresh liquid, which the Indians take
from it with great dexterity."[30] They did this by piling the fresh,
pulp-enclosed beans in a small, clean dugout canoe, in which from
its own gravity the pulp expressed "an abundant liquor of the
smoothest taste, between sour and sweet, which is of the most
refreshing coolness," especially for relief from the unrelenting heat
of the region. Although Fuentes y Guzmán fails to tell us this, the
drink was alcoholic, as the process he describes was part of the
usual fermentation involved in cacao production; indeed, such a
"wine" is still enjoyed in the Chontalpa.

We may conclude by reiterating that chocolate and the
remarkable tree from which it derives were thus *not* the invention
of the Aztecs, as most books on the subject would have us believe,
but of the remarkable Maya and their distant predecessors, the
Mixe-Zoquean-speaking Olmec. It was the Maya who first taught
the Old World how to drink chocolate, and it was the Maya who
gave us the word "cacao." They deserve recognition in the
culinary history of *Theobroma cacao*.

CHAPTER THREE

&

The Aztecs:
People of the Fifth Sun

Probably no other nation, past or present, has received such a bad press as the Aztecs (or the Mexica, as they usually called themselves). In the minds of the public at large, the Aztecs are almost universally viewed as a cruel and sadistic people, on a par with the Nazi Germans for their sadistic, bloodthirsty atrocities. Certainly the Spanish conquistadores and their apologists have fostered this image, to vindicate their own unjust invasion of Mexico and Central America, and the centuries of oppression, genocide, and ethnocide which followed in its wake. The deliberately distorted notion that "they had it coming to them" has entrapped even respectable historians of our own age.

Ironically, it is thanks to another group of Spaniards that we have an amazingly large and accurate body of information that allows us to construct a far less prejudiced and erroneous account of the native peoples of Mexico. This group consists of the mendicant friars who came early after the Conquest to win Indian converts to Christianity. They took the trouble to learn the Aztec tongue—Nahuatl—and to question closely the natives under their wing about life as it had been before the Conquest, with the idea of making conversion easier to accomplish. Another goal of the missionaries (particularly the Franciscans) was to build from the ruins of Mexican civilization a new Utopia, a millennial Kingdom of God, in which their converts would live a life uncorrupted by the lay Spaniards, whose sinful ways they despised.

The most remarkable among these mendicants was Fray Bernardino de Sahagún, rightly held by many in the anthropological profession to have been the world's first field ethnographer. Sahagún was in the second wave of Franciscan missionaries to follow the Conquest of 1521, and he quickly set to work to master Nahuatl, and then to interrogate the Aztec elite and intelligentsia—priests, nobles, merchants, and the like—on all details of their culture and religion as it had been on the eve of the Empire's destruction. His great encyclopedic *General History of the Things of New Spain* totalled 12 volumes of lavishly illustrated manuscript; and manuscript it stayed, at least until the end of the 19th century, for it was suppressed at the express order of the fanatical, bigoted Philip II of Spain. No other source on any native people of the Americas approaches it in completeness and accuracy, and we may place near-total reliance on what Sahagún's informants told him about every aspect of Aztec life, including the use of cacao and chocolate.[1]

There are, of course, many other sources on Aztec life and history, such as the conquistadores themselves (but these, especially Cortés, were very prejudiced observers), or members of the native nobility who wrote down their own histories in Nahuatl and sometimes Spanish. A particularly important source, somewhat later than Sahagún, is Fray Diego Durán, who compiled an account of the Aztecs from historical chronicles and ethnographic reports now lost to us.[2]

From all of these, and from the ritual books or codices (most of them actually pre-Conquest), one gets a picture of a vigorous, sympathetic, and ultimately tragic nation, far from the blood-crazed semi-barbarians depicted in modern popular and, we are sorry to say, scholarly history.[3]

Aztec Origins and Early History

According to Aztec traditions, there had been other worlds, called "Suns," before our own. Each had been created by the gods, had flourished, and then had been destroyed by the divine beings. The Aztecs, and all of humankind, including ourselves, exist in the Fifth Sun, which was supernaturally born in the great, ancient city of Teotihuacan. But one day even this Sun is to be annihilated, this time by monstrous earthquakes, and all living things will again perish in the final cataclysm.

Given such a powerful myth, the Aztecs were of necessity a nation of pessimists. Regarding their own origins during the epoch of the Fifth Sun, their beliefs belonged to the "born in a log cabin" school: like early United States politicians, and later ones too, the Aztecs liked to boast about their humble beginnings and their subsequent rise to eminence and power through their own mighty efforts. According to what they told the Spaniards, they themselves were not the original inhabitants of the Valley of Mexico, but had migrated there from a supposed homeland called Aztlan ("Land of White Herons"), said to be in the western or north-western reaches of Mexico. Another apparently conflicting legend had them emerging as seven tribes from a womb-like underground chamber called "The Seven Caves" (Chicomoztoc, in Nahuatl).

The Aztecs leave their ancestral home, Aztlan, located on a lake-bound island.
From the Tira de la Peregrinación.

Nevertheless, there is agreement among the sources that in their semi-desert homeland, they were little better than uncouth rustics: they wore skin clothing and killed game with the bow-and-arrow, and also eked out their existence with a little agriculture.

Their tribal god Huitzilopochtli ("Hummingbird on the Left") had given them a prophecy: they would leave Aztlan, and would eventually reach an island in a lake where they would see an eagle perched on a prickly-pear cactus, holding a serpent in its beak. On that island they were to found a city, and from that city they would come to rule the world. Led by four priests bearing the god's image. they tarried at a place called Coatepec, "Snake Mountain," where various mystic doings took place, including the birth of Huitzilopochtli from the womb of the mother goddess Coatlicue— a goddess who will later play a role in our story. By the beginning of the 14th century, the migrating Aztecs had reached the Valley of Mexico, which they found already occupied by the towns and cities of far more advanced peoples, the cultural descendants of the old Toltec civilization which had crumbled two centuries earlier.

At first, the Aztec immigrants lived as poor vassals and serfs for these overlords, whom they impressed by their warlike propensities. Following a series of vicissitudes, the intruders were expelled by the original inhabitants to several, small, swampy islands in the midst of the great lake, the Lake of the Moon, which once filled much of the Valley of Mexico. On one of these—lo and behold!— was the eagle sitting on the cactus with the serpent in its mouth, and there they established their soon-to-be-mighty capital, Tenochtitlan. It was not long before they had subdued all those city-states of central Mexico that had snubbed and oppressed them. By 1375, they had elected their first true king, Acamapichtli ("Handful of Arrows"). Within the short space of one hundred years, they had brought a large part of Mesoamerica under their sway, and their state could truly be called an empire.

The Aztecs had a genius for warfare; their large armies and their military ethos ensured that they would defeat almost all their adversaries. Their only major setback was at the hands of the Tarascans of Michoacan, on the west, and they wisely left these proud people alone for the rest of their history. To the east of the Valley was the Tlaxcallan state, hereditary enemies of the Aztecs; the Tlaxcallans were totally surrounded by Aztec armies, who eventually would have subdued them, but instead entered into a strange kind of pact called "The Flowery War," an agreement for perpetual hostilities which would guarantee a steady supply of sacrificial captives for both sides. As for the Maya of the highlands and lowlands to the east of the empire, they made no attempt to impose their rule on them. And why should they when they had such a lucrative trading relationship? It was in the interests of both peoples to maintain this, particularly through the mercantile port of Xicallanco, a great emporium controlled by those wily traders, the Chontal or Putún Maya.

For our story, the most significant Aztec conquest took place during the reign of Ahuitzotl (1486–1502): this gave to the Empire the province of Xoconochco (Soconusco), the Pacific coastal plain and adjacent piedmont of southeastern Mesoamerica, already famed for the high production and top quality of its cacao. This was of enormous interest to the Aztec long-distance merchants, or *pochteca*, and they played an important role in the campaign.

In retrospect, could there be any truth in the "born in a long cabin" legend, so carefully fostered by the upper echelons of the Aztec state? It could be true that a small band of migrants really *did* come into the Valley from the arid lands of the northwest, bringing with them their tribal cult of Huitzilopochtli, along with an austere, militaristic ethic which was so important in the Aztec state ideology. Yet it is undeniable that most of the people who lived in the heart of the empire had probably always been there, worshipping the old, pre-Huitzilopochtli gods. From these people, the Aztec rulers and intelligentsia absorbed their far more sophisticated culture, and perhaps even elements of Maya learning and culture which had penetrated into central Mexico during the turbulent times of the Terminal Classic. It is not unlikely that the most critical of these elements was the mercantile system of the Putún Maya, centered upon cacao.

The Aztecs on the Eve of the Conquest

Scholars are still debating the nature of the Aztec Empire. Was it a true empire in the modern sense? In the first place, it was technically an alliance between: (1) the island capital, Tenochtitlan; (2) Texcoco, an old and cultured city-state on the eastern side of the Lake of the Moon; and (3) Tlacopan, a minor principality on the mainland west of Tenochtitlan. Be that as it may, Tenochtitlan called all the shots when it came to military and political decisions. This was basically an alliance to divide up the tribute extracted from provinces which had been crushed by the Aztec war machine; naturally, Tenochtitlan got the lion's share of the booty, which poured into the Valley on a twice-yearly basis. This included vast amounts of foodstuffs, like maize and beans, as well as clothing, war costumes and shields, and all kinds of luxury items. By the time that the Spaniards arrived, the residents of Tenochtitlan were probably more dependent upon food coming in as tribute than upon what was being raised in the Valley's agricultural lands.

The size of the population of the empire can be debated, but the best estimates suggest that there were about 10 or 11 million people in central Mexico alone. It is extremely difficult to come up with a figure for the island capital itself, but Tenochtitlan (including the "sister city" of Tlatelolco, in the northern third of the island) may have had over 200,000 inhabitants, making it one of the largest cities in the world in its day.

The ordinary free citizens of every town and city, including the capital, were organized into *calpoltin*, localized, land-holding bodies with their own chiefs and lords, their temples, and their schools (education was universal, for both sexes). Each family held its land in usufruct, a man's land being taken away from him if he left it fallow for more than two years.

Yet this was a stratified, aristocratic society, in spite of its humble roots. A hereditary class of lords, or *teuctin*, had rights over the labor and tribute of the commoners; the lords also held private lands, generally worked by a large class of serfs. The very greatest of the lords belonged to the royal lineage, and the greatest of these was the *huei tlatoani* or "great speaker," the man we call emperor. He was chosen by a council of high nobles from a small list of candidates within the royal family, the succession passing either to sons or brothers. He ruled for life, and his person was sacred: none might gaze upon him or touch him (as Cortés had the effrontery to do). The later rulers lived in huge, luxurious palaces approaching in their organizational complexity and elaborate etiquette the royal courts of Baroque Europe. The palace compound housed not only the main arsenal of the Aztec state, but also the royal warehouses (including one devoted to cacao, as we shall see), important in a redistributive economy like that of the Aztecs.

Three social groups occupied special places in the Aztec order of things. Perhaps the most prestigious was the priesthood. To become a priest, one had to have graduated from the *calmecac*, a seminary for noble boys, and from a more advanced theological academy. It was no easy job, since one had to preside over the complex, calendrically fixed rituals of the temple (including human sacrifice), and keep vigils through the nights. Moreover, one was expected to be celibate *and* chaste.

Aztec religion, about which Sahagún and Durán give us vast amounts of information, was also enormously complex. The Aztecs were polytheists: there were literally dozens of gods and goddesses, many of them representative of natural forces and the agricultural round.[4] Some of these were quadripartite, being arrayed to the four directions. The most worshipped of these deities were Tlaloc, the god of rain; Tezcatlipoca, "Smoking Mirror," the dread, omnipresent patron of warriors, wizards, and the royal house;

Quetzalcoatl, "Feathered Serpent," Tezcatlipoca's adversary, and lord of the priesthood; and Xipe Totec, "Our Lord the Flayed One," god of springtime and the renewal of vegetation, represented by a priest garbed in the flayed skin of a captive.

The commoners participated in most of these cults. But while this multiplicity of deities may have satisfied the spiritual needs of the ordinary folk, we have evidence from Nahuatl poetry that the Aztec philosophers and thinkers had reconciled all this with the idea that the only, ultimate reality was an all-embracing supernatural residing in the topmost of the stratified heavens; this androgynous being or force, known as the Lord (and Lady) of Duality, embodied the concept of the unity of opposites. All else, including ourselves, was illusory and evanescent.[5]

Finally, we should mention the state cult of Huitzilopochtli, the ancient tribal deity of the Aztecs; he had taken on the attributes of the Sun God worshipped by the earlier inhabitants of the Valley. As the supreme war god, and as the sun itself, his worship demanded the daily sacrifice of brave captives taken in war, so that the solar orb could blaze forth at dawn each day. If this failed to happen, the Fifth Sun would end in universal disaster. This was the *raison d'être* of the Aztec human sacrifice—not blood lust, nor a predilection for cruelty, nor an obsession with death, but a fear lest the world and the life on it should perish. The number of victims who died under the knife was grossly exaggerated by the Spaniards, probably in an attempt to justify their

Image of Huitzilopochtli, patron god of the Aztecs and deity of war and the sun, from the Codex Borbonicus.

own reprehensible actions during and after their invasion of Mexico; at the most, a few thousand prisoners might have so ended their lives each year in the Aztec capital, as compared to the many tens of thousands claimed in the Spanish accounts.

The Great Temple at the center of the capital was actually divided into two halves: at the summit of one half was the temple of Tlaloc, god of rain and agriculture, while the other half was dedicated to Huitzilopochtli, patron of warfare and of the sun, its steps splattered with the blood of sacrificial victims. The Aztecs were fond of contrasts of this sort.

The warriors were the backbone of the Aztec state, and were graduates of the *telpochcalli*, the military academy. Armed with shield, darts to be hurled from spearthrowers, lance, and the *macuauhuitl* (the terrible, flat wooden war club set along the sides with razor-sharp obsidian blades), they were well-nigh invincible against their Mesoamerican enemies. When it was bent on conquest, which was the case through much of Aztec history, the state could field very large armies and keep them supplied for long periods of time. Armies travel on their stomachs, and the Aztecs army was no exception; the staple ration on campaigns was toasted tortillas, produced in great quantities by their women at home.

Prowess and valor on the field of battle, demonstrated by the taking of captives for sacrifice in the capital, was rewarded with both social and economic advancement. Although not of noble birth, valiant braves could ignore the sumptuary laws and wear the gorgeous attire usually restricted to the nobility.

The final group to be noted consists of the long-distance merchants. These are not to be confused with the market traders—the men and women who thronged the great market squares of Aztec towns and cities. Rather, these particular merchants constituted a kind of hereditary guild, and even had their own gods and rites. Their task was to mount expeditions, complete with porters, to distant "ports of trade" in the lowlands, above all to the Putún Maya emporium of Xicallanco, and to Xoconochco (Soconusco).

Aztec pochteca *merchants on the road, from Sahagún's Florentine Codex. This is the way that cacao was transported to the capital, Tenochtitlan.*

Their very name, *pochteca*, meaning "People from the Land of the Ceiba-tree," suggests their intimate connection with the tropical lowlands, where the ceiba flourishes. As we have said, the *pochteca* may have been instituted in central Mexico by the Putún overlords of Cacaxtla, centuries earlier.

Sahagún devoted an entire book of his encyclopedia to the *pochteca*.[6] From this we know that their main task was to procure from Xicallanco and Xoconochco exotic goods for the royal palace, such as resplendent feathers (above all, quetzal feathers), jaguar skins, and amber. Lest the enormous wealth that the *pochteca* caravans amassed excite jealousy and cupidity, the returning *pochteca* entered the city under cover of night. We shall come back later to this important group, for they were heavily involved in the cacao trade, and were themselves notable consumers of chocolate.

Such was the teeming world of the Aztecs in the Valley of Mexico, first seen by Old World eyes in AD 1519, and utterly destroyed at the hands of the Spaniards two years later. The Empire fell to the invaders not so much through the courage and resource-fulness of the conquistadores (as apologists for the Spaniards like to claim), or for the supposed superiority of European civilization over that of the Mexican "Indians," but by means of the hundreds of thousands of native allies which the Spaniards had gained from disaffected parts of the Aztec realm—allies which significantly included the fiercely anti-Aztec Tlaxcallans. But equally fatal to the Aztec cause was the introduction of epidemic diseases of Old World origin, such as smallpox and measles, which ravaged populations all over Mesoamerica, and which often traveled ahead of the Spaniards.

Attraction and Repulsion: The Case of Octli and Chocolate

There is a curious ambivalence in Aztec thought and culture regarding their two most important drinks, *octli* (the native "wine") and chocolate. This stems from an ambivalence in their society as a whole. On the one hand, as we have said, they firmly believed that through their bravery and hard toil, they had progressed from life as poor-as-dirt savages in the semi-deserts of northwestern Mexico to their present position of power and opulence—a Horatio Alger, "rags to riches" morality tale. On the other, by the close of the 15th century Tenochtitlan and the other cities of the Valley were rolling in luxury goods, and the elite class along with the warriors and merchants enjoyed a way of life that was unmatched in Mesoamerica. But there were heavy restrictions on the use and consumption of these luxuries, such as the rigid sumptuary laws about dress and ornament. There was, in fact, a strongly puritanical streak in Aztec life.

One of the reasons that the Aztecs were so interested in choco-late was that their native drink *octli* (known to the Spaniards as *pulque*, a word apparently of South American origin) was mildly alcoholic, and drunkenness was not looked upon favorably by

Aztec society. *Octli* was made of the juice of a few species of agave ("century plant" to us). When the agave plant had matured—not taking a century, to be sure, but perhaps ten to twelve years—under favorable conditions, and showed signs of shooting up a flowering stalk, the base of the stalk was undercut, the stalk removed, and the basin where the stalk had been was scooped out. Large quantities of juice resulted, and could be collected over a period of several months. This juice was allowed to ferment, and turn into *octli*.

The Aztecs considered chocolate a far more desirable beverage, especially for warriors and the nobility, but *octli* was not entirely prohibited. It was allowed for the elderly, although these are defined differently in various sources: some say that those with licence to imbibe *octli* were persons with children *and* grandchildren, but others give even more advanced ages. These old folks were permitted up to four cups every evening. As for the rest, there were certain feasts where everybody could drink *octli*, including one where even the children could tipple. But on the whole, the prohibitions were grim: the usual penalty for drunkenness was death. There is a considerable temperance literature among the Aztec; and the ruler, on his accession, often gave long harangues about the sins of drink. There were countless morality tales, such as the one about a corps commander who, to pay for his drinking habit, sold off his house piece by piece, and even his weaving women, ending up lying destitute and besotted in the road.[7] Another story told of how Nezahualcoyotl, the poet-king of Texcoco, while fleeing invaders who had butchered his father, encountered a woman during his wanderings in exile; infuriated to discover that she was cultivating agave so that she could sell *octli* to all comers, he slew her.[8]

Chocolate, then, became a highly successful and culturally acceptable replacement for *octli* among the upper echelons of Aztec society—but even then not all would accept it. The same kind of ambivalence operated here, too, since cacao was seen as a somewhat exotic, luxurious product, foreign to the austere life to which they so often looked back nostalgically. Perhaps they even associated chocolate with the luxury-loving people of the hot lands, that is, the Gulf Coast and the Maya lowlands from where it originated.

An extraordinary tale is recounted by Father Durán, one which highlights this ambivalence.[9] It goes as follows. The mid-15th-century ruler of the Aztecs was Motecuhzoma Ilhuicamina ("Motecuhzoma the Heaven-shooter"), one of the greatest of the emperors, who expanded the empire down on to the Gulf Coast by his victory over the Huaxtecs. Driven by curiosity about the origins of his own people, he dispatched an expedition of sixty sorcerers to seek out Aztlan, the mythical homeland from which his ancestors had supposedly migrated, led by their god Huitzilopochtli. At last the wizards arrived at Aztlan, which they found to be on an island in a lake, just like their own mighty capital. On being asked their mission, they told the natives of the place that they had a gift for Huitzilopochtli's mother, the goddess Coatlicue ("Serpent Skirt"); or, if she were dead, for her servants.

On the island was a hill, Colhuacan, where the old goddess still lived. The custodian of the hill told them to bring their gifts and follow him up the hill. But while the spry old man sped up the slope, the wizards found that they could barely walk, their feet sinking down in the sand.

> They called to the old man who was walking with such lightness that his feet did not seem to touch the ground.
> "What is wrong with you, O Aztecs?" said he. "What has made you so heavy? What do you eat in your land?"
> "We eat the foods that grow there and we drink chocolate."
> The elder responded, "Such food and drink, my children, have made you heavy and they make it difficult for you to reach the place of your ancestors. Those foods will bring death. The wealth you have we know nothing about; we live poorly and simply."[10]

The old man forthwith snatched up their bundles, and ushered them into the presence of the aged and ugly goddess herself. They urged her:

> "Accept the gifts, part of the wealth of your magnificent son, Huitzilopochtli."
>
> "Tell me children," said she, "what have you brought me, is it food?"
>
> "Great lady, it is food and drink; chocolate is drunk and sometimes eaten."
>
> "This is what has burdened you!" she told them. "This is why you have not been able to climb the hill."[11]

Their mission completed, the sorcerers went down the hill. But as their old guide descended, he became younger and younger, just as the farther he went up the hill, the older he became. Thus, he could control his age at will. This was the custodian's final homily to the imperial delegation, before their return to Tenochtitlan:

> Behold my sons, the virtue of this hill; the old man can climb to the point on the hill that he wishes and there he will acquire the age that he seeks. That is why we live to old age and that is why none of the companions of your ancestors have died since the departure of your people. We become young when we wish. You have become old, you have become tired because of the chocolate you drink and because of the foods you eat. They have harmed and weakened you. You have been spoiled by those mantles, feathers and riches that you wear and that you have brought here. All of that has ruined you.[12]

When all of this was reported to Motecuhzoma Ilhuicamina, he wept. But the Aztecs went on drinking chocolate, just as modern-day consumers go on smoking regardless of the dire warnings on cigarette packages.

The Aztec "Chocolate Tree": Cacahuacuauhuitl

One of the great works of Renaissance botany was compiled and written by Francisco Hernández, royal physician and naturalist to that unhappy monarch, Philip II of Spain. Sent by his sovereign in 1570 to the New World in a search for medicinal plants (of which more in Chapter Four), Hernández was in Mexico by 1572, remaining there until 1577. His *magnum opus* on the plants of New Spain (Mexico) contained descriptions of over 3000 species, along with their Nahuatl names, and was illustrated by native artists. Unhappily for posterity, the original went up in flames in 1671, in the fire that destroyed Philip's library in the Escorial; but it had a partial survival in a poor copy that was finally published with woodcuts based on the native watercolors.[13]

His Aztec informants gave Hernández the general name for the cacao tree: *cacahuacuauhuitl*, compounded from *cacahuatl*, "cacao," and *cuauhuitl*, "tree." They told him about four cultivated varieties; most modern botanists believe they were all of the *criollo* variety. From the largest in overall size and size of fruit, to the smallest, they were:

(1) *cuauhcacahuatl*: "wood cacao" or perhaps "eagle cacao."
(2) *mecacahuatl*: "maguey cacao."
(3) *xochicacahuatl*: "flower cacao," said to have a seed reddish on the outside.
(4) *tlalcacahuatl*: "earth cacao," the smallest. This name was also confusingly given to the peanut, a South American native which probably was taken to Mexico following the conquest of Peru.

Of course, none of these varieties grew in the frost-prone central highlands of Mexico—cacao was brought in as either trade or tribute, or both. True to his medical calling, Hernández dwells on the supposed therapeutic virtues of the cacao tree and its products,

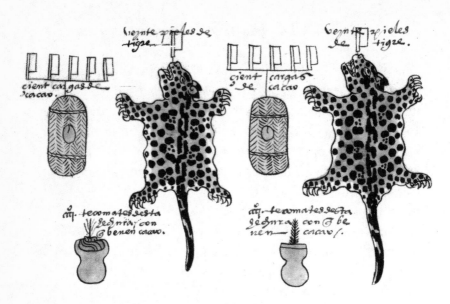

One page of the Codex Mendoza covers the tribute extracted by the Aztecs from Xoconochco. This detail shows 200 loads of cacao beans, 40 jaguar skins, and chocolate jars.

but this is a subject that we shall cover in detail in the next chapter, for this was a prime concern of the medicine-poor Europeans.

To return to the pre-Conquest Aztecs, their prize possession was surely Xoconochco (Soconusco). In a conflict instigated and abetted by the *pochteca*, the long-distance merchants, the Aztec war machine had extended the empire to its farthest frontier, and ensured a steady flow of premium cacao and other elite goods into the imperial storehouses. Other, lesser sources of tribute-cacao for the Aztec state were the Huaxtec lands of coastal Veracruz, also seized by Ahuitzotl, the emperor under whose rule Xoconochco was conquered; and the torrid coast of what is now the state of Guerrero.

It is not clear whether the great entrepot of Xicallanco in the Chontalpa of Tabasco was entirely dominated by the Putún Maya, or whether the Aztec merchants exercised some kind of control over it. But this was never part of the empire, and the produce of the huge Chontalpa cacao plantations had to be procured through

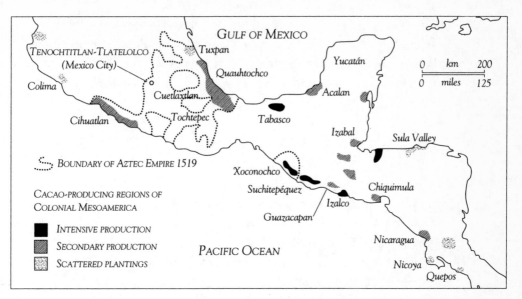

Map of the cacao-producing regions of Mesoamerica during the early Colonial period. The province of Xoconochco (Soconusco) was the major cacao producer in Mesoamerica at the time of the Aztec supremacy.

trade, not through the exaction of tribute. In this, the *pochteca* were on the same footing as the Maya traders coming from Yucatán. There was probably a babble of tongues in the marketplace of Xicallanco, a sort of Mesoamerican Constantinople. The *pochteca*, there to buy luxury goods along with cacao for their imperial master in Tenochtitlan, spoke Nahuatl among themselves, but almost certainly were fluent in Chontal Maya, for they were trained to pick up foreign intelligence on their travels. Also present must have been ordinary traders from the cities of the Valley of Mexico, for we know that cacao was sold in the huge general market of Tlatelolco, in the northern part of the island capital.[14]

To get to these hot lands of the southeast—known collectively to the Aztecs as *Anahuac*, "Near the Sea"—the human caravans of the *pochteca* started from their staging and warehouse center of Tochtepec, "Rabbit Mountain," in northern Oaxaca just above the Gulf Coast plain. The traders and their many hundreds of porters then split into two groups, one heading for Xicallanco, and the other for Xoconochco and coastal Guatemala. On their way back from Xoconochco, they may have mingled with Aztec tribute collectors, along with their porters, returning to the imperial storehouses with cacao and other goods extracted from the local chiefs.

The Royal Coffers

In a society in which the seeds of *Theobroma cacao* served both as money and as the source of a very elite beverage, the sheer amount of cacao held in the royal storehouses of the three cities within the Triple Alliance is astounding. These depositories shared some of the characteristics of Fort Knox, on the one hand, and Louis XIV's wine cellars, on the other. We have some interesting figures on this subject, but before we give them we should point out that all transactions in pre-Conquest Mesoamerica were measured in terms of numbers rather than weight or bulk (scales, for instance, were unknown until the Spaniards introduced them, but for the next three centuries, cacao was still counted). The basic Aztec count was vigesimal, or base 20, rather than decimal. Thus, a *tzontli* was 400 of anything, while a *xiquipilli* was 20 times this, or 8000; and this is the way cacao beans were reckoned. The normal load of cacao in the backpack of a trader or porter was three *xiquipillis*, or 24,000 beans.

We are told by one source[15] that to maintain the palace and court of Nezahualcoyotl (the king of Texcoco), his majordomo had to supply, among other items of food, no less than four *xiquipillis* of cacao on a daily basis—this is 32,000 beans.[16] This amounts to 11,680,000 beans annually, or just over 486 loads. This figure may be exaggerated, for according to Juan de Torquemada,[17] quoting information from Nezahualcoyotl's nephew, the palace account books listed the annual expenditure at 2,744,000 beans, still a huge amount. Some of these dried beans were probably consumed in the chocolate drink, and some as salaries and other payments.

It goes without saying that Motecuhzoma Xocoyotzin ("Motecuhzoma the Younger," the familiar "Montezuma" of popular histories) in Tenochtitlan was far wealthier than his Texcocan cousin. The chronicler Francisco Cervantes de Salazar[18] informs us that the Emperor's cacao warehouse held more than 40,000 loads, which would mean 960,000,000 beans! Whether inflation has crept in here we shall never know, but Bernal Díaz del Castillo states that more than

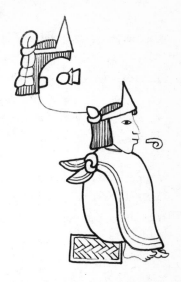

*Motecuhzoma II (reigned 1502–20),
after Sahagún's* Primeros Memoriales.

2000 containers of chocolate beverage, with foam, were daily destined for the soldiers of Motecuhzoma's guard alone.[19]

We have some idea of what Motecuhzoma's warehouse, or at least a part of it, looked like thanks to the depredations of the cruel and avaricious Pedro de Alvarado, the Heinrich Himmler of the Conquest.[20] One night, when the Aztec ruler was held captive in his own palace, about 300 Indian servants of the Spaniards broke into the storehouse, and worked until sunrise to cart off as much cacao as they could. This came to Alvarado's ears, and he enlisted the aid of one Alonso de Ojeda, who was guarding Motecuhzoma: "When you have turned over your watch and see that it is time, call me, for I also want part of that cacao." They went there with fifty persons, presumably also Indian servants.

The cacao was in some bins like great cubes, made of wicker, so huge that six men could not span them, coated with clay inside and out, all placed in order, which was something to see. They serve as granaries, for maize as well as for other needs; much of what they put into them is conserved; sometimes they are closed on top and opened on one side;

they serve as protected houses, though mostly as granaries, underneath a flat roof. Alonso de Ojeda, on seeing that daylight was on its way, before their time ran out, cut the bands of those bins with a broadsword; then those looking for cacao stuffed their skirts and mantles; they emptied three bins, in [each of] which were 600 loads, each load having 24,000 beans.[21]

What Alvarado and his fellow thieves made off with that night was 43,200,000 beans, not even a twentieth of the Emperor's cacao stock, if we can believe our figures.

How the Aztecs Made Chocolate

The basic Aztec method of preparing chocolate (which, like cacao, is universally called *cacahuatl* in our early sources) was about the same as that prevalent among the Maya; the only real difference is that it seems to have been drunk cool rather than hot as seems to have been the case among the Maya of Yucatán. One of the earliest notices of this drink is by the hand of a man known to scholars as the Anonymous Conqueror, described as "a gentleman of Hernán Cortés," whose description of Tenochtitlan was published in Venice in 1556:

These seeds which are called almonds or cacao are ground and made into powder, and other small seeds are ground, and this powder is put into certain basins with a point [whatever that may mean], and then they put water on it and mix it with a spoon. And after having mixed it very well, they change it from one basin to another, so that a foam is raised which they put in a vessel made for the purpose. And when they wish to drink it, they mix it with certain small spoons of gold or silver or wood, and drink it, and drinking it one must open one's mouth, because being foam one must give it room to subside, and go down bit by bit. This drink is the healthiest thing, and the greatest sustenance of anything you could drink in the world, because he who drinks a cup of this liquid, no matter how far he walks, can go a whole day without eating anything else.[22]

To this encomium the Anonymous Conqueror adds the comment that "it is better in hot weather than in cool, being cold in its nature." Cold in its nature? What did he mean by this strange statement? We shall return to this subject later.

According to Sahagún's native informants, fine chocolate was called *tlaquetzalli* ("precious thing"), and was prepared by the seller in this way:

> She grinds cacao [beans]; she crushes, breaks, pulverizes them. She chooses, selects, separates them. She drenches, soaks, steeps them. She adds water sparingly, conservatively; aerates it, filters it, strains it, pours it back and forth, aerates it; she makes it form a head, makes foam; she removes the head, makes it thicken, makes it dry, pours water in, stirs water into it.[23]

The inferior product, the informants tell us, was mixed with *nixta-malli* and water—in other words, a chocolate-with-maize gruel drink. On the bad stuff, they go on to say, the bubbles on the froth burst. Yet many must have taken it this way, or as *pinolli* (pinole), for Fray Toribio Motolinia, whose account of the Aztecs is even earlier than Sahagún's, says: "Cacao is a very common drink. When ground and mixed with corn and other seeds, which are also ground, it serves well as a beverage and is consumed in this form. In some sections they prepare it well. It is good and they consider it a nutritious beverage".[24]

There is no mention in these primary sources of the grooved wooden beater or swizzle stick (Spanish *molinillo*) for the production of the much-prized foam, nor does any word for it appear in the first Nahuatl-Spanish dictionary, that of Alonso de Molina, published in Mexico City in 1571. This item, so important later on

Europeanized but accurate watercolor of a high-ranking Aztec woman pouring chocolate to raise foam, from the late 16th-century Codex Tudela.

in chocolate preparation in America and Europe, must have been introduced from Spain during the 16th century. By the time the Jesuit Francesco Saverio Clavigero published his detailed report on native Mexican life and history (in 1780, in Italian), he describes the use of the *molinillo*, but totally omits the pouring from one vessel to another to produce a good head on the drink.[25] Yet during the pre-Conquest past, this was the exclusive method, all over Mesoamerica. In the 16th-century Codex Tudela, there is a lovely drawing in European style, showing an Aztec woman doing just this, a scene which recalls the palace tableau of the Princeton Vase, painted some eight centuries earlier in the Maya lowlands.

There is, however, ample mention of stirrers or stirring spoons. These were fashioned from tortoise or sea-turtle shell. Some of these survived the Conquest, for among the confiscated goods of two Aztec sorcerers arrested by the early Spanish Inquisition were many of these stirrers, along with cacao and the cups from which chocolate was drunk. Which brings us to the cups themselves. A reading of our sources indicates that these were small, hemispherical bowls which could be of polychrome ceramic; calabash gourd (from the *Crescentia cujete* tree), painted or lacquered with designs; and even gold, in the case of the *huei tlatoani*.

Flavorings, Spices, and Other Additions

We have described in the previous chapter some of the myriad ways in which cacao was prepared among the Maya. The same variation existed among the Aztecs: there was not just one chocolate beverage, but many.[26] Our almost exclusive devotion to taking our chocolate "straight" is singularly unimaginative. Maize could be added, as well as the ground seed of the ceiba or silk-cotton tree (*Ceiba pentandra*), but apparently, before these "cacao-extenders" were put in, the foam was removed, then later replaced. However, these adulterated drinks were not in the *tlaquetzalli* class, the highest rating of the cacao drink, the kind served to the lords.

Universally popular throughout Mesoamerica was the addition to the drink of chilli (*Capsicum annum*), dried and ground to a powder. The Molina vocabulary calls the drink *chilcacahuatl*; of course, given the extraordinary array of chillis grown in Mexico, it could be anywhere from mildly pungent to extremely hot. We ourselves have prepared chocolate this way, and can assure our readers that it is very good indeed; in fact, chilli powder makes a very tasty component to chocolate ice cream, giving a pleasant "afterburn" to each spoonful.

Sahagún's native informants gave him a menu of chocolate drinks served to the ruler, which comes at the end of his chapter on the food of the lords (the *tlatoque*).[27] Before this, Sahagún gives a description of the maize breads, the soups, the casseroles of fish and meat, the fruit, the "seeds that they consider fruit" (which include corn on the cob and stringbeans), as well as tamales containing maize tassels and the pits of ground-hog plum (*Spondias* sp.) After that, we hear of the many people who were fed from the kitchen of the ruler, starting with the visiting nobility, through the guards, the priests, the singers, and the pages, and down to the feather-workers, the cutters of precious stones, the mosaic-workers, and the barbers who kept the ruler well-groomed. Only then do we get to the fine chocolate beverages: "Then, by himself in his house, his chocolate was served: green cacao-pods, honeyed chocolate, flowered chocolate, flavored with green vanilla, bright red chocolate, *huitztecolli-*flower chocolate, flower-colored chocolate, black chocolate, white chocolate".[28] We have no idea how the "green cacao-pods" were taken, but it may be that one merely ate the sweet pulp surrounding the seeds; Sahagún claims that these made one drunk, which could have been true if they had been fermented. In our culture, we insist on taking our chocolate sweet, so the notion of "honeyed" chocolate is welcome. We are not told what might have been in the colored chocolate, but achiote or annatto (*Bixa orellana*) is a likely guess for the red drink. The flowers and the vanilla would have been dried and ground, or pounded into a power, before being added to the chocolate.

Francisco Hernández gives us a chocolate recipe which he asserts excites the venereal appetite; the probably baseless claim that chocolate has aphrodisiac properties was one that was to arise again and again in Europe, and obviously also appeals to modern authors.[29] What is interesting about Hernández's recipe is that it contains three flavorings which we know were highly prized by the Aztecs. The first is *hueinacaztli*, the thick, ear-shaped petal of the flower of *Cymbopetalum penduliflorum*, a tree of the *Annonaceae* or custard-apple family, which grows in the tropical lowland forests of Veracruz, Oaxaca, and Chiapas; this was one of the most highly valued products brought back by the *pochteca* merchants from their expeditions. It is a confusing plant, because it has at least three Nahuatl names: it may be called *hueinacaztli* ("great ear"), *teonacaztli* ("divine ear"), or *xochinacaztli* ("flowery ear"). The distinguishing feature is the ending *nacaztli*, meaning "ear." A minority opinion considers this plant to be *Chiranthodendron pentadactylon*, but the Mexican botanist Maximino Martínez[30] is probably correct in identifying the latter as the Nahuatl *macpalxochitl* ("hand flower"), also a chocolate flavoring, named from the resemblance of the flower to a tiny hand.

Be that as it may, *Cymbopetalum penduliflorum* was the premier chocolate flavor among the Aztecs. When a *pochteca* merchant had returned from his dusty and dangerous trading trip to the low country, and wished to celebrate by giving a feast for his colleagues, the first step in the preparations was to obtain cacao and *hueinacaztli*. These may well have been part of the merchandise in his caravan, for they are listed among the most treasured things of the Aztecs, up there with the glistening tropical bird feathers, the jade and jewels, and the gold and shell.

What did this flower taste like, once it had been turned into powder and added to the fine cacao? Sahagún as usual cautions against taking too much of it, warning that excess could lead to drunkenness. The American agronomist Wilson Popenoe said that it tasted like black pepper, with a hint of resinous bitterness;[31] and in many cases, when he wrote in the early part of this century, the Maya who were making *batido* (described in the last chapter) could replace the *hueinacaztli* called for in this beverage with black pepper. Other sources compare it variously with nutmeg, all spice, and cinnamon. Shall we just agree that it must have tasted spicy?

The second of Hernández's reputedly aphrodisiac trio was *tlilxochitl* ("black flower"), none other than our familiar vanilla (*Vanilla planifolia*). In contradiction to its Nahuatl name, the vanilla flower is actually greenish yellow; the plant is a climbing orchid, and it is the pod that is black. Vanilla was another spice of the tropical lowlands, and was extensively cultivated along the Gulf Coast, particularly by the Totonacs of Veracruz, where it is still grown commercially. There is not a hint that the Aztecs considered it to be an erotic stimulant, but they did put it into their chocolate.

The last in Hernández's trio of chocolate flavorings is *mecaxochitl* ("string flower"). This is a member of the genius *Piper*, probably *Piper sanctum*, and therefore actually related to black pepper. The flowers, said to be white by some and black by others, are tiny and packed on to an inflorescence. According to Hernández, "taken with *cacahuatl* [cacao] it gives an agreeable taste, is tonic, warms the stomach, perfumes the breath . . . combats poisons, [and] alleviates intestinal pains and colics." Martínez, on the other hand, denies that the flowers were used to flavor chocolate, despite the name, and assigns that function to the leaves and the pulp of the small fruit. The heart-shaped leaves of this plant, known today as *acuyo* in Veracruz, are used on the Gulf Coast to wrap and flavor foods, especially fish; having eaten such dishes many times, we can testify that they impart a pleasant, tarragon or anise-like taste to the food.

This by no means completes the inventory of Aztec chocolate flavorings. Two varieties of *Magnolia mexicana* could be added, although drying the flowers causes them to lose their fragrance while at the same time retaining their astringency. The flowers are shaped like a heart, hence the Nahuatl name *yolloxochitl* ("heart flower"). In this case, the medieval Doctrine of Signatures (the idea that like produces like) appears to be correct. The "heart flower" tree, like the rest of the *Magnolia* family and genus, contains alkaloids; if the seeds and flowers of *Magnolia mexicana* are cooked in water and administered to a patient, they are supposed to augment the pulse and regularize the heartbeat, but an overdose causes arrhythmia. Hernández, on the other hand, recommends dropping a petal of the beautiful *eloxochitl* (*Magnolia dealbata*) into our chocolate, but as usual Sahagún cautions that too much will "intoxicate, derange, [and] disturb."[32]

Izquixochitl ("popcorn flower") can be any one of several species of *Bourreria* in the borage family. It is a tall, fine-looking tree with a white flower that looks like a dog-rose, and has a rose scent and flavor (Francisco Ximénez, writing in 1615, remarks that it is fit to be "the pride of the garden of His Majesty the King"). Sahagún directs us to use it in chilled chocolate.[33]

There were still other things that the Aztecs added to their chocolate. Achiote, which could be used for flavor as well as color, and chillis have already been mentioned, and allspice (*Pimienta dioica*), a New World contribution to the spice shelf, was also used.

When Hernández gives us his recipe for what he claims is aphrodisiac chocolate, he appends to it a recipe approved of as being cooling, refreshing, sweet, and fattening, and having no untoward side-effects. One took equal parts of roasted cacao beans, and the heart of the seed of the sapote (*Pouteria sapota*), ground them both, and added some ground maize, mixing and beating in the approved Mesoamerican manner. This, Hernández specifies, is what is called *chocolatl*—an intriguing piece of evidence in the convoluted puzzle of this word's origin (see Chapter Four). The large sapote seed, which comes in a shiny, brown, hard shell within the creamy, orange-red flesh of the fruit, contributes a taste which is merely bitter to some, and like bitter almonds to others. This *chocolatl* could then be elaborated with any one of the three principal spices, or with honey. The last step in its preparation was to beat it until a foamy head was formed; given that the technique of pouring to produce the foam is not mentioned, the recipe and its name may well not be pre-Conquest in origin (certainly the name was not, as we shall see).

In summary, given all of the foregoing information, we should be convinced that the Aztecs rang many more changes on the chocolate theme than do we, who are so indissolubly tied to drinks that are sweet. The mere idea of chocolate without sugar seems incomprehensible to most of us.

The Drink of the Elite

In our more-or-less democratic society, chocolate is something that is taken in liquid or solid form by members of every social level (although the most expensive, finest-quality chocolates are necessarily consumed only by those with well-lined pockets). Not so among the Aztecs and other Mesoamericans: our sources unanimously declare that the drinking of chocolate was confined to the Aztec elite—to the royal house, to the lords and nobility, to the long-distance merchants, and to the warriors. The only commoners who had a chance to try this luxury seem to have been soldiers on the march. Priests are not mentioned as consumers, and almost surely they were not, for they were expected to lead lives of high austerity and penance. We ourselves would perhaps be shocked to learn that our ministers or priests regularly took champagne with their dinners.

One other point should be mentioned. At banquets and at the more ordinary meals of the elite, chocolate was never sipped or drunk during the repast—it was served at its end, along with smoking tubes of tobacco, just as the port, brandy, and cigars appear only at the close of a very formal dinner in Western society. It was an ambrosia from the rich and exotic lands of Anahuac, not something to wash down one's food.

The most famous eye-witness account of an Aztec banquet must surely be that of the emperor himself, Motecuhzoma Xocoyotzin, in the lively, if slightly inaccurate at times, memoirs of the conquistador Bernal Díaz del Castillo. The Emperor's meal was a colossal event, with over 300 dishes prepared especially for him; but most of this food was passed to the staff of the royal household, since he ate frugally. In Bernal Díaz's version, the ruler's chocolate was served intermittently, rather than as the meal's finale—but it should be kept in mind that these are the recollections of an old man in his eighties, written down while he was in retirement in Guatemala. At any rate, here is what Bernal Díaz has to say:

> . . . and from time to time they brought him some cups of fine gold, with a certain drink made of cacao, which they said was for success with women; and then we thought no more about it; but I saw that they brought more than 50 great jars of prepared good cacao with its foam, and he drank of that; and that the women served him drink very respectfully . . . .[34]

The caution with which this testimony should be received is highlighted by the dubious statement about the aphrodisiacal

In this detail from the Codex Nuttall, a Mixtec book from Oaxaca, Mexico, the great Mixtec King 8 Deer receives a pot of frothy chocolate from his bride Princess 13 Serpent, in the year AD 1051. Chocolate was always present in Mesoamerican wedding ceremonies.

property of Motecuhzoma's cacao. While the *huei tlatoani*, like other Mesoamerican rulers, had a large harem, the idea that he needed sexual stimulants has no factual basis. This was a Spanish obsession, as was the chronic constipation with which the invaders were afflicted, through a diet which was almost all meat and lard, with few if any fruits and vegetables. The conquistadores searched for native Mexican laxatives as avidly as they did for aphrodisiacs.

Fray Bartolomé de las Casas was among the first Dominicans in the Americas, and reviled by his compatriots for his sympathy for the Indians and for his fierce denunciations of the injustices which had been visited upon them by the Spaniards. Probably relying on information from a conquistador less removed in time from the events than was Bernal Díaz, his account of "the emperor's banquet" is more detailed and convincing. The cups for drinking chocolate were not golden, as claimed by Díaz, but of calabash, and were painted inside and out; Las Casas states that "any lord would drink out of them as if they were gold and silver." Such cups, called *xicalli* in Nahuatl, were the usual vessels for quaffing chocolate throughout Mesoamerica. Las Casas than goes on to say, "The drink is water mixed with a certain flour made of some nuts called cacao. It is very substantial, very cooling, tasty, and agreeable, and does not intoxicate."[35]

The banquets held by the *pochteca*—the long-distance traders—regularly included large amounts of the chocolate drink. There were twelve *pochteca* guilds in the heart of the Empire; membership in them was hereditary, and each had its own head-quarters and warehouses. An aspiring merchant could rise in rank within his guild, but this was a very expensive business: to climb up the socio-economic ladder, an individual was obliged to host a large and expensive banquet for his fellow merchants at each rung of the ladder. These were increasingly costly as one rose higher, with vast expenditures of food, cacao drink, slaves bought for sacrifice, and even hallucinogenic mushrooms (with which the guests could foretell their fate in this very risky profession). Sahagún goes into great detail on what kinds of food were served at these affairs, and how, as usual, the coda to these mighty meals was chocolate:

> And then they ended with the chocolate [*cacahuatl*, as always in Sahagún's original]. To carry it one placed the cup in this right hand. He did not go taking it by its rims, but likewise went placing the gourd in the palm of his hand. And the stirring stick and gourd rest he went bearing there in his left hand.
> These were to pay honor to the lords. But those who followed, all [were served with] only earthen cups.[36]

This glimpse of chocolate etiquette among the *pochteca* tells us that the fine gourd and calabash cups were for the higher echelons of the organization, while lesser mortals drank theirs from clay cups.

The warriors, the backbone of the Aztec state, were another group permitted chocolate. Cacao, in fact, was a regular part of military rations. Durán informs us that ground cacao was made into pellets or wafers and issued to every soldier on a campaign, along with toasted maize, maize ground into flour, toasted tortillas, ground beans, and bunches of dried chillis.[37] The Elder Motecuhzoma—Motecuhzoma Ilhuicamina—had laid down in the sumptuary laws that he who does not go to war, be he the son of a king, may not wear cotton, feathers, or flowers, nor may he smoke, or drink cacao, or eat rare viands. So how was it that the *pochteca* could do all these things? Because they, too, were considered warriors: they were often armed, they traveled through very dangerous lands to reach their markets, and often fought pitched battles with hostile foreign groups.

"Happie Money"

"When Money Grew on Trees" is the wonderful title of René Millon's pioneering Ph.D. thesis on cacao in Mesoamerica. The Spaniards first learned that cacao beans were "coin of the realm" as well as the source of food and drink from the Maya of Yucatán. It was not long before Cortés and his henchmen found out that the beans could be used to buy things, and to pay the wages of their native laborers, such as the all-important porters. This information came to the ears of the ever-curious Milanese chronicler Peter Martyr (Pietro Martire D'Anghiera, who coined the phrase "the New World"); a wonderful passage on the subject appears in his *De Orbe Novo*, and here it is, as it was published in 1612 in English translation:

> But it is very needfull to heare what happie money they use, for they have money, which I call happy, because for the greedie desire and

gaping to attaine the same, the bowelles of the earth are not rent a sunder, nor through the ravening greediness of covetous men, nor terrour of warres assayling, it returneth to the dennes and caves of the mother earth, as golden, or silver money doth. For this groweth upon trees.[38]

Sadly, there are very few data on the value of cacao currency in pre-Conquest times, but throughout the Colonial era there is extensive documentary information, since many market and wage transactions continued to be conducted with cacao beans. We also know about rates of exchange between cacao and the gold and silver coinage of the Spanish Crown—but of course these fluctuated with the availability of cacao, and with changes in the value of metallic currency.

We have already seen in the last chapter what Oviedo had to say about the purchasing power of cacao beans in Nicaragua, shortly after the Conquest. Motolinia tells us that in his day (not long after the fall of Tenochtitlan), the daily wage of a porter in central Mexico was 100 beans, which puts into perspective the following partial list of commodity prices in Tlaxcala, in a Nahuatl document in 1545:

- One good turkey hen is worth 100 full cacao beans, or 120 shrunken cacao beans.
- A turkey cock is worth 200 cacao beans.
- A hare [jackrabbit] or forest rabbit is worth 100 cacao beans each.
- A small rabbit is worth 30.
- One turkey egg is worth 3 cacao beans.
- An avocado newly picked is worth 3 cacao beans; when an avocado is fully ripe it will be equivalent to one cacao bean.
- One large tomato will be equivalent to a cacao bean.
- A large sapote fruit, or two small ones, is equivalent to a cacao bean.

- A large *axolotl* [larval salamander, an Aztec delicacy] is worth 4 cacao beans, a small one is worth 2 or 3 cacao beans.
- A tamale is exchanged for a cacao bean.
- Fish wrapped in maize husks is worth 3 cacao beans.[39]

Any time coinage achieves any sort of value, clever individuals are going to start practicing deception, and the Aztecs were no exception. The counterfeiting of cacao beans is thus described by Sahagún's informants:

The bad cacao seller, [the bad] cacao dealer, the deluder counterfeits cacao. He sells cacao beans which are placed in [hot] ashes, toasted, made full in the fire; he counterfeits by making fresh cacao beans whitish; he places them in [hot] ashes—stirs them into [hot] ashes; then he treats them with chalk, with chalky earth, with [wet] earth; he stirs them into [wet] earth. [With] amaranth dough, wax, avocado pits [broken into pieces which are then shaped like cacao beans] he counterfeits cacao; he covers this over with cacao bean hulls; he places this in the cacao bean shells. The whitish, the fresh cacao beans he intermixes, mingles, throws in, introduces, ruins with the shrunken, the chilli-seed-like, the broken, the hollow, the tiny. Indeed he casts, he throws in with them wild cacao [*Theobroma bicolor*] beans to deceive the people.[40]

So adept were the Aztecs at this practice, that their talents began to shift to the gold and silver coins of the invaders, to the consternation of the first Spanish viceroy of New Spain, Antonio de Mendoza, who wrote to his sovereign in 1537 of his inability to put a stop to this deception.

Yet each time an Aztec took a drink of chocolate from the brightly painted gourd cups in which it was served, he was, so to speak, drinking real money; the only equivalent to this in our own culture would be to light one's cigar with a twenty-dollar bill. Small wonder that its consumption was the prerogative of the elite.

Page from the Codex Féjérváry-Mayer, a pre-Columbian book from an unknown region of the Aztec Empire. It depicts the four quarters of the universe, four world-trees, and nine gods, along with the sacred calendar. The cacao tree of the south can be seen on the right.

Cacao in Symbol and Ritual

Cacao had not only economic and gastronomic value among the Aztecs, but deep symbolic meaning as well. Open the pre-Conquest ritual book known as the Codex Féjérváry-Mayer and you will see. On one of the screenfold pages of this book—painted somewhere within the confines of the empire during the Late Post-Classic— the cacao tree appears as part of a cosmic diagram (a mandala, if you wish) laid out to the four directions and to the center. It is the Tree of the South, the direction of the Land of the Dead, associated with the color red, the color of blood. At the top of the tree is a macaw bird, the symbol of the hot lands from which cacao came;

while to one side of the tree stands Mictlantecuhtli, the Lord of the Land of the Dead.

The intelligentsia—the priests, poets, and philosophers—liked to speak in metaphors composed of two words or phrases which, when uttered in sequence, had a third, hidden meaning. One of these metaphors was *yollotl, eztli,* "heart, blood," an esoteric figure of speech for chocolate. Sahagún's informants (who definitely belonged to the intelligentsia) enlarged upon the theme thus:

> This saying was said of cacao, because it was precious; nowhere did it appear in times past. The common folk, the needy did not drink it. Hence it was said: "The heart, the blood are to be feared." And also it was said of it that it was [like] jimson weed [*Datura* sp., a powerful hallucinogen]; it was considered to be like the mushroom, for it made one drunk; it intoxicated one. If he who drank it were a common person, it was taken as a bad omen. And in past times only the ruler drank it, or a great warrior, or a commanding general, a general. If perhaps two or three lived in wealth [i.e. the merchants], they drank it. Also it was hard to come by, they drank a limited amount of cacao, for it was not drunk unthinkingly.[41]

This passage has puzzled scholars, since there is no evidence that chocolate, apart from the stimulating effects of theobromine and caffeine, has any mind-altering or inebriating properties whatsoever. Quite possibly these admonishments were part of the puritanical view of the Aztecs about this exotic drink, told for the purpose of underlining the sumptuary laws regulating its consumption.

Moreover, the cacao pod was a symbolic term, used in ritual, for the human heart torn out in sacrifice. Eric Thompson, who wrote a vanguard study of cacao among the Maya and Aztecs, suggested that this might have arisen because of the vague resemblance in shape between the two objects, but that a more likely explanation would be that "both were the repositories of precious liquids—blood and chocolate."

In one spectacular ritual that took place annually in Tenochtitlan, cacao was directly associated with heart extraction. Once a year, a slave perfect in body was chosen to impersonate the great god Quetzalcoatl. For 40 days he went around dressed in the raiment and jewels of the god, during which time he was treated as the god himself (however, he was locked in a cage at night lest he escape!) Then, on the eve of his sacrifice, he was warned by the temple elders that he was to die, after which he had to perform a dance, which had to be carried out as though he were completely happy about his fate. And if he were not? Diego de Durán describes the macabre remedy:

> . . . and if they saw that he became melancholy, that he stopped dancing joyously, with the happiness that he had shown, and with the gaiety they desired, they prepared a heathen, a loathsome spell for him: they went immediately to procure sacrificial knives, washed off the human blood adhering to them (the result of past sacrifices), and with that filthy water prepared a gourd of chocolate, giving it to him to drink. It is said that the draught had this effect upon him: he became almost unconscious and forgot what he had been told. Then he returned to his usual cheerfulness and dance. . . . It is believed that he offered himself for death with great joy and gladness, bewitched by the beverage. This drink was called *itzpacalatl*, which means "water from the washing of obsidian blades." They gave him this beverage because if a man became sorrowful owing to the warning it was held as an evil omen or sign prognosticating some future disaster.[42]

As Juan de Torquemada later commented, the *itzpacalatl* left him "blazing with spirit and courage."[43] This sanguinary symbolic meaning for chocolate might have spilled over into the military sphere, accounting for its inclusion in war rations for the army (a sort of precursor of "Dutch courage," although there is no proof for this). Be that as it may, chocolate was served at the installation ceremony for a new Eagle Knight or Jaguar Knight, who had undergone penances as long and severe as that suffered by any knightly hero in a Wagnerian opera. Being symbolically blood, it was the right and true potion for Aztec warriors.

But there was a further layer of symbolic reference to cacao and chocolate. Aztec royalty and nobility were devoted to music, song, dance, and poetry. Great poems—and many have survived from Aztec times—were recited to the sound of drumbeats in palace courtyards; and some of the finest are by Nezahualcoyotl, the poet-king of Texcoco. While many of these poems express a deep pessimism and an aching awareness of the transitoriness of life, many celebrate life's pleasures. In the latter, chocolate—especially *xochicacahuatl*, "flowered chocolate"—was a metaphor for luxuriousness and sensuality; yet even in these poems it was made painfully clear that we all must perish from this earth. We shall end our exploration of the Aztec world with a song by Nezahualcoyotl himself:

> My friends, stand up!
> The princes have become destitute,
> I am Nezahualcoyotl,
> I am a singer,
> head of macaw.
> Grasp your flowers and your fan.
> With them go out to dance!
> You are my child,
> you are Yoyontzin.
> Take your chocolate,
> flower of the cacao tree,
> may you drink all of it!
> Do the dance,
> do the song!
> Not here in our house,
> we do not live here,
> you also will have to go away.[44]

A late 15th-century Spanish caravel, from a contemporary woodcut illustrating
Columbus's First Voyage.

CHAPTER FOUR

èa

Encounter and Transformation

It was thanks to Christopher Columbus that Europeans first set eyes on the seed of the chocolate tree. Exonerated by the *Reyes Católicos* (the "Catholic Monarchs," Ferdinand and Isabella) from the unjust charges and imprisonment with which his third great voyage had ignominiously ended, the Admiral of the Ocean Sea was determined to make one more exploratory trip to the New World which he had "discovered." This time his goal was to find a strait which might lead westwards to that part of Asia already reached and exploited by Spain's principal competitor, Portugal.

Few ships that ever sailed the seven seas could have looked more ungainly than the three-masted caravels used by the Spaniards and the Portuguese on their astonishing voyages of exploration. With their huge rudders, towering poops and even higher forecastles, they looked more like houses than boats; in fact, the first caravel to be spotted off the shores of Motecuhzoma's realm was reported by his spies to be "a house that moved on the water." In their general tubbiness, they resembled the Chinese sea-going junks that Marco Polo had so admired. Yet few more seaworthy vessels have ever been designed than the caravel and the junk.

First Encounter: Guanaja, 1502

Columbus set sail on his fourth voyage on 9 May 1502, with four caravels and 150 men. Forbidden by Hispaniola's Spanish colonists to land on that island, he nevertheless weathered a hurricane in which those selfsame rivals went down with their ships (for which the pious admiral gave thanks to God). He next headed for Jamaica but, missing it, he continued on a WSW course across the reef-strewn open sea. At last he made land at the island of Guanaja, some 30 miles (50 kms) north of the Honduran mainland, in what are now known as the Bay Islands. There they anchored; in the limpid, transparent waters that surround the island, the caravels must have seemed as though floating on blue-green air.

Until now, the Spaniards had encountered in their "New World" only scantily-clad subjects of small chiefdoms—in the simplicity of their culture, these bore little resemblance to the civilized subjects of the mighty Khan of the Cathay which Columbus was so intent on reaching.

On the fateful day of 15 August 1502, these latter-day Argonauts came across something very different. The admiral had sent a reconnaissance party ashore at Guanaja, where they found people like those of other islands, but with "narrower foreheads" (whatever that might signify). What happened next is to be found in the account penned in Jamaica in 1503 by Columbus's second son Ferdinand . This work was eventually translated into Italian and finally reached print in Venice in 1571, by which time it had become somewhat corrupted by later material (for example, a statement that cacao beans were used for money in "New Spain," a fact which could only have been known by the year 1518).[1] Nonetheless, this is the only text we have regarding these events, the Spanish original having been lost.

Here is what transpired on that day. There suddenly appeared a tremendous dugout canoe, said by Ferdinand to have been as long as a galley; the standard Venetian galley of the period being between 141 to 164 feet long (40 to 50 m).[2] Even if its size was exaggerated, it must have indeed been an impressive vessel. The chronicler Peter Martyr tells us that there were not one but two such canoes, each rowed by slaves with ropes around their necks, and that they came from a land called *Maiam*, almost surely the

Maya lands of the Yucatán Peninsula.[3] As for the canoe described by Ferdinand Columbus, amidships it had a shelter fashioned of palm leaves, "not unlike those of Venetian gondolas," under which were placed the children, the women, and the cargo. The admiral immediately ordered its capture, which was effected without resistance. By this adroit move, he gained an excellent idea "of all the goods of that country without exertion or exposing his men to any danger."

The vessel he had captured was a great Maya trading canoe, most likely belonging to the Chontal-Maya-speaking Putún; its cargo consisted of fine cotton garments, flat war clubs set with razor-like stone blades along the edges (the formidable *macuauhuitl* of Aztec warriors), and small axes and bells of cast copper. Ferdinand goes on to say:

> For their provisions they had such roots and grains as are eaten in Hispaniola [these would have been maize and manioc], and a sort of wine made out of maize which resembled English beer; and many of those almonds which in New Spain [Mexico] are used for money. They seemed to hold these almonds at a great price; for when they were brought on board ship together with their goods, I observed that when any of these almonds fell, they all stooped to pick it up, as if an eye had fallen.[4]

Lacking an interpreter, the admiral had no way of knowing that these "almonds" were used to manufacture the New World's most esteemed beverage, nor could he have realized cacao's use as money, but he must surely have been impressed with the high value put on these strange seeds.

Columbus never tasted chocolate, nor did he ever again encounter those civilized people of whom he had dreamed. Instead, he turned his little fleet in the wrong direction, towards the southeast and to what is now western Panama, where he did at last find some of the gold which he had so coveted. Four years later he died in Spain. The discovery of the fabulous wealth of the Indies was to be made by others.

Crossing the Taste Barrier

From the initial invasion of Yucatán, beginning in 1517, and of Mexico in 1519, it took the Spaniards little time to grasp and take advantage of the monetary value of cacao beans in the native economy: witness the shameless plundering of Motecuhzoma's warehouse, described in the last chapter. This was "happie money" that retained its function as small currency through virtually all of the Colonial period.

But although they appreciated cacao as money, the conquistadores and those who followed them into the newly conquered

lands of Mesoamerica were at first baffled and often repelled by the stuff in the form of drink. While the open-minded Italian Peter Martyr on the other side of the Atlantic could sing the virtues of chocolate as a drink worthy of kings, lords, and nobles, it is highly doubtful that he ever tried it. His compatriot Girolamo Benzoni, who was in the New World, certainly did, and his reaction to the strange, murky, sinister-looking beverage was probably typical of Europeans encountering it for the first time. In his *History of the New World*, published in 1575, Benzoni comments sourly:

The Milanese historian and voyager Girolamo Benzoni (1518–70), one of the first Europeans to describe cacao and the chocolate drink.

108

Woodcut from Benzoni's 1565 La Historia del Mondo
Nuovo, *depicting a cacao tree and cacao beans spread out to
dry; the artist has naively shown the pods growing from
the tips of the branches, instead of the trunk.*

It [chocolate] seemed more a drink for pigs, than a drink for
humanity. I was in this country for more than a year, and never
wanted to taste it, and whenever I passed a settlement, some
Indian would offer me a drink of it, and would be amazed when I
would not accept, going away laughing. But then, as there was a
shortage of wine, so as not to be always drinking water, I did like
the others. The taste is somewhat bitter, it satisfies and refreshes
the body, but does not inebriate, and it is the best and most expensive merchandise, according to the Indians of that country.[5]

Gonzalo Fernández de Oviedo, an enemy of Bartolomé de las Casas
and one who despised the natives of the New World, had run across
chocolate during the Spanish conquest of Nicaragua, and, not
surprisingly, found it obnoxious: when the drink was quaffed with
its usual lacing of achiote, it turned the Indians' mouths, lips, and

whiskers red, as though they had been drinking blood.[6] Fernández de Oviedo had better things to say about cacao's by-product, cacao butter. In this account, he meets an Italian friend who fries up a mess of eggs in this substance for his troops, converting cacao to a use utterly foreign to the fat-free native cuisine. For Fernández de Oviedo, the butter also had medicinal virtues, for, on cutting his foot on a rock, he cured the wound by covering it with bandages soaked in the oil.

Yet the Spanish aversion to the chocolate drink was eventually to change. How did this come about? Initially, the invaders would have little to do with the foodstuffs which they found in 'New Spain', unless there was no alternative. Maize-based bread in the form of tortillas and tamales had no attraction for them; nor did the wide variety of vegetables and pot herbs, for the traditional Iberian cuisine was heavily weighted toward meat and starch, as it is today, with an emphasis on frying with lard and olive oil. In contrast, the Mesoamerican housewife never cooked with oils and fats. To make matters worse, cheese was totally absent from the native table (in fact, they didn't even *have* tables).

Soon after the Conquest, the new settlers went about remedying this deplorable situation, importing beef cattle, milk cows, sheep, goats, pigs, and chickens, and forcing their native laborers— treated little better than slaves—to plant wheat, chickpeas, and Old World fruit trees like peaches and oranges. Cane sugar was also a novelty to Mesoamerica, and was grown on a vast scale on the private estates of the Marqués del Valle (as Cortés was by now styled). Although sweetenings in the form of honey, agave syrup, and other substances existed in the native diet, the Maya and the Aztecs had nothing approaching the European sweet tooth induced by the medieval introduction of sugar into the western part of the Old World. The Spaniards craved it.

In time, though, a kind of hybridization or creolization between the two cultures began to take place, as the Spaniards, for instance, found themselves consuming less wheat and more maize, or absorbing Nahuatl words for local plants and animals into their own language. Likewise, the abused and long-suffering Indians willingly adopted their oppressors' domestic animals and fruit trees into their way of life (while rejecting the Iberian wheat and chickpeas). The poorer Spaniards perforce married native women, while the richer ones took them as concubines; thus in many a "Spanish" kitchen of early Colonial Mexico, the housewife was an Aztec. And it was not long before an entire generation of Spanish Creoles was to be born in the old Aztec realm, never to set foot in the old country from which their parents had come. Thus, an entirely new, creolized culture was taking form that partook of elements from both cultures, but was different from both. This was the context in which chocolate was taken into the Colonial cuisine of New Spain, and was eventually transplanted to Old Spain and the rest of Europe.

Imaginary scene purporting to show Aztecs making chocolate, from John Ogilby's
America, *of 1671. The artist has misunderstood the use of the* metate, *and
has mistakenly included the post-Conquest* molinillo.

It may not have been just the Aztec women in the back kitchens who were responsible for the adoption of the chocolate drink by the invaders—Spanish women may also have been agents of change, becoming "chocoholics" before their menfolk, if we examine an episode recounted by Bernal Díaz.[7] In 1538, a huge banquet was staged in the Great Plaza of Mexico City (newly built over the ruins of the Aztec capital); this was to celebrate the signing of a peace treaty between those two arch-enemies, Charles V of the Holy Roman Empire and Francis I of France. In sheer ostentation, expense, and gaudy display of valuables, it was one of the most lavish examples of "conspicuous consumption" the New World has ever witnessed. Among other vulgar extravagances, there were actually fountains of wine. Allowed to gaze on the all-male revelers from windows and corridors, the Spanish ladies were chivalrously regaled with sweetmeats and other costly viands, along with wine. But they were also served chocolate in golden goblets. Was this a taste that they, and not their husbands, had picked up from their female servants?

That the Spanish appetite for chocolate may have been at first biased towards the distaff side is confirmed by somewhat jaundiced remarks made by the Jesuit José de Acosta in his *Natural and Moral History*, published in 1590:

> The main benefit of this cacao is a beverage which they make called Chocolate, which is a crazy thing valued in that country. It disgusts those who are not used to it, for it has a foam on top, or a scum-like bubbling. . . . It is a valued drink which the Indians offer to the lords who come or pass through their land. And the Spanish men—and even more the Spanish women—are addicted to the black chocolate.[8]

To cross the ethnocentric taste barrier and be accepted as a normal beverage by the Spanish-born and the Creoles, the cold, bitter, usually unsweetened drink had to undergo its own process of

Through fermentation and drying, the cacao pod's pulp-surrounded seeds are converted into nibs ready for roasting and grinding into chocolate liquor.

The Maya god of merchants approaches a fantastic cacao tree, on a mural from Cacaxtla, in central Mexico, far from the Maya area (right). Terminal Classic period, c.AD 800–900.

Detail of a palace scene on a Late Classic Maya vase (below). The ruler gestures towards a pot of foaming chocolate; below the throne is a dish heaped with sauce-covered tamales.

hybridization. The first transmutation was that the whites insisted on taking chocolate hot rather than cold or at room temperature, as had been the custom among the Aztecs. We shall see that this custom may have been adopted from the usage of the Yucatec Maya, from whom they first learned of chocolate as a drink. Secondly, it came to be regularly sweetened with cane sugar. Thirdly, Old World spices more familiar to the invaders, such as cinnamon, anise seed, and black pepper, began to be substituted for native flavorings like "ear flower" and chilli pepper (this never could have been too popular with the invaders, anyway). And finally, while certain modes of preparation remained the same as before, such as grinding the shelled cacao beans on a heated *metate* (curved grinding-stone), the froth was now obtained by beating the hot chocolate with a large, wooden swizzle-stick called a *molinillo* (about which, more below), instead of pouring the liquid from a height, from one vessel into another.

One further innovation deserves mention, for it was important to the transmission of chocolate drinking to Spain and its dissemination throughout Europe and the British Isles. This was the manufacture of the finished beverage from a wafer or tablet of ground cacao to which hot water and sugar could be added. Although one source ascribes this invention to Guatemalan nuns, we have already seen that Aztec warriors were issued such wafers to be turned into a kind of "instant chocolate" which was drunk during military campaigns. The Spaniards merely seized on these wafers as a convenient way to store and ship the cacao liquor as a dried product.

Crossing the Language Barrier

The military adventurers who brought down the Aztec Empire may have been able to deal with the formidable Aztec military machine, but they were helpless before the phonetic complexities of the

Nahuatl language spoken by their adversaries. The Spaniards consistently refused to stress Nahuatl words on the next-to-last syllable, as all Nahuatl words required, and they could not— or would not—properly pronounce the sound *tl*, which so often ends Nahuatl words as a noun marker, making it sound like *te* (or *tay*, the way English speakers would write it). Cortés had a "tin ear" for the niceties of Nahuatl, on the evidence of his *Letters* to Charles V: he wrote the name of the capital as "Temistitan" instead of Tenochtitlan, and the tribal god Huitzilopochtli as "Uichilobos". He probably did not care what such barbarians called them.

But the new settlers from the Iberian peninsula had to deal on a day-to-day basis with these people following the Conquest, whether constructing a new capital on the rubble that was once Tenochtitlan, or forcing tribute from unwilling vassals, or harnessing native labor on the newly founded cattle ranches and plantations that were usurping traditional lands everywhere in "New Spain." This was truly frontier country, and as on any frontier a kind of hybrid way of life took form. Nahuatl words for plants, animals, and even for prepared dishes previously unknown to the Spaniards were adopted wholesale, after they had undergone linguistic transformation to fit Spanish mouths. Thus, the wild dog *coyotl* became the *coyote*; an ear of corn, *elotl*, turned into an *elote*; *xicalli*, the gourd drinking bowl, was hybridized into the *jícara*; and so on.

Chocolate and its appurtenances for preparation and consumption went through the same process of linguistic hybridization, matching the "creolization" of the drink itself. The Spanish (and English) word *chocolate* is a case in point.[9] Our Merriam Webster

Dictionary, 1993 edition, in agreement with most books and articles on chocolate, simply states that this is derived from the Nahuatl word *chocolatl*. This seems logical given the mutation from *-tl* to *-te* endings for so many other nouns which have entered Mexican Spanish. But the real story is far more complex and ambiguous than this.

We must first of all tell you that *chocolatl* appears in no truly early source on the Nahuatl language or on Aztec culture! You can search in vain for it in the first Nahuatl-Spanish dictionary, that of Alonso de Molina (published as early as

Four wooden molinillos or chocolate-beaters (this page and opposite), from a 1687 French treatise of Nicolas de Blegny.

1555); or in Sahagún's great encyclopedia; or in the *Huehuetlatolli,* "The Sayings of the Ancients," preserved in several versions. In those pristine sources, the word for the chocolate drink is *cacahuatl*, "cacao water," a reasonable compound since the drink was made of ground cacao beans and water. Cortés himself always uses for the chocolate beverage the word *cacao*, which the Spaniards almost surely picked up from the Maya of Yucatán and Tabasco. But some time in the latter half of the 16th century, the Spaniards began using a new world, *chocolatl*. It is also used by the Royal Physician Francisco Hernández who, as we have seen, was carrying out his researches in Mexico during the decade of the 1570s.[10] According to him, this was a drink made up of equal parts of *cacahuatl* ("cacao beans," in this case) and ground *pochotl* (seeds of the ceiba tree), frothed up with a wooden *molinillo*. It was probably simultaneously that *chocolatl* was transformed into *chocolate*, by the white population, and employed by them for every kind of drink made from cacao; at any rate, this is what José de Acosta and his contemporaries called these beverages.

The noun *chocolate* had even spread beyond the confines of New Spain to the province of Yucatán, for it appears as a gloss to the native Yucatec Maya name for the drink in early Maya-Spanish dictionaries, such as the one now in Vienna's National Library. Yet it is clear that *chocolate* is what the Spaniards called it, not the natives.

Exactly what is the origin of this neologism? Here we enter the murky realm of supposition. The authoritative *Diccionario de la lengua española* of the Royal Spanish Academy claims that it derives from the Nahuatl *chocolatl* (thus agreeing with Merriam Webster), which, in turn, is based on *choco*, "cacao," and *latl*, "water." Mexican linguists rightly hold this etymology in derision, since neither of the latter exist in Nahuatl. A more informed school of thought would have it transformed from a hypothetical *xocoatl*, based on *xoco-*, the root for "bitter," and *atl*, "water." This is possible, but unlikely, since there is no strong justification for altering the sound *x* (like English *sh*) to *ch*, and inserting an *l*.

Now let us recall that the invaders first became familiar with cacao and the chocolate drink in the Maya lowlands, and turn again to the Vienna and other very early Maya vocabularies: there "the drink called *chocolate*" is glossed *chacau haa*, literally "hot water," with the implication that these people drank theirs hot, not cold. Another word for "hot" in Yucatec is *chocol*, so that an alternative way of saying the same thing would be *chocol haa*. We are now getting very close to *chocolatl*.

Then there is a possible derivation of *chocolate* from the Quiché Maya verb *chokola'j*, which, as we have seen in Chapter Three, means "to drink chocolate together." This is a clue which needs further research.

It was the distinguished Mexican philologist Ignacio Dávila Garibí who first proposed that the Spaniards had coined the new word by taking the Maya word *chocol* and then replacing the Maya term for "water," *haa*, with the Aztec one, *atl*.[11] Thus we get first *chocolatl*, then *chocolate*. Miguel León-Portilla, the greatest living authority on Nahuatl, has told us that this is a reasonable explanation, and we agree. The vast majority of Iberians who had poured into Mesoamerica had settled in the old Aztec realm, not in the gold and silverless Yucatán, and they needed a new term that could be applied to a beverage that they had learned to drink hot and sweetened with cane sugar—not the cold, bitter, water-based *cacahuatl* of the native Aztecs. *Chocolatl* and *chocolate* suited them perfectly.

Be that as it may, there must have been an even more compelling reason for the sudden switch among its white users for *cacahuatl* to *chocolate*, and we think we know what it is. As we can see in this modern world of instant, global communication, words and word roots that are innocuous in one language often become exceedingly embarrassing when they are transferred into another cultural and linguistic setting. This can be seen in its most acute form in the case of certain Korean and Cantonese personal names which sound like four-letter words in English; often the bearers of such names are forced to adopt new spellings and even new pronunciations when moving into the international marketplace.

The *caca* of *cacahuatl* falls into this category. In most Romance languages, and in the Latin from which they descend, this is a vulgar or nursery word for feces, and is often compounded to make other words and even verbs describing defecation. Spanish is definitely one of these languages (we can even find the term *cacafuego*, "shitfire," in an early 18th-century Spanish-English dictionary). It is hard to believe that the Spaniards were not thoroughly uncomfortable with a noun beginning with *caca* to describe a thick, dark-brown drink which they had begun to appreciate. They desperately needed some other word, and we would not be at all surprised if it was the learned friars who came up with *chocolatl* and *chocolate*.

Yet there are always nagging doubts about hypothetical etymologies. For example, just to confuse matters even further, the modern residents of the Chontalpa—the rich, cacao-growing region of Tabasco—call themselves *Chocos*, and claim (perhaps through local chauvinism) that the word *chocolate* comes from this!

We have seen that the Creole Spaniards altered the indigenous method of producing foam on top of their chocolate by the introduction of the *molinillo* or rotary whisk, a vertically grooved stick spun back and forth between the hands. It is usually thought that this word is a straightforward Spanish diminutive meaning "little mill," derived from *molino*, "mill." But, like *chocolate*, the story is not so simple. As Dr León-Portilla has pointed out,[12] the twisting, back-and-forth motion is not that of a European mill at all, but something quite different, for which some other term was necessary. He has shown that *molinillo* is probably one more creolized Nahuatl noun, derived from the verb *molinia*, "to shake, waggle, or move"; its more immediate progenitor is likely to be *moliniani*, "something which moves or waggles."

As for the gourd cup out of which the native Aztecs and early Colonial Spaniards drank their foamy chocolate, this was originally *xicalli* in Nahuatl, but was soon creolized to *jícara*, a term that came

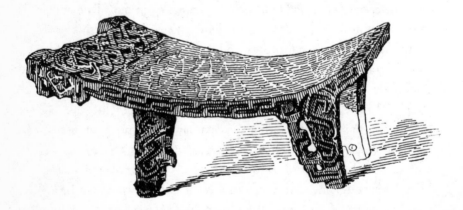

A pre-Conquest metate from southern Nicaragua, of a type that was probably used to grind cacao.

to be applied to pottery bowls or cups for quaffing chocolate throughout the New World and also in Spain (once the habit had become established there).

Crossing the Medical Barrier

Was chocolate good, bad, or indifferent for one's health? This was a vital topic for the Spaniards, who were at the mercy of a worthless and often destructive constellation of medical theories which had held the Western world in its grip for almost two millennia. Full acceptance of the exotic beverage held in such esteem by the defeated Mesoamericans meant fitting it into this fallacious scheme.

The basis of pre-modern European medical practice was the humoral theory of disease and nutrition, originated by the Classical Greeks, and not to be extinguished in the West until the advent of modern medicine and physiology in the first half of the 19th century. The invention of the theory is accredited to Hippocrates, who lived from 460 to 377 BC; he held that the body contains four humors—blood, phlegm, yellow bile, and black bile. The right proportion and mixture of these results in health, while disease is caused by an imbalance. This theory was taken up by Galen, a Greek born about AD 130, who expanded it by adding the notion that humors, diseases, and the drugs to cure disease could also be hot or cold, and moist or dry. Blood, for instance, is hot and moist, while phlegm is cold and moist.

Galen achieved great fame as a physician, and even doctored Roman emperors, including Marcus Aurelius and his dreadful son Commodus. His main principle was curing by contraries, so that a "hot" fever called for a "cold" drug. By extension, since nutrition was an integral part of his health regime, foods were forced into this rigid classification. Like two other towering figures from the Classical past, Aristotle and Ptolemy, Hippocrates and Galen were held in such awe by Europeans throughout the Dark Ages, medieval times, and even the Renaissance, that this scheme was never seriously challenged and was held to be dogma in the best medical schools. Other fanciful ideas adhered to it, such as the Doctrine of Signatures, which held that one must cure like with like: thus, if you want to cure an earache, seek out an herb, flower, or seed pod which resembles a human ear.

Add to this a large helping of magic, of belief in judicial astrology, and of downright quackery, such as the use of bezoar stones (calcoli found in the gastrointestinal tracts of animals), and you will appreciate that the medical knowledge brought by the Spaniards to the New World was largely ineffectual.

In contrast, while the Aztec *ticitl* or doctor used a good deal of magic in his or her cures, and while Aztec disease etiology also had an overall theoretical scheme made up of contrary principles (such as "hot" vs. "cold"), native medical practices were light years ahead of the Spaniards'. This was due in large part to their incredible knowledge of the plant world included within the empire's frontiers. They had, as the anthropologist (and chemist) Bernard Ortiz de Montellano has shown,[13] an excellent empirical understanding of the actions of hundreds of plants in effecting real cures; the emperor even had a botanic garden at Huaxtepec in Morelos, where many of these plants were grown and tested.

Word of this pharmacopeia reached the ears of Philip II, and that is why he sent his Royal Physician Francisco Hernández across the Atlantic in 1570. In his great work, described in the last chapter, Hernández classified the plants of Mexico as either "hot" or "cold," and "wet" or "dry" (please bear in mind that this has nothing to do with their actual temperature or humidity). Thanks to his slavish application of Galenic theory, it is almost impossible to find out how the Aztecs actually classified these same plants, or even how they used them in their own pharmacopeia: one has to get these data from other sources.

Cacao and chocolate naturally attracted Hernández's attention. The cacao seed is "temperate in nature," he says, but leaning to the "cold and humid"; on the whole, it is very nourishing (a virtue that would generate its own controversy in Europe, as we shall see in the next chapter). Because of its "cool" nature, drinks made from it are good in hot weather, and to cure fevers. Adding the *mecaxochitl* flavoring to chocolate not only gives it an agreeable taste, but because it, like most cacao spices, is "hot" by nature, it "warms the stomach, perfumes the breath . . . [and] combats poisons, alleviates intestinal pains and colics," and so on. However, composite chocolate drinks, as we have seen already, "excite the veneral appetite"— which must have made them even more attractive to the Spaniards.

As Ortiz de Montellano tells us,[14] the plants and plant derivatives that Hernández puts under the "hot" rubric are those with a strong odor or taste, or with a bitter flavor; while those with little odor or taste were "cold". How, then, did the strongly flavored and quite bitter chocolate become classified as "cold"? We suspect that it was because the Aztecs themselves held it to be "cold," and Hernández did not contradict them in this case (although he did in many others). According to Aztec belief, their other great drink, *octli* wine, was also "cold"; to the bewilderment of the Spaniards, the natives usually took it before undertaking hard labor, to avoid tiring the body by overheating it. But Aztec disease etiology bore little resemblance to the Galenic nonsense of the Europeans: for instance, fevers were not necessarily "hot," and were often cured not by administering "cold" medicines but by giving the patient "hot" medicines to induce sweating—excellent medical practice, as we now know.

Published in 1591, a treatise on New World foods by Juan de Cárdenas[15] takes Hernández's Galenic analysis of chocolate one step further (this treatise was later to be studied by European "experts"). After warning that "green" chocolate harms the digestion, and causes alarming symptoms like paroxysms, melancholy, and irregular heartbeats, Cárdenas goes on to assert that cacao, if toasted and ground and mixed with a bit of *atole* gruel, is fattening and sustaining, aiding the digestion and making one happy and strong. According to him, chocolate has three parts:

(1) A "cold", "dry", and "earthy" part.
(2) An oily part which is "warm and humid," and associated with air. There is more of this part in chocolate made from old cacao; oil is likewise increased with more toasting.
(3) A very "hot" part, with a bitter taste; this gives one headaches [perhaps not so far off the mark, as this is a symptom of caffeine, and possibly theobromine, withdrawal].

The native chocolate flavorings are all "hot"; he is high in praise of *hueinacaztli*, "ear flower," which comforts the liver, stimulates digestion, and extirpates windiness. Cárdenas's advice was that "hot" (overheated) persons should cool off by drinking chocolate with *atole* and sugar, or with honey and hot water.

Most of this was very welcome news to the Spaniards, who were as obsessed with health and diet as we are. During the course of the 16th century, cacao had been accommodated into the Spanish system as tribute, as coin, and as the first American foodstuff to have been accepted by the invaders for reasons of taste rather than necessity; but it had also passed the linguistic and health barriers. For full acceptance by Europe, it had one further barrier to surmount: the ecclesiastical. We shall look into this and other matters in the following chapter.

CHAPTER FIVE

᠊᠊

Chocolate Conquers Europe

I wait upon the Lieut Governour at Dorchester, and there meet
with Mr. Torry, breakfast together on Venison and Chockalatte;
I said Massachusetts and Mexico met at his Honour's Table.

The Diary of Samuel Sewall

Thus did Samuel Sewall, (a judge at the infamous Salem witch
trials of 1692 and by now heartily repentant of his role), write on
an autumn day of the year 1697.[1] How exactly did it come about
that "Massachusetts met Mexico"? What was the roundabout route
that took cacao from its point of origin in Mesoamerica across the
Atlantic to Spain; then throughout Europe as far as the British
Isles; and then back again across the ocean to Britain's American
colonies? Who took it, and when, and how? This is the tale that we
shall tell in this chapter, and the reader will see that it is one filled
with certainties as well as uncertainties, with well-established facts
as well as with conjecture (not always unfounded). We shall
make every effort to separate fact from fiction, but we may not be
entirely successful.

While cacao and chocolate had been "discovered" by
Europeans of the Renaissance, it was during the Baroque Age that
the beverage made its major journeys, and it was in Baroque palaces
and mansions of the wealthy and powerful that it was elaborated
and consumed. It had been an elite drink among the copper-
skinned, befeathered Mesoamericans, and it stayed that way among
the white-skinned, perfumed, bewigged, overdressed royalty and

nobility of Europe. This was the age of the Sun King, Louis XIV; of profligate and decadent Tuscan dukes; of enormous Counter-Reformation churches; of theatrical operas and churchly oratorios, produced by composers of genius like Lully and Couperin; of intriguing princes of the church such as Mazarin and Richelieu; of courtly banquets, receptions, and levees; of Charles II of England and the Restoration.

In this heady environment traveled the chocolate drink. We have learned that the Spaniards had stripped it of the spiritual meaning which it had for the Mesoamericans, and imbued it with qualities altogether absent among the Aztecs and Maya: for the invaders, it was a drug, a medicine, in the humoral system to which they all adhered. It is hardly surprising to find that it was under this guise that chocolate traveled in Europe, from one court to another, from noble house to noble house, from monastery to monastery. But it soon became a medicine that was appreciated for its taste, its filling nature, and its stimulation. Are we shocked to learn that a medicine or drug with supposedly curative powers was converted to recreational use? We should not be, since the same transformation has taken place a number of times in modern Europe and America. The most famous case is that of Coca-Cola, which began life as a patent medicine in the American southland—a sweet, carbonated drink with a hearty dose of caffeine from the cacao-related kola nut, and a measure of cocaine (gone from today's drink, but the seed pod of the coca shrub is memorialized in the traditional shape of the bottle). The list of such potions includes tonic or quinine water; bitters; and a host of after-dinner liqueurs and other alcoholic drinks (such as absinthe). Even coffee and tea, which arrived in extra-Peninsular Europe at about the same time as chocolate, were considered medicines and classified accordingly. In the end, whatever the ailments that initially caused people to take them as a cure, these potions engendered a craving for them.

Perhaps this is an opportune moment, before we immerse ourselves in the tangled early history of chocolate in Europe, to remind

A 16th-century German woodcut of the four temperaments—phlegmatic, sanguine, choleric, and melancholic—according to the humoral system devised by Hippocrates and Galen. These were related to the seasonal states of cold, moist, hot, and dry, and to the four elements and their zodiacal signs.

THE GALENIC HUMORAL SCHEME IN BAROQUE EUROPE					
Fluid [humor]	**Properties**	**Organ**	**Temperament**	**Time of day**	**Season**
Blood	Warm and moist	Liver	Sanguine	9 p.m.–3 a.m.	Spring
Yellow bile	Warm and dry	Gall bladder	Choleric	3 a.m.–9 a.m.	Summer
Black bile	Cold and dry	Spleen	Melancholic	9 a.m.–3 p.m.	Autumn
Phlegm	Cold and moist	Kidneys	Phlegmatic	3 a.m.–9 p.m.	Winter

ourselves of the European medical theory of the time, since so much of the Baroque Age commentary on chocolate is couched in these terms. It will be recalled that in Galen's theory and practice, the body contained four humors, and that good health depended on a balance between them. Each of these humors had specific properties—"hot" or "cold," and "dry" or "moist." Each humor was seated in an organ of the body, and that organ's function was to produce its humor. For example, before Harvey's discovery of the circulation of the blood, it was thought that blood was generated in the liver, and taken by the arteries to all parts of the body. We might well laugh at this Galenic notion, but we still talk of love being seated in the heart.

In the European Baroque Age, the humoral theory was extended to include all sorts of phenomena and conditions, such as the divisions of the day, the four seasons, and even the cardinal points. Shown on the previous page is just part of the scheme on which everyone relied, including even the Royal Physician of the mighty Sun King himself.

As we said in the last chapter, Galen's theory ruled in prescribing medicines and foods to be given the patient, so that if the disease was essentially a warm and dry one (that is, associated with too much yellow bile), a cold and moist medicine and/or food were prescribed. So over-elaborated and detailed did this useless system become that drugs, foods, spices, and so on, had their properties divided up into degrees; thus, according to one Dr. Piso,[2] in a tract published in Amsterdam in 1658, vanilla is "hot in the 3rd degree," and the *mecaxochitl* spice "hot in the 4th degree" and "dry in the 3rd degree." Those who had the nerve to add these to their chocolate had first to check the state of their own humors.

We can afford (at times) to chuckle over the naiveté of this theory and practice, but consider the medical horrors that were faced by our Baroque Age Europeans. No one had any real idea of disease etiology—what caused infections, epidemics, and plagues, why women often died of childbed fever, and so forth. Knowledge of anatomy and physiology was just beginning, but had little effect so far on medical practice. Surgery was carried out without anesthesia or antiseptics, necessarily at great speed, and if patients failed to succumb to loss of blood or from shock, at least half of them later fell victim to septecemia and gangrene. As we have said, European knowledge of plants which might have been efficacious in some diseases was pathetic compared to that of the New World natives whom they had fairly well destroyed by this time. In these circumstances, it was only natural that sick persons and those treating them would grasp at straws, in this case the much-flawed system of Hippocrates and Galen—and pray to the saints. The introduction and spread of chocolate in Europe can only be understood in this context.

Cacao in Spain: "Chocolate Brought to Perfection"

No one knows for sure exactly when cacao first reached Spain. Many books and articles have given credit for the introduction to Hernán Cortés, but there is absolutely no historical basis for this. The first opportunity which he *might* have had would have been in 1519, before he had even laid eyes on the Aztec capital, Tenochtitlan. From the headquarters which he had established on the coast of Veracruz, the future conqueror of Mexico dispatched a ship to Spain, laden with the Royal Fifth—the fifth part of the booty which he had thus far accumulated in Mesoamerica, which by law was

Bronze medallion of Hernán Cortés at age 43. There is no evidence that the famous conqueror introduced chocolate to Europe.

due his sovereign. We have fairly detailed descriptions and lists of what was in this shipment, such as gold and silver objects (which excited the admiration of Albrecht Dürer when he saw them in Brussels) and even native books. But there is no mention whatsoever of cacao.

The next window of opportunity would have been in 1528. Towards the end of that year, eager to receive the honors and privileges which he rightly felt were owed to him after his great conquest, Cortés presented himself at the court of Charles V, by now Holy Roman Emperor.[3] With him was a dazzling sample of Mexico's riches and wonders. These included one of Motecuhzoma's sons, "many gentlemen and nobles of Mexico," eight tumblers, ballplayers with their miraculously bouncing rubber ball (something previously never seen in Europe), several albinos, dwarfs, and "monsters" (whatever these might have been). Cortés brought an entire zoo with him: jaguars, albatrosses, an armadillo, and an opossum are mentioned in our sources. Among the gifts offered to the ruthless Habsburg ruler were feather and hair mantles, fans, shields, plumes, and obsidian mirrors. But there was no mention of cacao, or any other seeds or plant products. Cortés finally did receive his patent of nobility, along with titles to vast territories in Mexico, but it was apparently not for introducing the pleasures of chocolate drinking to his sovereign.

The first documentary evidence for the initial appearance of chocolate in Spain (and, by extension, Europe) comes from an entirely different quarter, and concerns the Maya, who are usually overlooked in the story of cacao. The Kekchi Maya of Guatemala live in the Alta Verapaz, a beautiful and prosperous region of cloud-forested mountains and fertile valleys, bordering on the Petén lowlands. The Spaniards called it *Verapaz*, "True Peace," because this is where well-meaning Dominicans led by Bartolomé de las Casas had begun an experiment to win over the rebellious Kekchi by kindness and understanding rather than by violence. Their efforts were largely successful, and in 1544 the Dominican friars

Chocolate pot with molinillo and drinking cups of 17th-century Spain; the bread was dipped into the chocolate.
Detail of a painting by Antonio de Pereda y Salgado, 1652.

Detail of an early 18th-century painted tile panel depicting a chocolatada *(chocolate party) in Valencia, Spain.*

took a delegation of Maya nobles to visit Prince Philip in Spain, presumably to thank him for his magnanimity (a virtue which he seldom displayed after he became Philip II).[4]

The Kekchi visitors seem to have arrived in their native costumes, for the prince expressed his concern about how scantily they were clad for Spain's cold winter climate. We have a list of the presents they brought him from their distant land; most precious (to them) were 2000 quetzal feathers, from the resplendent bird that was (and still is) to be found in their cloud forests. Also included were clay vessels and lacquered gourds, as well as plant products, such as chillis of various kinds, beans, sarsparilla, maize, liquidambar (a plant of the witch hazel family) and copal (resin) incense. They also brought to court receptacles of beaten chocolate; as far as we can tell, this marked the debut of chocolate in the Old World, and we can only hope that Philip politely sampled the exotic beverage at this historic moment.

These are the facts, as we presently know them. But it should be kept in mind that throughout the 16th century there was constant intercourse between Spain and its New World possessions, as military men, civilians, and the clergy passed back and forth across the Atlantic. It could be that our notice of the Kekchi episode is an accident of history, and that the true transmission of chocolate was via the lines of communication between monasteries and convents in Mesoamerica, and the parent communities in Spain. Be that as it may, true transoceanic commerce in cacao came relatively late, for it was not until 1585 that the first official shipment of the beans reached Seville from Veracruz.

Regardless of how and when chocolate actually got to the Iberian Peninsula, there is general agreement that it became acclimatized in the Spanish court during the first half of the 17th century, where it was specifically the same hot beverage that had taken shape among the Creole Spaniards of Mexico.

In 1701, an English traveler (one E. Veryard) published his "Choice Remarks" concerning his voyage in Spain during the latter

half of the 17th century. His account of how the Spaniards manufactured their chocolate is detailed and clear, and worthy of being
repeated here in its entirety:

The *Spaniards* being the only People in *Europe*, that have the
Reputation of making *Chocolate* to perfection, I made it my
Business to learn the manner, which is as follows. Take twenty
pounds of *Cacao-Nuts*, and dividing them into four or five parcels,
dry each apart in an Iron-pan pierced full of holes, over a gentle
Fire without the least flame, stirring them continually and without
the least intermission. The coming off of the Husks is no argument
of their being sufficiently dried, but you are to continue it 'till the
Kernels slip between your Fingers, and being lightly pressed
crumble into pieces, but not so as to turn into Dust. The *Cacao*
being thus prepared, put it into a Box or other Vessel, stopping it
up close, and stirring it every two Hours, and twice or thrice during the Night-time, for otherwise it's apt to take fire. The next Day
work it gently on the Stone with a Roller, that the Husks may
come off, which are to be separated by winnowing, and such as
remain afterwards must be carefully pickt out, and the Dust separated by a Searce [sieve]; when it is thoroughly cleansed, grind it
on the Stone with a little Fire under it in a Chafendich [chafing-
dish], 'till it be wrought into a Mass. Weight the whole, and add to
it as much Sugar finely powder'd as will make up twenty five
Pound, with four Ounces of Cinamon, working them all together
very well with your hands, 'till they are mixt and united. Then you
must grind it as before, but with greater force and longer, 'till it be
well incorporated, and look as if it were all *Cacao*. Next you are to
add twenty-five *Bainillas* [vanilla pods] (more or less according to
every one's palate) finely powder'd, proceeding to mix and grind it
again as you did before with the Sugar. After this some put in a
Drachm of Musk powder'd in a Mortar with a little dry Sugar, and
to work it over again. Others add a small quantity of *Acciote*,
which is a sort of red Earth brought from the West Indies, and

serves to give it a Colour; but neither of these two latter ingredients are necessary. Lastly, you may form it into Cakes, Bricks, or Rolls, according to your fancy. The Rolls are made by dividing a Sheet of brown Paper into four parts, and laying as much of the Mass on each as you think sufficient (which you may regulate by weight) shaking and rolling it from side to side 'till it be formed. You may make the Cakes by putting about ten or twelve parcels on a sheet of the same Paper, and beating it against the Table to make it run abroad. For making the Bricks, the Paper must be forced into that shape, and the *Chocolate* put in. It must remain in the Papers 'till it be cold and dry.[5]

Apart from the musk (an exotic flavoring probably introduced by the Italians), this method—which was apparently standardized in late 16th-century Mexico—became universal throughout Spain and Europe, and stayed that way until Van Houten's revolutionary discoveries in the early 19th century.

However, Veryard's recipe for the "cacao mass" seems minimalist compared to the way many Spaniards of the time preferred their chocolate. A very good idea of the ingredients that were common in more exalted circles is given in the 1644 account by Antonio Colmenero de Ledesma (a work widely distributed in translation in the rest of Europe and even in England). After cautioning us that cacao by itself is "very cold and dry" (and thus, in the grim logic of the humoral system, apt to produce melancholy), he presents a recipe:[6]

RECIPE OF ANTONIO COLMENERO DE LEDESMA, 1644

100 cacao beans
2 chillis (black pepper may be substituted)
A handful of anise
"ear flower"
2 mecasuchiles [mecaxochitl]

(lacking the above two spices, powdered roses of
Alexandria may be used)
1 vanilla
2 oz [60 g] cinnamon
12 almonds and as many hazelnuts
½ lb [450 g] sugar
Achiote to taste

In all cases, the dried mass in the form of cakes, rolls, or bricks was placed with hot water in a special jug or chocolate pot fitted with a lid pierced in the middle to hold the handle of the *molinillo*, and given the usual, froth-producing beating. Colmenero de Ledesma knows of other ways of preparing chocolate, including with cold water; but he warns against the latter method, since it gives one stomach aches, and opines that the Indians drink it like this because of the intense heat in their country.

There is a misconception among some food writers that solid chocolate confectionery is a fairly modern invention, being unknown until the 19th century. Yet there is evidence that such sweets were being manufactured early on in Mexico by Spanish cloistered and missionary nuns; according to one modern writer, these Mexican convents amassed fortunes through the sale of these delicacies. They almost certainly graced many a banquet table in Baroque Europe, accompanied by a multitude of candied fruits, sorbets, and other sugar-laden delights.

Naturally, Spanish physicians had their say about this, since chocolate, as we know, was considered medicinal. We have already heard from Dr. Juan de Cárdenas of Mexico, who in 1591 promulgated the notion that while chocolate by its nature was "cold," the New World spices that are added to it are all "hot," so that the end result is likely to be neutral; according to him, "hot" persons (presumably in New Spain) drink it with atole and sugar to make themselves "cooler," or drink it with honey and hot water. An interesting fictitious dialogue on this subject was published in

1618 by one Bartholomeo Marradón,[7] and is set in either Mexico or Spain (it is not sure which). The protagonists are a doctor, an American Indian, and a "bourgeois," and they are arguing about chocolate. The physician takes a very dim view of the stuff: cacao beans have "an astringent and bitter taste . . . so disagreeable that one does not marvel that those who taste them have a horror of the beverage made of them." He goes on to claim, "I hold without difficulty that the principal causes of the obstructions, opilations, and hydropsies which are familiar in the Indies must be attributed to Chocolate and to Cacao, being of an earthy and cold nature." The Indian, unsurprisingly, stoutly defends his native drink; while the sensible bourgeois is inclined toward compromise, and says to use one's reason.

The Spanish royals, and the noble men and women dancing attendance on these exalted persons, must initially have sipped their foamy chocolate in the traditional Mesoamerican way, from gourd or clay *jícaras* (small, open bowls), but to do this with the delicacy required by court etiquette could not have been easy. The solution came from overseas, in the form of the *mancerina*, which became a standard part of the Spanish chocolate service by the mid-17th century. Its origin and name can be traced to the Marques de Mancera, Viceroy of Peru from 1639 to 1648.[8] Horrified at seeing one of the ladies present at a viceregal reception accidentally spill a *jícara* of chocolate on her dress, he determined to find a better way to take the drink. He had a Lima silversmith make a plate or saucer with a collar-like ring in the middle, into which a small cup would sit without being able to slip. Thus was born the *mancerina*, eventually to be manufactured in porcelain by European potters.

Chocolate not only reigned supreme in the courts of Spain's Habsburg rulers all through the 17th century, but it radiated out to those great public displays and pageants that were so typical of Baroque Spain: the bullfight and the *auto-da-fé*. In a typical ceremonial visit of the day, Cosimo de' Medici was in Spain and

Portugal in 1668 and 1669, a few years before he became Cosimo III, Grand Duke of Tuscany (of whom, more later).[9] He was royally received by the Spanish king, and taken to a bullfight, during which Cosimo and his gentlemen were served with candied fruit in basins, with cold waters, and with chocolate in "huge cups." Cosimo probably drank it all up, as he was one of the greatest "chocoholics" of all time.

Joseph de Olmo describes an *auto-da-fé* held in Madrid in 1680;[10] the terrible proceedings, in which the "secular arm" punished and dispatched those deemed guilty by the Inquisition, went on all day, watched by the king himself (the weird, fanatical Charles II) from a balcony. Refreshments were provided for the high-ranking officials who were required to attend the spectacle— ecclesiastics, officials of the "secular arm", commissioners of the Holy Office, foreign ambassadors, and others; these consisted of biscuits and chocolate, as well as sweets and sweet drinks. While de Olmo does not tell us whether the victims received chocolate or not, other sources suggest that those being held for investigation by the Inquisition did.

One foreign onlooker at this particular event was repelled by the horrible execution suffered by Jews (always prime targets for the Holy Office). This was Marie de Villars, wife of the French ambassador in 1680. Like other French visitors to Spain, Mme. de Villars took a jaundiced view of many of its customs and in particular its garlic-laden cuisine. Here is what she had to say about chocolate, in a letter written to a friend in that same year:

> I observe my chocolate diet, to which I believe I owe my health. I do not use it crazily or without precaution. My temperament would seem incapable of accepting this nourishment [presumably her temperament was melancholic or phlegmatic]. However it is admirable and delicious. I have it made at home, which can do no harm. I often think that if I should see you again, I would make you take it methodically, and make you confess that there is nothing better for the

health. There's an encomium of chocolate! Remember that I am in Spain, and taking it is almost my only pleasure.[11]

Her compatriot Mme. D'Aulnoy, a noted writer of fables, was in Spain at the same time, and published a narrative of her stay after her return to France. Aside from the usual French ethnocentricism, Mme. D'Aulnoy's account contains some acute observations on chocolate-taking at court and among the Spanish nobility, and describes a collation to which she was invited by one of the princesses in 1679. After being given some *confitures* (sweet preserves),

> . . . they presented next the Chocolate, each cup of porcelain on a saucer of agate garnished with gold [this is what the *mancerina* had become], with the sugar in a bowl of the same. There was iced chocolate, another hot, and another with Milk and Eggs; one took it with a Biscuit, or rather with dry small Buns . . . besides this, they take it with so much pepper and so many spices, that it is impossible they don't burn themselves up [the reader will recall that spices were considered to be "hot"].[12]

Mme. D'Aulnoy further comments on the women she went among:

> Their teeth are good, and would be white if they took care of them, but they neglect them. Besides the sugar and the chocolate which spoil them, they have the bad habit, men and women alike, of cleaning them with a toothpick, in whatever company they are; it is one of their common postures.[13]

It had been discovered in Baroque Spain, and in fact all over Europe, that the strong taste of chocolate made it an effective disguise for poisons. An unusual case of overt poisoning is cited by Mme. D'Aulnoy.[14] A Spanish "lady of quality" took revenge on a lover who had left her without cause: she got him to her house, where she offered him the choice of a dagger or a poisoned cup of chocolate. He chose the latter, and drank it to the last drop, complaining that it lacked enough sugar to cover up the poison's bitterness. The unfortunate lover died in agony within the hour; the woman "had the barbarity of not leaving him until he was dead."

Chocolate in Italy: "A More Exquisite Gentility"

To trace chocolate's progress through the mansions, villas, brocaded palaces, and ecclesiastical establishments of Europe's elite during the Baroque Age is no easy matter. This was the era of the religious wars, when the continent was convulsed in ferocious struggles between Catholics and Protestants, between the Reformation and the Counter-Reformation, when the map of Europe often looked more like a series of battlegrounds, and alliances shifted from one week to another.

While Protestant potentates kept no armies in Italy, everyone else's seemed to be there. It should be kept in mind that until the final unification of the Kingdom of Italy in 1870, there was no such thing as an Italian nation. For centuries, the southern part of the Italian "boot," as well as Sicily, was a Spanish possession; the Papal States were more or less in the middle of the peninsula and on the Adriatic coast; while in the north there was a collection of usually independent states that at times might lose their autonomy as France and the Holy Roman Empire (and its successor, Austria) sent their troops into Italy. Each of these states retained its own culture and language, its own royal or noble house, and its own army—even the Pope had an army, and often fought bitterly with his secular rivals. Powerful ruling families like the Medici found it expedient to link themselves by marriage to various of these powers, since at the highest levels marriage was a standard method of cementing important alliances. As these exalted women moved from one Italian state capital to another, and to the courts of foreign lands, important items of elite culture, particularly culinary, often traveled with them.

It seems certain that Italy followed Spain and Portugal in adopting the chocolate drink, but the history of its introduction there and in the rest of Europe is as ambiguous and clouded as that of the other great novelty of post-Columbian Europe, syphilis. There are several rival theories there.[15] One would have it that chocolate was brought into Italy by Emanuele Filiberto of Savoy (1528–80), Captain General of the Spanish army, who returned to Italy following the victory of San Quentin over the French. There is no confirmatory evidence for this, nor for the rival notion that it was imported by Catherine of Austria, daughter of Spain's Philip II and wife of Carlo Emanuele I, Duke of Savoy from 1580 to 1630. So much for the Savoy connection.

A far more serious contender for the honor of having inaugurated chocolate drinking in Italy is Francesco d'Antonio Carletti, who is given credit for it by most historians of the subject. Carletti was a Florentine businessman, a sort of latter-day Marco Polo, who undertook a remarkable circumnavigation of the globe in search of new markets and new products (some say that he was also a slaver, as was Columbus). Having left his native Florence in 1591, by the year 1600 he found himself in a place called S. Jonat, which from his description must have been on the Pacific coast of El Salvador, close to the Guatemalan border. There he saw rich cacao plantations (although he realized that the main zone of cacao production lay to the west, in Guatemala). In his report Carletti describes all stages of cacao growing and processing, including the use of the *molinillo* in making the drink. On Carletti's return to Florence in July 1606 he presented the manuscript to Ferdinando I de' Medici, Grand Duke of Tuscany, but that potentate did nothing about it; it was not to see the light of print until 1701. Nevertheless, the MS was consulted by the extraordinary poet-scientist Francesco Redi some time before 1666, and Redi included a long section from it concerning chocolate in the notes to his *Bacco in Toscana*

("Bacchus in Tuscany").[16] We shall return to Redi later, as he plays an important role in our history.

Yet nowhere in his journal does Carletti say anything about returning to Italy with cacao or chocolate; nor is there any shred of truth, as Redi and other patriotic Tuscans would have it, that Italians first learned of the drink from Carletti. As we have seen in Chapters Three and Four the Milanese Girolamo Benzoni and Pietro Martire d'Anghiera had "scooped" him on this story by about a century.

Setting aside the otherwise deserving Carletti, a far more convincing bit of evidence is supplied by a Roman physician, Paolo Zacchia, in a book of 1644 with the odd (to us) title *De' Mali Hipochondriaci* ("Of Hypochondriacal Sicknesses"). At that time, Dr. Zacchia clearly knows of chocolate, but only as a drug: "But I do not wish to forget to mention a medicine, which was brought here from Portugal not many years ago, to which it was sent from the Indies, and it is called Chacolata."[17] In defiance of those who said that the cacao seed was "very cold," Zacchia maintains that the potion made from it is "very hot"; but this switch in Galenic properties may stem from the flavorings and additions which he recommends, and which—with the notable absence of chilli peppers, never very popular with Italians to the north of the Spanish possessions in Italy—are basically the same as those we have already encountered in Spain and Mexico. Taken early in the morning, says Zacchia, chocolate comforts the stomach and aids digestion; but, thanks to its "hotness," it must be used cautiously. Based on what he tells us, then, chocolate was a novelty at the time in Rome; and, by extension, probably in much of Italy outside the Spanish territories, where we can expect Spanish officials to have been devoted to the drink.

Chocolate could well have been disseminated to central and northern Italy through the international religious network of monasteries, convents, and priestly orders that now linked Europe with Latin America. In this century of religious conflict, the most active of these groups was the Society of Jesus (or Jesuits), the shock troops of the Counter-Reformation. Founded by the Spaniard Ignatius Loyola in 1540, the Jesuit order was dedicated to strengthening the Catholic Church from within, crushing the heretics without, and championing papal supremacy over kings, princes, and nations. To pass through the portals of their two great churches in Rome, the Gesù and San Ignazio, is to walk into the Baroque Age: their 17th-century interiors are a riot of twisted Berninian columns, gold, silver, gilt-bronze, stuccowork, lapis lazuli, and rare marbles—the Jesuits believed not only in the Church militant but the Church triumphant. The ceilings are frescoed with vertiginous perspectives of Baroque heaven, with Jesuit saints rising in glory, while heretics, infidels, and apostates are hurled down from on high with their detested books.

There were 16,000 Jesuit priests in 1624; they were politically strong not only in Europe but throughout Spain's American colonies where, like the monastic orders before them, they excited the jealousy and suspicion of colonists and viceroys alike. They were not in the long run sympathetic to the native populations in their charge, and eventually promulgated various decrees regarding the unsuitability of the Indians for the priesthood that can only be described as racist. Nevertheless, one native custom was gladly adopted by them: chocolate drinking. And they found it extremely lucrative to become cacao traders themselves ("to the great glory of God"), as will be seen in the next chapter.

Florence, the capital of Tuscany, bears far less witness to the glories and extravagances of the Italian Baroque than does Rome— there is little approaching the opulence of the great Jesuit churches of Rome, or Bernini's amazing Baldacchino and dazzling colonnade at St. Peter's, or his St. Theresa melting in marble ecstacy. The last of the Medici, the Grand Dukes of Tuscany during the 17th century, were the perfect example of a once-great family in disastrous decline, largely through their own much-flawed characters. Matters were not so bad in the first half of the century: the

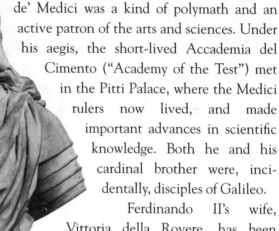

easy-going, bulbous-nosed Ferdinando II de' Medici was a kind of polymath and an active patron of the arts and sciences. Under his aegis, the short-lived Accademia del Cimento ("Academy of the Test") met in the Pitti Palace, where the Medici rulers now lived, and made important advances in scientific knowledge. Both he and his cardinal brother were, incidentally, disciples of Galileo.

Ferdinando II's wife, Vittoria della Rovere, has been described as "a prim and interfering woman, plain and fat".[18] Their son, the future Cosimo III (whom we last saw on a trip to Spain), inherited all of his mother's bad traits, including her enormous double chin, and few of his father's good ones.

Marble bust of Cosimo III de' Medici, the gluttonous, bigoted Grand Duke of Tuscany. By the time this was carved (c.1717), Cosimo had slimmed down under a diet imposed by Redi.

In 1661 the heir-apparent was forced into a supremely unhappy marriage with Margaret Louise of Orleans, the niece of Louis XIV. She loathed Florence, loathed Italy, and above all, loathed her husband to the point of insanity. Even when he had become Grand Duke (he succeeded his father in 1670), she tried to get the marriage annulled but failed. She finally returned to France.

In just about every respect, Cosimo III was deserving of his admittedly tiresome wife's hatred. The Italian historian Luigi Villari has described him as "weak, vain, bigoted and hypocritical."[19] He was, according to Sir Harold Acton, "intolerant of all free thought . . . his existence [was] a round of visits to churches and convents, a daily routine of prostration at different altars".[20]

So fanatical was he that he decreed the most savage punishment for "mixed marriages," that is, between Catholics and Jews. Sir Harold had this further to say about this most unworthy prince:

> After the departure of Margaret-Louise [in 1675], Cosimo's first impulse, we are told, anxious to improve the reputation for avarice his wife had given him, was to introduce into his life a new system of what Balzac would have called insolent luxury, such as had not been seen in Florence for many a year. Regardless of calamities, he spared no expense to summon the rarest and most precious condiments from all sections of the globe to his table. . . . The richness and extraordinary magnitude of his repasts were the admiration of all that were admitted to them, albeit the Grand Duke's intemperance somewhat diminished their esteem of his person. The "paragon of purity" preached the virtue of abstinence to others, and taxed his subjects heavily so that they might practice it, but himself remained a conspicuous gourmandizer. Strangers of every country were admitted to these banquets, to publish an account of them, but few of his subjects.[21]

Christopher Hibbert, another chronicler of the House of Medici, comments: "He himself [Cosimo III] consumed gargantuan platefuls of the richest delicacies, becoming fatter than ever with a complexion not so much ruddy as inflamed."[22]

Cosimo's extravagances, disastrous administration, and enormous taxes bankrupted what had once been a prosperous and enlightened land, and it never recovered. On this, Villari has a final word: "So ruin fell upon Tuscany. Crime and misery increased, and the poor, who only asked to work, were given alms and sent oftener to church."[23] Historians have painted this unpleasant, profligate Grand Duke as a monster, yet even monsters and tyrants can be discerning patrons: Nero had Seneca as his tutor and Petronius as his "arbiter," Stalin encouraged Prokofiev, and Cosimo III de' Medici had his Redi. Born in 1626 to a well-to-do-

G. Benagha inc.

Francesco Redi.

Francesco Redi (1626–97), scientist, poet, philologist, and physician to his patron Cosimo III de' Medici. Redi was the inventor of the renowned jasmine chocolate of the Tuscan court.

family of Arezzo, Redi took a doctorate in medicine and "natural philosophy" (that is, science) at the University of Pisa. Eventually, he became physician to Ferdinando II, and continued in this office under Cosimo III.

Redi was extraordinarily talented in many fields, and was encouraged in these endeavors by the Grand Dukes. As a biologist, he virtually founded the field of parasitology, writing a notable book on the subject; but his greatest achievement in this field was his experiment disproving the notion of spontaneous generation—widely held since Aristotle. He did this by carefully enclosing exposed meat with screening to protect it from flies, thus demonstrating that maggots could only appear when these flies were allowed to lay their eggs on the meat. Redi's experiments foreshadowed Pasteur's two centuries later.

As a philologist, Redi did outstanding work on the Italian language through his membership in Florence's Accademia della Crusca, the Academy of Letters, which was then and still is dedicated to producing the definitive dictionary of the Tuscan dialect, now the national tongue. For this academy, for his friends, and for the Grand Duke, he began to write poetry, some of great merit. And he continued to doctor his patron—in fact, he probably saved Cosimo's life by putting and keeping him on a strict diet (the wretched man lived on until he was 80, confirming the adage that the good die young).

Among the works which Redi produced for the Accademia della Crusca was a dithyramb, that is still admired, entitled *Bacco in Toscana* ("Bacchus in Tuscany").[24] What is a dithyramb? In Classical antiquity, it was a poem recited in honor of Bacchus as god of wine, which got wilder and wilder as it progressed, reflecting the increasing drunkenness of the god and his devotees. Redi's entire poem is in high praise of the vineyards and wines of the Grand Duke's domain, but it has this to say about three exotic, non-Classical drinks (in Leigh Hunt's English version of 1825):

> Cups of chocolate,
> Aye, or tea,
> Are not medicines
> Made for me.
> I would sooner take to poison,
> Than a single cup set eyes on
> Of that bitter and guilty stuff ye
> Talk of by the name of Coffee.[25]

Admittedly, this is not much, but Redi has quite a lot to say about chocolate in the extensive footnotes which follow the poem, which dates to about 1666. We have already seen that he had consulted Carletti's manuscript, and thought that it was that voyager who had introduced chocolate to Florence in 1606. But this hypothesis is contradicted by a passage in the journal of one Tomasso Rinuccini: "1668, was introduced in Florence in this year rather widely a drink used in Spain called *ciocolatto*, and one of the above-mentioned shops sells this in little earthen beakers, and hot as well as cold, according to taste.[26] Chocolate may have been consumed by Florentines in previous years, but if so, then it was surely confined to the Grand Ducal family in the Pitti Palace. In all events, in the notes to *Bacco in Toscana*, Redi says:

Chocolate was first introduced from America by the court of Spain, where it is made in all perfection. And yet, to the Spanish perfection has been added, in our times, in the court of Tuscany, a certain I know not what of more exquisite gentility, owing to the novelty of divers European ingredients; a way having been found out of introducing into the composition the fresh peel of citrons and lemons, and the *very genteel* odour of jasmine; which, together with cinnamon, amber, musk, and vanilla, has a prodigious effect upon such as delight themselves in taking chocolate.[27]

Now the introduction of novel, perfume-laden flavors into chocolate was truly an innovation in its history, and there can be little doubt that Redi, as the physician and apothecary to the Grand Duke, was responsible. The "amber" that is mentioned here is ambergris, a solid, fatty substance that occurs as a biliary concretion in the intestines of sperm whales, and is occasionally found washed up on tropical beaches. Once employed extensively in medicine, it is now used mainly in perfumery for its floral, violet-like fragrance. Equally exotic is musk, a perfume ingredient derived from a strong-smelling glandular secretion of the musk deer, native to the Himalayas, Tibet, Siberia, and northwest China. Musk is one of the most powerful odors known: one grain will scent millions of cubic feet of air.[28]

So strong is musk that it does not enter into the making of the famous and delicate jasmine chocolate, a speciality of Cosimo III's court. Redi guarded this recipe jealously; in a letter to Sig. Cestoni, written from Florence in 1680, Redi says: "I am sorry that you have asked something which I have an expressed order not to reveal, that is, how one concocts Chocolate with the odor of jasmine."[29] Redi does, however, caution his friend against trying to make it with jasmine water, as this will not combine with cacao. After Redi's death in 1697, the naturalist Antonio Vallisnieri came into possession of the hitherto secret recipe for this most Baroque of all chocolate drinks; here, for those who would like to recreate it, is the formula:[30]

THE RENOWNED JASMINE CHOCOLATE
OF THE GRAND DUKE OF TUSCANY

Ingredients
10 lb [4.5 kg] toasted cacao beans, cleaned and coarsely crushed
Fresh jasmine flowers
8 lb [3.6 kg] white sugar, well-dried
3 oz [85 g] "perfect" vanilla beans
4 to 6 oz [115–170 g] "perfect" cinnamon
2 scruples [$^1/_{12}$ oz, 2.5 g] ambergris

Method
In a box or similar utensil, alternate layers of jasmine with layers of the crushed cacao, and let it sit for 24 hours. Then mix these up, and add more alternating layers of flowers and cacao, followed by the same treatment. This must be done ten or twelve times, so as to permeate the cacao with the odor of the jasmine. Next, take the remaining ingredients and add them to the mixed cacao and jasmine, and grind them together on a slightly warmed metate; if the metate be too hot, the odor might be lost.

While Redi was still alive, not even his Jesuit friend Father Tommaso Strozzi of Naples, who had penned a Latin poem on chocolate, could get his hands on this recipe.

Many years later, in 1741 to be exact, another Florentine named Marcello Malaspina (1689–1757), a lawyer, senator of Florence, and, like Redi, a member of the Florentine Academy of Letters, published another dithyramb in imitation of *Bacco in Toscana*. The rather silly plot of *Bacco in America*[31] goes like this: the gods Bacchus and Silenus and their followers have left Tuscany by ship, but get caught up in a great storm and are shipwrecked on the coast of Guatemala (of all places); there they encounter a grove of cacao trees, and have the bright idea of making a drink from its fruit; so taken are they by this chocolate beverage that they unanimously decide it is far superior to wine. The whole troop then sings in ecstacy:

Oh Bevanda delicata	Oh, delicate Beverage!
Oh tremenda Cioccolata!	Oh, awesome Chocolate!

They conclude by making the beach resound with their hymn of praise:

Viva viva il nostro Nume	Long live, long live our Deity . . .
Ne più appelisi il Toscano	No more should he be called the Tuscan,
Ma il Gran Bacco Americano	But the great American Bacchus;
Mentre in bevendo omai sentenziamo,	While in drinking now we judge,
Ciascheduno pregando a darci fe,	Everyone praying to give us faith,
Che il CIOCCOLATTA *d'ogni Beva è il Re.*	That chocolate is the king of drinks.[32]

Crossing the Ecclesiastical Barrier

For Catholic countries like Spain and its overseas possessions, France, and the various states that made up Italy, there was a distinct fly in the ointment—or chocolate-pot. This was the perennial question of whether the taking of chocolate broke the ecclesiastical fast. In short, was chocolate a drink, or was it a food? Did it merely quench the thirst, or was the body also nourished by it? If it was a food, as well as a drink, then it could not be taken by practicing Catholics during the hours which ran from midnight until Holy Communion (in 1958, Vatican II shortened this period to one hour); nor could it be taken on fast days, which included the forty days of Lent.

The arguments for and against this question raged among ecclesiastics and laymen for over two and a half centuries, and even involved popes: the literature on it is enormous and for the most part tiresome, and we shall not burden the reader with more than a glimpse of its highlights. In many respects, much of it was simply a rehash of similar arguments that had been made about wine. Even the religious orders entered into the fray, with the Jesuits (who were far from uninterested parties since they traded in chocolate) usually holding that it did *not* break the fast, and the puritanical Dominicans, generally their adversaries throughout the period, taking the opposite view. For example, we learn from the memoirs of the duc de Saint-Simon that Louis XIV was told by his Jesuit advisors to drink chocolate on fast days, as they did themselves, but to desist from his custom of dunking bread into it.[33]

The first shot in this war was fired in Mexico in 1591 by Juan de Cárdenas.[34] He argued that there are two ways of interpreting the word "drink" (*bevida* in Spanish): (1) as anything drinkable; (2) as liquids which are intended to refresh and to allay thirst. All kinds of nourishing materials could be ground up and added in the case of (1). As for (2), plain water does a better job. Since, according to Cárdenas, the idea of "fast" is to mortify the flesh by denying it food and thirst-quenching liquids (incidentally, a concept close to that of the Muslim Ramadan), then chocolate in any form, at any time, breaks the fast.

This did not satisfy many in Mexico, including the viceroy; the latter asked Fray Agustín Dávila Padilla for his opinion, which was that neither chocolate nor wine broke the fast.[35] Eventually, at the instigation of the Procurator of the Province of Chiapas ("where this drink began" according to our source), a high-ranking cleric consulted Pope Gregory XIII, a militant Counter-Reformationist who celebrated the news of the St. Bartholemew's Day Massacre with a *Te Deum* in St. Peter's. The Supreme Pontiff said it did *not* break the fast. Throughout the centuries that followed, other popes were similarly asked their advice on this weighty matter—Clement VII, Paul V, Pius V, Urban VIII,Clement XI, and Benedict XIV—and they all said the same thing.

Even that failed to stop the more puritanical clerics from trying to ban chocolate during the fast. The usual argument was that it nourishes because a person can subsist on it for quite a long time: and, of course, because all sorts of substances could be ground up and added to it. Extra ammunition was provided or those who would ban it by the Spaniard Juan de Solorzano y Pereyra around the year 1629; from Bernal Díaz's suspect description of Motecuhzoma's "banquet," Solorzano made the usual claim that chocolate excited the venereal appetite, "by which it will be understood that it runs counter to the fast, which is undertaken principally to lessen these lascivious desires."[36]

The author most quoted in the later literature on this never-ending debate is another Spaniard, Antonio de León Pinelo, who produced a book on the question in 1636.[37] This work transcends its subject, however, since León Pinelo gives details on production as well as recipes for the drink; he is also extremely knowledgeable about cacao, chocolate, and various writers on chocolate. He comes to the reasonable conclusion that the solution to the theological problem depends on how much nourishing material is added: if it is a lot, then it is nourishing, but if the chocolate is concocted with plain water, then it is merely a drink and therefore licit during the fast. A similarly middle-ground stance was taken in 1645 by another Spaniard, Tomás Hurtado, who held a chair in theology at the University of Seville: as long as only water is added, and not milk or eggs, then it is all right. Interestingly, Hurtado maintains that the addition of ground maize is permissible, but not "foreign flours" (that is, foreign to chocolate's native Mexico) like broadbeans and chickpeas—the only reference we have found to chocolate adulteration during the Baroque Age.[38]

Title page of the treatise by León Pinelo, Madrid, 1636, discussing whether chocolate breaks the ecclesiastical fast.

This more liberal view was taken up again in 1664 by the Italian Francesco Maria Brancaccio.[39] Chocolate is definitely nourishing, said he, if things like breadcrumbs are added to it (as was the case in

Spain), or if eaten in solid form. But if mixed only with water, it is clearly a drink, just like wine which had been permitted during the fast by the Western Church for ten centuries. The beverage is a beneficial medicine which "restores natural heat, generates pure blood, enlivens the heart, conserves the natural faculties," and so on. Fasting is not divine law, but ecclesiastical law, and thus subject to change—and it should be changed to accommodate this fine beverage. For these comforting words, Brancaccio was given a cardinal's hat.

Before leaving this debate, we must end with what strikes us as the most telling argument against banishing chocolate from the table during the fast. This is related by Giovanni Batista Gudenfridi, in a work published in Florence in 1680, specifically in answer to an anti-chocolate tract by one Francesco Felini, who claimed that it was both a food and an aphrodisiac. Here the astute Gudenfridi counters with a story in the life of that holy Dominican, St. Rose of Lima, "Virgin of Peru":

. . . we are told that one day, after many hours of an ardent elevation of spirits, the Holy Girl [*Santa Fanciulla*], feeling herself languish, lacking breath, and weakened in body, had at her side an Angel, who presented her with a little cup of chocolate, with which she regained her vigor and her strength returned. I ask the Sig. Cav. Felini what he thinks of this angel? Does he think it is an angel of darkness, or of light? Bad or good? He cannot think it bad without offense, to say the least, of the trust due to the historian. But, if it was a good one, does he think that if Chocolate be the poison of chastity, that the Angel would have brought it to a Virgin of Christ? If Chocolate injects into the veins of those that drink it the spirit of las- civiousness, does he think that the good Angel would have given even a sip to a maiden who was a Temple of the Holy Spirit? Does he think, if Chocolate merits the name of a diabolical liquid, that God would command, or permit, that by the hand of his Angels such a drink be given to one of his Brides?[40]

Chocolate in France

Regarding the introduction of chocolate to France, we are confronted with the same story of confusion and conjecture that we have already seen for Spain and Italy. Here we have three rival theories.[41] The first (and the most popular with food writers) is that it was taken there by Anne of Austria (1601–66), daughter of Philip III of Spain and Margherita of Austria-Stiria. Born at Valladolid, Spain, the Infanta was forced into a political marriage with Louis XIII of France in 1615 , when both where only 14 years old, and an unhappy marriage it proved to be. The boy-king was sickly, uninterested in women throughout his life, and dominated by the Queen Mother, the formidable Marie de' Medici, and by her unpopular chief minister, the Italian adventurer Concino Concini. Up to the death of Louis XIII in 1642 (when Anne became regent for the young Louis XIV), the king's attitude toward her has been described as "morbidly cold"; "yet he expected an heir to be born from his infrequent and ceremonious approaches."

The court intrigues of the period appear in the novels of Alexandre Dumas (1802–70); a major figure in these events was the mighty Armand Jean du Plessis, Cardinal de Richelieu (1585–1642). When Richelieu became Minister in 1624, he decided that Anne was opposed to his anti-Spanish policy, and he raised suspicions against her. Thus, her influence was always weak at best, and usually non-existent. All this makes for fascinating reading, but unfortunately for our story, there is no real evidence that the unfortunate Anne of Austria brought chocolate with her to the French court.

According to a second theory, the transmission from Spain took place when Spanish monks sent gifts of the stuff (presumably cacao tablets or bricks) to their French *confrères*. This is possible, but again we are dealing with pure conjecture.

The final theory at least has some documentary evidence to increase its plausibility; it becomes even more credible when we learn from it that chocolate could have entered France as a medicine; this would have been typical of the period. Here are the data upon which this theory is based. In his *Mélanges d'Histoire et de Littérature*, published in 1713, Bonaventure d'Argonne makes the following assertion:

> We know that Cardinal Brancaccio wrote a treatise on Chocolate, but perhaps we do not know that the Cardinal of Lyon, Alphonse de Richelieu, was the first in France to use this drug. I heard from one of his servants that he used it to moderate the vapors of his spleen, and that he had the secret from some Spanish monks who brought it to France.[42]

Even more precise is a passage in Alfred Franklin's important 1893 history of tea, coffee, and chocolate: "This assertion is even more likely in that René Moreau, celebrated physician of Paris, recounts having been consulted, before 1642, by the Cardinal of Lyon, on the therapeutic properties of chocolate.[43] Alphonse de Richelieu was the elder brother of the famous Cardinal de Richelieu, master politician, and there is reason to believe that the latter took up chocolate drinking on a regular basis on the advice of his sibling.

Alphonse de Richelieu (1634–80), may have been the one who first brought chocolate to France, as a medicine for his spleen.

The equally formidable Cardinal Mazarin—actually an Italian, born Giulio Mazarini—succeeded Richelieu as Minister in 1643, and exercised power in the name of the Queen Regent,

Anne of Austria, until his death in 1661. He smashed the Fronde
uprising of the French nobility (paving the way for Louis XIV's
absolutism) and crushed the Jansenists, whom the Pope had
excommunicated for heresy. In 1654, he and the duc de Gramont,
Marshal of France, brought from Italy two cooks experienced in
the art of preparing coffee, tea, and chocolate, according to both
Alfred Franklin and Albert Bourgaux. However, Bourgaux tells us
that Italian chocolate came to be disliked by the French, who
considered it over-roasted, too bitter, and providing too little
nourishment. This may be in part true, yet there are overtones
of the Tuscan court taste in some French recipes for chocolate
surviving from the Baroque Age.

We are certain that it was thanks to the chocolate-loving
Mazarin's interest that on 28 May 1659, letters patent were given at
Toulouse to Sieur David Chaliou, granting him the exclusive
privilege to make and sell chocolate throughout the kingdom.
The document reads thus:

> LOUIS, etc.
> Our dear and well-loved David Chaliou has very humbly
> represented to us that he has made various voyages in Spain, in
> Poland and other places of Europe, during which he has applied him-
> self to the search for secrets which might be useful to the human
> body; he had among other things become acquainted
> with a certain composition which is called chocolate, the use
> of which is very healthful.[44]

Chaliou was permitted to sell this "composition" as liquor, as tablets,
or in *boëttes* (boxes). But the letters of patent did not actually
become final until the king signed them on 9 February 1666.

Mazarin died in 1661, and the young king became absolute
monarch of France, a position of supreme power that he held
through a very long and brilliant reign (the Sun King died in
1715). In 1659, the duc de Gramont had journeyed to Madrid to

ask the hand of the Infanta María Teresa for the king of France, and the royal couple were wed in 1660. This was hardly a marriage of love (Louis was enamored of Mazarin's niece), but served rather to ratify peace between France and Spain. Naturally, the Infanta brought with her from Madrid her own retinue of Spanish women to serve her at court, and they, like the new queen, were all chocolate drinkers. In her memoirs, the duchesse de Montpensier relates that the queen's chocolate habit did not meet her husband's approval, and so she took it in secret, at first with one of her women named La Molina, then, after the departure of La Molina, with another named "La Philippa" (presumably La Felipa).[45] Whether this account is true or not, at that time chocolate-drinking was obviously not something that decent Frenchwomen were allowed to do (at least in public).

Ten years later, all that had changed. Marie de Rabutin-Chantal, marquise de Sévigné (1626–96), was one of the great letter-writers of the age. Over 1500 of her letters to her family and friends survive, and they reveal much of the aristocratic and intellectual life of the times, including Louis XIV's enormous court at Versailles. Mme. de Sévigné was an affectionate mother, and often wrote to her daughter, who was married to a royal official in Provence. Her correspondence of 1671 tells us, firstly, that the taking of chocolate was now widespread among the aristocratic women of France, and, secondly, that she was thoroughly inconstant regarding the virtues of chocolate. On 11 February she writes: "But you are not well, you have hardly slept, chocolate will set you up again. But you do not have a *chocolatière* [chocolate-pot]; I have thought of it a thousand times; what will you do? Alas, my child, you are not wrong when you believe that I worry about you more than you worry about me."[46] Yet on 15 April she can write this:

> I want to tell you, my dear child, that chocolate is no longer for me what it was, fashion has led me astray, as it always does. Everyone who spoke well of it now tells me bad things about it; it is cursed, and

accused of causing one's ills, it is the source of vapors and palpitations; it flatters you for a while, and then suddenly lights a continuous fever in you that leads to death. . . . In the name of God, don't keep it up, and don't think that it is still the fashion of the fashionable. All the great and the less [great] say as much bad about it as they say good things about you . . . .[47]

Here is even worse, in a letter of 25 October: "The Marquise de Coëtlogon took so much chocolate during her pregnancy last year that she produced a small boy as black as the devil, who died."[48] But three days later Mme. de Sévigné writes: "I have reconciled myself to chocolate, I took it the day before yesterday to digest my dinner, to have a good meal, and I took it yesterday to nourish me so that I could fast until evening: it gave me all the effects I wanted. That's what I like about it: it acts according to my intention."[49]

In court circles, there was clearly some confusion about the medical merits and demerits of chocolate, but all that should have been settled in March 1684, when a Paris physician named Joseph Bachot sustained his thesis on this beverage.[50] So much did he favor it that he indulged in hyperbole, saying that "chocolate, well known, is an invention so noble, that it should be the nourishment of the gods, rather than nectar or ambrosia." It has even been conjectured that Linnaeus was familiar with Bachot's thesis, leading to his adoption of the generic name for cacao, *Theobroma*, "food of the gods." And nourishing it was, if we can believe an item in the memoirs of the Versailles court by Primi Visconti, who recounts the woes of the lovelorn Chevalier de Vendôme, despondent over an Italian lady: "His love for her was such that he shut himself in his room for months on end, with the windows closed, with a guitar, paper and ink to write verse, without sleeping, without eating, drinking barely enough cups of chocolate to sustain him."[51] Those chocoholic clerics who claimed that chocolate was only a drink and did not break the fast would not have like this passage at all!

Louis XIV's Versailles, to which he moved his court, was on a scale that defies the imagination: its façade alone was a third of a mile long. Versailles was a virtual ant-palace thronged by the French elite; in it, at his constant beck and call, were about 10,000 officials, noblemen, and attendants. At one time, chocolate was regularly served at all public functions, levees, and the like. But in 1682, María Teresa died, and the king secretly married the puritanical Mme. de Maintenon, under whose influence he had been for some time. Life in the court of the Sun King grew more frugal, abstemious, and hypocritically pious; so it comes as no surprise to learn that in 1693, for reasons of economy, the king suppressed the serving of chocolate, which previously had been put at the disposition of guests at his thrice-weekly receptions.[52] But in truth he had never particularly cared for it himself.

18th-century French silver chocolatière, *The lid would once have held the handle of a wooden* moulinet (molinillo).

The French are usually credited with the invention of the *chocolatière*, the chocolate-pot, at least as we know it from the end of the 17th through the 18th centuries. The roots of particular piece of equipment can be traced back to Mexico. It will be recalled that in pre-Spanish times, the native Mesoamericans prepared their chocolate by pouring the drink from one vessel to another. It will also be remembered that the 16th-century Spanish colonists introduced the *molinillo*, which was twirled between the hands to produce the foam-topped beverage, in tall vessels of pottery and probably wood. They discovered that a better result could be obtained by covering the pot with a wooden lid, with a hole in the middle for the *molinillo* handle. Such chocolate-frothers, made of lathe-turned wood, can be bought in many rural markets in today's Mexico, and were probably common in the Iberian peninsula.

Similar chocolate-pots were perhaps already being made in copper in Baroque Age Spain and Italy. But the French innovation seems to have been to fix a straight wooden handle to the metal pot at right angles to the spout; this handle was usually unscrewed clockwise so that it would remain tight while pouring from the pot in a counter-clockwise motion.[53] At the top was a hinged lid, with a central hole under the swiveling (or hinged) finial to take the handle of the *moussoir* ("froth-maker"), as they called the *molinillo*. Such was the *chocolatière* whose absence from her daughter's table so worried Mme de Sevigné. Of course, this would have been in silver, as would the *chocolatières* of all the nobility.

The exact date of the first appearance of the silver (and gold) *chocolatière* in France involves a very strange episode in the relations of Baroque Age Europe with Asia, and centers on a shady Greek adventurer named Constantine Phaulcon, chief minister to King Narai of Siam, a country coveted both by the Dutch and by Louis XIV. In 1686, as a counterweight to the Dutch, Phaulcon had persuaded his lord and master to send an embassy to Versailles.[54]

Porcelain cups and saucers for chocolate, called trembleuses; *18th-century Viennese descendants of the 17th-century Spanish* mancerina.

When the Siamese mission duly arrived in Louis XIV's court, with the wily Phaulcon as its guide and interpreter, they came bearing some very impressive presents, consisting largely of equipment in gold and silver for producing and consuming the chocolate drink. The Dauphin, for example, was given two *chocolatières* in silver, one with golden flowers, and the other japanned; while the Siamese queen had sent to the Dauphine no less than five chocolate-pots, one of them entirely in gold. It was not that the Thai had suddenly turned into chocolate drinkers (they never did so), but that Phaulcon had obviously instructed the royal metalsmiths to turn out something that would appeal to the French court.

Alfred Franklin was of the opinion that this marks the origin of the silver chocolate-pot. However, since we know of a dated 1685 chocolate-pot made by the English silversmith George Garthorne,[55] this hypothesis is untenable. If such objects are a French invention, as we believe they are, then they must predate the Siamese mission by some time. But regardless of its origin, the silver *chocolatière* would prove to have a long and distinguished career in many European countries as well as in the British American colonies. Its decline would only come when Van Houten invented his method for defatting cacao in the early 19th century; after that, the chocolate-pot, which had been necessary to stir and beat the heavy liquid, no longer was of use in making a palatable drink.

We will leave this section on Baroque France with some chocolate recipes published in 1692 by one M. St. Disdier.[56] In his commentary, St. Disdier shows a remarkably accurate knowledge of the whole chocolate business, including the New World spices. He knows, for example, that the correct name for vanilla is *tlilxochitl* (which so many of his contemporaries got wrong), and that one has to use only the best vanilla beans, which are long and thin and come in packets of fifty; these must be fresh, oily (but beware of unscrupulous merchants who anoint them with oil), pliant, and with an excellent odor. One should also be aware that in some chocolate tablets, the merchants have spared the vanilla and added too much sugar—with sometimes more sugar than cacao in the product. St. Disdier gives three recipes, with his own ratings; measurements are in apothecaries' weights.

St. Disdier's Chocolate

Recipe 1 (very good)
2 lb [900 g] prepared cacao
1½ lb [680 g] cassonade (sugar)
6 drachm [³⁄₄ oz: 20 g] powdered vanilla
4 drachm [½ oz: 14 g] powdered cinnamon

Recipe 2 (excellent)
2 lb [900 g] prepared cacao
1¼ lb [570 g] sugar
1 oz [28 g] powdered vanilla
4 drachm [½ oz: 15 g] powdered cinnamon

Recipe 3 (high taste, for those with no fear of overeating)
2 lb [900 g] prepared cacao
1 lb [450 g] fine sugar
3 drachm [⅓ oz: 9 g] cinnamon
1 scruple [¹⁄₂₄ oz: 7 g] powdered cloves
1 scruple [¹⁄₂₄ oz: 7 g] Indian pepper [chillis]
1¼ oz [35 g] vanilla

St. Disdier informs us that Recipe 3 is "Spanish style." For those who want their chocolate perfumed, one may add to this recipe 8 grains of ambergris and 4 grains of musk; if one wants ambergris without the musk, use 12 grains. Although he does not say so, "perfumed" chocolate must reflect the Baroque refinements introduced at the decadent court of the Grand Duke of Tuscany.

Method

Grind the roasted cacao nibs with the sugar on a heated stone [pierre d'Espagne, i.e. a metate], them mix the spices in with the paste. To make the drink in one's chocolatière, boil 5 to 7 oz [140 to 205 ml] of water with 1/4oz [35 g] sugar (the higher the heat the better), throw in the broken-up chocolate tablet, and beat. Letting the mixture simmer after boiling will make it foam better.

Five years earlier, his compatriot Nicolas de Blegny published an almost equally complete and authoritative account of chocolate, and gave a recipe virtually identical to the "perfumed" version of St. Disdier's Recipe 3; he makes the interesting comment that this was the formula "most common among us," with the caveat that most users omit the chilli pepper.[57] In all events, we may be sure that it was the "stepped-up," Baroque, Tuscan version that was served to and drunk by all those heavily-bewigged aristocrats at the court of Versailles.

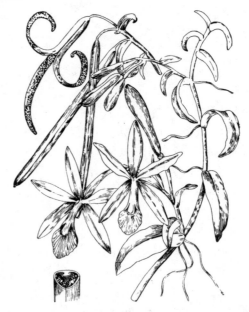

The source of vanilla flavoring is the fermented and dried pod of this climbing orchid.

Chocolate and the English: From Pirates to Pepys

The initial English contact with cacao seems to have been via the pirates and adventurers—many sailing under Elizabeth I's Letters of Marque—who preyed on Spanish shipping, and who terrorized Spanish ports during the latter half of the 16th century. They had not the slightest interest in these strange, bitter seeds, nor did they care to know what they were, for we are told that in 1579 English buccaneers contemptuously burned a shipload of the stuff, thinking the beans were but sheep droppings.[58] In his *Natural and Moral History* of 1590, José de Acosta notes: ". . . and in this year, an English corsair came by and burned in the port of Guatulco in New Spain [Mexico] more than 100,000 loads of Cacao."[59] Remembering that a load consisted of 24,000 beans, this was indeed a fortune in cacao.

Cacao finds a place in the 1633 edition of John Gerard's famous *Herbal or General History of Plants*, but he obviously knew it only at second hand. According to this pioneer botanist, "Cacoa," as he calls it, is a fruit "well known in divers parts of America"; and he is aware that in some places they use it as money, "and to make a drinke, of which, though bitter, they highly esteeme." Gerard goes on to say that the fruit is "of an astringent and ungrateful taste," an opinion that he may have picked up by reading Benzoni.[60]

When the chocolate drink finally did reach England, in the 1650s, the "scepter'd isle" was a tumultuous place, racked by political and social upheavals the likes of which were not to be seen on the other side of the Channel until the final decades of the next century. In 1646, that stubborn Stuart champion of the "divine right of kings," Charles I, was taken prisoner by Parliamentary forces in a civil war that had begun four years earlier; he was executed on 30 January 1649. England became a Puritan republic, bearing more resemblance to the Iran of the ayatollahs than to the Baroque Age states of France, Italy, and Spain. From 1653 until his death in 1658, the virtual dictator of England was Oliver

du Caffé, & du Chocolat. 247

pag. 247

X iij

S.H. fec.

Posture d'vn homme faissant la paste de chocolat.

Grinding cacao beans on a heated metate, from de Blegny's 1687 treatise. This technique, used by the pre-Conquest Mesoamericans, persisted for centuries in Europe.

Cromwell, who bore the title of "Lord Protector." Anglicans were pitted against Calvinists of every stripe, Puritans against "papists" both within England and without, and landed gentry against the more radical revolutionaries.

With Cromwell safely in his grave (until he was later exhumed and hanged in chains), Charles II returned in 1660 from his exile in France and Holland; the Restoration had begun, with renewed friction between king and parliament. Charles's brother James II, on succeeding to the throne in 1685, had every intention of returning England to the Catholic fold. This was too much for Protestant England; James was deposed by the "Glorious Revolution," and William of Orange, invited from Holland to be crowned in 1689 as joint sovereign with Mary, his wife and the daughter of James II. Unlike the Puritan Revolution, this one was bloodless.

Yet in spite of all this mayhem, religious bigotry (on all sides), and personal and public tragedy, the 17th century was in some respects the most brilliant in all English history, with towering figures in many fields—art, architecture, literature, music, philosophy, and, not least, science. Unfettered by the Papal Inquisition which hampered their great Italian contemporaries, such as Galileo, English scientists like Isaac Newton were free to explore the macrocosm (the universe) and the microcosm (the human body). Newton discovered gravitation and the secrets of the solar system, while William Harvey began the demolition of Galenic medicine by discovering the circulation of the blood.

Such was the context in which English men and women first took up the three great alkaloid-bearing drinks: tea, coffee, and chocolate. Although these drinks originated in three different continents—Asia, Africa, and America respectively—and came to England by different routes, they arrived virtually simultaneously (coffee being the earliest by only a few years).

Thus far we have said very little about coffee and tea, which were beginning to conquer continental Europe and which would

Fanciful depiction of a Turk, Chinese, and Aztec indulging in their respective drinks, from Dufour's 1685 treatise on coffee, tea and chocolate. The chocolatière *and* molinillo *are post-Conquest.*

in time oust chocolate as Europe's most popular hot drink. Let us begin with coffee. Its source, *Coffea arabica*, is a shrub native to northeastern Africa, and probably was domesticated for its caffeine-loaded berries in the Ethiopian highlands, but by the 14th and 15th centuries the plant was being cultivated around the shores of the Red Sea. In Europe, Venice was always the great commercial gateway to the markets of the Middle East, where Arab merchants drank coffee avidly, so it comes as no surprise to learn that the coffee habit had reached "The Most Serene Republic" from Constantinople and Cairo some time early in the 17th century. By 1638, coffee was being sold in Venice at exorbitant prices, as a medicinal product imported from Egypt. Thus, as was the case with chocolate, coffee travelled as a medicine once it arrived in Europe, where it was classified by the medical establishment as "hot and dry" (and was therefore connected with the gall bladder and the choleric temperament).

The very first coffee drinker in England is supposed to have been a Cretan student in Balliol College, Oxford, who was brewing it in his chambers in 1647, soon after the end of the Civil War. For medicine or for recreation, or for both? We are not told. It was also in the town of Oxford that the earliest English coffee-house was opened in 1650, by a Jewish proprietress;[61] Cromwell had allowed Jews into England, from which they had been expelled by Edward I almost four centuries earlier. Most of those Jews arrived from Holland, where coffee and tea drinking were already well known. Two years later, a coffee-house was opened in London by a Greek servant of an English merchant; he obtained his coffee from Smyrna, in the land of the Ottoman Turks. By 1663, during the early years of the Restoration there were no fewer than 82 coffee-houses in the English capital, most of them near the Exchange (the association of coffee-drinking and business is an old one). But, as we shall see, it was not only coffee that was being served in these establishments.

The tea bush is really a camellia (its scientific name is *Camellia sinensis*), and was domesticated for the brew which could be prepared from its leaves many millennia ago in China; by about AD 800, it was known in Japan. During the 16th-century, Europeans could read about this beverage in Portuguese and Venetian writings, but had little idea of what it was. When a very exotic delegation of four young converted samurai was brought to Rome from Japan by the Jesuits in 1585, to be presented to Pope Sixtus V, the Italians witnessed them preparing and drinking their tea, but thought it to be merely hot water—this dumbfounded them as much as seeing them eat their food with wooden or ivory sticks.[62]

It was the Dutch East India Company that finally imported tea into Europe as a commodity, the first consignment arriving in 1610. As was the case with both coffee and chocolate, this had to be fitted into the medical theory of the time: in 1687, for instance, one

John Jacob Mangetus proclaimed that tea was "moderately hot and dry," and good for colds, headaches, asthma, palpitations, podagra (gouty toe), and kidney stones—and for keeping one from getting drunk. He goes on aver that it was abused by Belgian women, whatever that might mean.[63]

The first English advertisement for tea appeared on 6 September 1658, the year of the Lord Protector's death. But because of its very high price then and throughout the century, it was sold and used only in small quantities. It would be a long time before England became a nation of tea drinkers. On 25 September 1660, Samuel Pepys wrote in his diary (begun on 1 January of that year): "And afterwards did send for a Cupp of Tee (a China drink of which I had never drank before) and went away."[64] You may be assured that this ever-curious and wonderful man was one of the first in England to taste this exotic beverage.

Chocolate did not lag long behind tea and coffee in getting to England—if, in fact, it did lag. Cromwell's forces took the island of Jamaica from the Spaniards in 1655; cacao plantations were already flourishing there, and Jamaica became England's main source for chocolate from that year. By 1657, an entrepreneur was advertising chocolate in an English newspaper. In its issue of 12–23 June 1659, *Needham's Mercurius Politicus* printed the following:

> Chocolate, an excellent West India drink, sold in Queen's-Head-alley, in Bishopsgate-street, by a Frenchman, who did formerly sell it in Gracechurch-street and in Clement's-churchyard; being the first man who did sell it in England. There you may have it ready to drink, and also unmade at easie rates, and taught the use thereof, it being for its excellent qualities so much esteemed in all places. It cures and preserves the body of many diseases, as is to be seen by the book, who hath it there to be sold also.[65]

This was the very same year that Louis XIV granted a country-wide royal monopoly for chocolate to Daniel Chaliou, pointing up a profound difference between the two nations: England was a land of shopkeepers and enterprising private businessmen, while France was a highly centralized, authoritarian kingdom with vast, tightly regulated state monopolies. In France, chocolate was strictly for the aristocracy, while in England it was available to all those who had the money to pay for it, and it was on offer to all who patronized coffee-shops. Chocolate was becoming democratized.

Samuel Pepys (1633–1703) the great diarist is revealed to us as one of the most sympathetic men of his age. Completely honest, frank about his own foibles and those of others, Pepys was a man of very high ability. Of middle-class origins, by hard work and native intelligence he rose to become England's first Secretary of the Admiralty, doubling her naval strength by the time he retired. Friend and confidant to Charles II, he knew everybody in England who counted, including her scientists (he was president of the Royal Society when it published Newton's *Principia*). His *Diary*, written in cipher, is a virtual window into the age, and into his own life.

Chocolate-taking was one of his pleasures. Although Pepys may have tried it before 1660, when his diary began (and when he went with the fleet that brought Charles II back from exile), it is in that year that we find this entry: "When I came home I found a Quantity of Chocolate left for me, but I know not from whom."[66] For 6 January 1663, he says: "Up, and Mr. Creede brought a pot of chocolatt ready made for our morning draught."[67] Here is the entry for 26 February of the following year: "Up; and after dressing myself handsomely for riding, I out & by water to Westminster to Mr. Creeds chamber; and after drinking some Chocolatte and playing on the vyall . . ."[68] Typically honest is the entry for 3 May 1664; "Up; and being ready, went by agreement to Mr. Blands and there drank my morning draught in good Chocolatte, and slabbering my band sent home for another."[69] In another entry, made on 24 November of that year, one can savor Pepys' gloriously free spelling: "About noon out with Commissioner Pett, and he and I into a Coffee-house to drink Jocolatte, very good!"[70]

The coffee-house had already become one of the greatest English institutions, retaining its social and political importance well into the next century, when it was transformed into the English club. The coffee-houses of the time are well described by the Italian Lorenzo Magalotti, who lived in London from 1668 to 1688. He tells us that they were places

> . . . where coffee is sold publicly, and not only coffee, but other drinks, like chocolate, tea, sherbert [then a sweet fruit drink], cock ale [ale with pieces of boiled fowl!], cider, and others, according to the season. In these houses there are various rooms . . . where one hears what is and what is believed to be new, be it true or false. In winter, sitting at a great fire and smoking two hours costs no more than two *soldi*; drinking, one pays for what one has drunk.[71]

Interior of a typical London coffee or chocolate-house c.1700. Charles II had unsuccessfully tried to suppress these establishments which he considered hotbeds of sedition.

As the historian Richard Dunn reminds us,[72] this was exactly the period that the two great political parties were forming: the Tories, who were "divine right" royalists, and the Whigs, who were generally anti-Stuart. Charles II greatly admired Louis XIV's absolutism (and secretly took a subsidy from the Sun King), but Whitehall was not Versailles—as he found out when he promulgated his "Proclamation for the Suppression of Coffee Houses" on 29 December 1675, which he described as places of licence and seditious libel (probably because they were frequented by Whigs). From now on, said Charles, it would be forbidden "to keep any Public Coffee House, or sell by retail, in his, or her or their house or houses (to be spent and consumed within the same) any Coffee, Chocolate, Sherbet, or Tea."[73] There was a tremendous outcry, and the monarch let them stay open another six months. But this was relatively democratic England, not absolutist France, and Charles's futile decree was soon forgotten.

Those coffee-house customers who were less than affluent had to think of their purses: chocolate was dearer than coffee, but tea was the most expensive of all. Coffee provided the most stimulation for the least outlay, which is probably why these were "coffee-houses" rather than "chocolate-houses."

England's chocolate-lovers of the late 17th century had access to some very detailed, English-language treatises on their favorite beverage. One of the best was *The American Physician*, published in London in 1672, by William Hughes;[74] this included an accurate description of cacao production and cacao preparation for an English audience, based upon the author's own experience in the New World tropics, as well as upon Spanish-language authors. Another was published by Philippe S. Dufour, who must have been one of the many Huguenot refugees who so enriched English life and commerce. After telling us about its origins and its popularity at the Spanish court, Dufour goes on to say that chocolate has been "lately much used in England, as Diet and Phisick with the Gentry" (ignoring the probability that most of it was consumed in coffee-houses). As compared with the ways that it is prepared and drunk in the Indies and in Spain, Dufour is decidedly unhappy with English methods of fixing their chocolate:

> But we in *England* usually boyl the *Chocolate* with the water, and some to make it more dainty, though less wholesome, use therein Eggs and Milk. There is yet another way, something different from this former, for they boyl both the *Chocolate* and water together till there swims at the top a fat buttery substance, taking care, that there is not too great a fire to make it boyl over. But this way I do in no wise approve of, for the fat separating it self from the earthy parts, this sinks to the bottom, and the other keeps on top, so that being thus drunk, the first [cacao butter] loosens the stomach, and takes away the appetite, and the latter causes melancholy.[75]

We are a long way from the Baroque splendors of Tuscan chocolate! The luxurious, unhurried methods elaborated by Redi for Cosimo III would never do for a "nation of shopkeepers." England was fast becoming the greatest commercial power of the world, and its people were in a hurry. Here, then, is Dufour's quick and wholesome way of preparing chocolate, suitable, as he assures us, for "men of business."

DUFOUR'S METHOD

Take a cake of chocolate, and either pound it in a mortar or grate it into a fine powder. Mix this with sugar, and pour it into a little pot in which water is boiling. Then, take the pot from the fire and "work it well with your little Mill; if you don't have a mill, pour it a score of times from on pot into another [shades of the Classic Maya!], but this is not as good." Finally, let it be drunk without separating the "scum" from it.[76]

173

A distinctly negative view of coffee, tea, and chocolate, especially the latter, was taken by Martin Lister in his *Journey to Paris in the Year 1698*. Why do Parisians, especially the women, become so corpulent? One reason is that they are too given to "Strong-waters" and strong wines. But the other is that they daily take coffee, tea, and chocolate with lots of sugar; this is what he has to say against such beverages:

> Mighty things indeed are said of these Drinks, according to the Humour and Fancy of the Drinkers. I rather believe that they are permitted by God's Providence for the lessening the number of Mankind by shortening Life, as a sort of silent Plague. Those that plead for Chocolate, say, it gives them a good Stomach, if taken two hours before Dinner. Right; who doubts it? You say, you are much more hungry, having drunk Chocolate, than you had been if you had drunk none; that is, your Stomach is faint, craving, and feels hollow and empty, and you cannot stay long for your Dinner. Things that pass soon out of the Stomach, I suspect, are little welcome there, and Nature makes haste to get shut of them. There are many things of this sort, which impose upon us by procuring a false hunger.
>
> The wild *Indians*, and some of our People, no doubt digest it; but our pampered Bodies can make little of it; and it proves to most tender Constitutions perfect Physick, at least to the Stomach, by cleaning that into the Guts; but that wears it out, and decays Nature.[77]

One of the most widely respected and quoted English authorities on chocolate was Dr. Henry Stubbes (or Stubbe or Stubbs; 1632–72), a friend of the philosopher Thomas Hobbes. Stubbes was said to have been a great master of the "chocolate art"; he opined that the cacao bean by itself was harmless, while most of the ingredients added to chocolate were not.[78]

When he prepared chocolate for Charles II, he doubled the usual quantity of cacao kernel in relation to the others. However,

Stubbes recommended that "cold" constitutions should add all-spice, cinnamon, nutmeg, and cloves to the concoction (the Spanish authorities had already deemed these to be "hot"). He is also aware of those aromatic Tuscan embellishments—musk, ambergris, citron, and lemon peel. Stubbes suggests adding sack (sherry) to chocolate made with milk and eggs, one spoonful to a dish (the English of the day often drank their coffee and chocolate from dishes rather than cups). With such additions, small wonder that Stubbes claimed one ounce of chocolate equal in nourishment to one pound of beef.

Dr. Stubbes was convinced, as were most of his contemporaries in England and on the Continent, that chocolate was an aphrodisiac. His encomium on the alleged erotic property of the substance is so good that we quote it in its entirety:

The great Use of *Chocolate* in Venery, and for Supplying the Testicles with a Balsam, or a Sap, is so ingeniously made out by one of our learned Countrymen already, that I dare not presume to add any Thing after so accomplished a Pen; though I am of Opinion, that I might treat of the Subject without any Immodesty, or Offence. *Gerson*, the grave *Roman* Casuist, has writ *de Pollutione Nocturna*, and some have defended Fornication in the Popish Nunneries; hysterical Fits, hypochondriacal Melancholy, Love-Passions, consumptive Pinings away, and spermatical Fevers, being Instances of the Necessity hereof, natural Instincts pointing out the Cure. We cannot but admire the great Prudence of *Moses*, who severely prohibited that there should be no Whore among the Daughters of *Israel*, yet that most wise Legislator took great care for their timely Marriage; upon these very Accounts the Casuists defend the Protestant Clergy in their Marriages. And *Adam* is commanded in Paradise to increase and multiply, therefore I hope this little Excursion is pardonable, being so adequate to this Treatise of *Chocolate*: which, if *Rachel* had known, she would not have purchased *Mandrakes* for *Jacob*. If the amorous and martial *Turk* should ever taste it, he would despise his Opium. If the

Grecians and *Arabians* had ever tried it, they would have thrown away their Wake-robins and Cuckow-pintles; and I do not doubt but you *London* Gentlemen, do value it above all your Cullisses and Jellies; your Anchovies, *Bononia* Sausages, your Cock and Lamb-stones, your Soys, your Ketchups and Caveares, your Cantharides [Spanish fly], and your Whites of Eggs, are not to be compared to our rude *Indian*; therefore you must be very courteous and favorable to this little Pamphlet, which tells you most faithful Observations.[79]

We would imagine that chocolate sales in London rocketed after this essay was published. Incidentally, it provides a fairly complete list of what other foods and substances were then believed to promote the venereal appetite, some of them smacking of the magical Doctrine of Signatures (like produces like).

Beyond Europe

Thus did chocolate make the long journey from Mesoamerica to Spain, and thence to other European countries, including England. It was probably not very long after Pepys first tasted it in London that it went back across the Atlantic to England's North American colonies (although it is possible that it traveled there directly from Jamaica after that island had been wrested from Spanish control). The most likely explanation is that high Colonial officials carried it with them when they were assigned to their administrative posts in places like Virginia and Massachusetts. At any rate, by the end of the 17th century, Judge Sewall could have witnessed Massachusetts meeting Mexico at the table of one of those officers of the King.

Chocolate never made any real inroads in the coffee-loving Near East: Dr. Stubbes's "amorous and martial Turk" spurned it. Giovanni Francesco Gemelli Carreri was another of those adventurous Italian merchants who voyaged around the world, leaving home in 1693, and returning in 1699. At one point he was in the

city of Smyrna, on the Turkish coast, and had a near-disaster on
account of chocolate:

> Thursday the Aga of Seyde came to see me. I gave him some choco-
> late, but this savage had never tasted it, or perhaps he was drunk, or
> the tobacco smoke produced the effect; he became very angry with
> me, saying I had made him drink a liquid to disturb him and take away
> his judgement. In short, had his anger lasted it would assuredly have
> gone badly with me, and it would have served me right, to have
> regaled such a coarse person with chocolate.[80]

We asked our friend Charles Perry, an authority on the cuisines of
the Near East and Central Asia, why chocolate has never really
been accepted in that part of the world. He writes us:

> I've often been puzzled about why this should be. The bittersweetness
> of chocolate confections ought to appeal in a part of the world where
> nut-filled pastries are popular. Possibly the cult of coffee and the way
> of life that revolves around the coffee house prevented the establish-
> ment of a popular taste for drinking chocolate at an early date, and
> later on there would have been the factor of the climate, which isn't
> friendly to tempered[81] chocolate. Perhaps cultural conservatism is the
> main reason; witness the peanut, which has made only trivial inroads
> on the traditional nuts in pastries.

We think Charles Perry's last explanation probably hits the mark:
cultural conservatism. The subject is still somewhat of a mystery.

Nor did chocolate ever "conquer" India, Southeast Asia, or
the Far East (with the exception of the Catholic Philippines).
Portuguese merchants and Jesuit missionaries took it with them on
their eastern enterprises, but the natives had little interest in the
substance. In 1993, in clear hopes of converting Chinese palates,
Cadbury Schweppes began construction, in a joint venture, of
a chocolate factory near Beijing; but the news magazine that

reported this came up with the sobering information that the Chinese eat only one bar of chocolate for every 1000 consumed by the chocoholic British![82]

As we have said, chocolate's one Asian success was the Philippines, conquered by the Spaniards in 1543, and a Spanish possession until annexed by the United States in 1898. Gemelli Carreri noted: "They have brought from New Spain to the Philippines the Cacao plant, which has multiplied so well, although it has degenerated a bit, that in a short while they can do without that of America."[83] In his day, a cup of chocolate was a common feature of "the best tables". The Philippines were the source of the chocolate that Jesuit missionaries and Portuguese businessmen found a necessity of life for their survival in such places as Siam. And the hot, thick chocolate drink is still part of the Spanish heritage, being taken by Catholic Filipinos throughout the islands as part of their traditional Christmas breakfast. Even a century of Americanization has not been able to change this.

But Baroque Europe was always chocolate's real conquest.

CHAPTER SIX

æ

The Source

In 1493, with the stroke of a pen on a piece of vellum all of the New World was divided into two parts. The pen was held by the hand of that most corrupt Renaissance pope, Alexander VI Borgia, he of the pious tonsure, sensuous lips, and scandalous personal life. Readjusted the following year by the Treaty of Tordesillas, this papal bull gave everything to the west of an imaginary north–south line to Spain, and everything east of it to Portugal; needless to say, not one of the inhabitants of these distant lands was consulted about his or her fate. Portugal's share became Brazil, while Spain got everything else, at least for the time being.

At first, this was largely a theoretical apportionment, but subsequent conquests carried out by Cortés, Pizarro, and others made it a reality for Spain. It did not take long for the Spanish Crown to impose on this vast territory a huge administrative, military, religious, and mercantile bureaucracy in which power flowed down from the royal Council of the Indies, whose headquarters were in Seville, through the regional viceroys. The Spanish commercial enterprise in the Americas was in effect a gigantic monopoly, on a scale never witnessed before or after, with a single set of rules and a single currency. Henceforth, the native "Indians" were to be harnessed as labor by means of the *encomienda*, a system administered by local Spanish land barons, mostly former conquistadores; the colonies were to provide gold, silver, and agricultural products to the mother country; and all manufactured goods used in the colonies were to be imported from Spain. All trade of any sort between Europe and America was to go through the Mediterranean port of Cádiz, where it could be rigidly controlled. And finally, foreigners were to be strictly excluded from this all-encompassing mercantile network; even the colonies were discouraged from trading with each other. It was in this context that cacao was grown, used, and traded.

New Spain and Central America: The Colonial Enterprise Begins

We have seen that the origins of domesticated cacao and its product, chocolate, lie wholly within Mesoamerica; until AD 1521, neither was known elsewhere in the world. We have also learned that the novelty and high value of cacao beans as "happie money" had enormously impressed the rapacious invaders right from the beginning of their enterprise: witness Alvarado's outrageous looting of Motecuhzoma's cacao warehouse. Since a copy of the Aztec tribute list had been made by order of the first Spanish viceroy in New Spain (Mexico), the very able Antonio de Mendoza, the Spaniards were quite aware of cacao's economic importance to the empire they had destroyed. Accordingly, they began to demand cacao tribute from those same regions—especially Soconusco (the former Xoconochco)—that had furnished the Aztec emperor with his cacao, this time for the benefit of the Spanish Royal Treasury. In fact, even before the arrival of Mendoza on Mexican soil, Hernán Cortés was demanding and receiving cacao tribute for himself.

Now the Spaniards, like other Europeans, had always bought and sold their goods by weight, but the Mesoamericans had never possessed scales and conducted their transactions by counting. Although some of the Spanish bureaucrats opined that cacao beans should be weighed in the market, it was soon found that for each load sold, the shrewd natives had shortchanged them by several hundred beans; accordingly, the *cabildo* (town government) of the newly-founded Mexico City issued ordinances that cacao transactions were always to be by number rather than by weight. This was *money*, and surely one would not sell gold coins by weight, would one? We are told that whites, Indians, and mestizos (those of mixed blood) used cacao beans as tender for small trans- actions all over Mesoamerica, right through the Colonial era. In his 1858 book *The States of Central America*, the American traveler and pioneer archaeologist Ephraim G. Squier has this to say about cacao: "It is, in fact, still used as a medium of exchange in the mar- kets of all the principal towns of Central America, where the absence of a coin of less value than three cents makes it useful in effecting small purchases. Formerly, and I believe still, two hundred nuts were valued at a dollar."[1]

In early post-Conquest Mexico and Guatemala (which then included Chiapas), the drinking of chocolate was pretty much confined to the natives, since many of the Spaniards found it unpalatable. But with the changes effected by the Peninsular and Creole Spaniards from the mid-16th century on (which we have treated in Chapter Four), there was an enormous increase in cacao consumption, particularly in Mexico. Through the next two centuries, chocolate-drinking—which in both pre-Conquest Mesoamerica and in Europe was the costly prerogative of the elite—was spread through all classes, including even the religious clergy. In a letter of 1779, a viceroy noted:

> In this country [New Spain] cacao is a primary food not only for persons of means as in other countries, but also among the poor people, especially servants both rustic and urban, who are given a ration of chocolate. It breaks your heart to hear the laments of the inhabitants of these vast regions, and particularly the poor male and female religious, whenever cacao hits an excessive price because of monopoly or poor harvest.[2]

As we saw in the last chapter, chocolate-drinking became a craze in 17th-century Europe, during the Baroque Age, and while its use was confined to the middle and upper social strata, it was virtually continent-wide. Thus, demand was doubled through the addition of the European market. At the same time, the Indian population of Mesoamerica—by whose labor chocolate was produced in the first place—plummeted. This was part and parcel of the greatest demographic catastrophe the planet has ever known, as all the native peoples of the Western Hemisphere were attacked by epidemic diseases of Old World origin, against which they had not the slightest resistance. Mistreatment by the Spaniards in their newly established mines, plantations, and cattle ranches also had its lethal effect. By the close of the 17th century, when the fat, decadent Cosimo III de' Medici was contentedly sipping his perfumed chocolate, only 10 percent of the original Indian population of the Americas had survived this holocaust. This human cataclysm was to have a profound effect on the geographic distribution of the cacao plant, and on how cacao traveled the trade routes within the Americas and across the Atlantic to Europe. Mesoamerica's role in this story was to be one of steady and irreversible decline.

Soconusco—long home to the world's premier cacao—is actually part of a large, Pacific lowland plain which runs all the way from the Isthmus of Tehuantepec down to the border country of Guatemala and El Salvador. We devoted some of our younger years to archaeological projects on this plain; for those unused to truly hot climates, the high humidity and constantly high temperatures (both day and night) can come as something of a shock. Yet where this oven-hot plain meets the foothills of the volcanic highlands, although the rainfall is higher, the heat is mitigated and the surroundings are far more pleasant. This is the coffee country of Mexico and Central America, but before the latter half of the 19th century, it was where cacao was grown. So rich was this piedmont zone in this product that highland Maya kingdoms had vied for control of these lands, and the Aztecs had made their most profitable conquest by taking over Soconusco. Lured by the cacao, the Spaniards were here soon after the Conquest. Initially, the rapacious conquistadores tried enslaving the Indians of Soconusco: a slave was valued at 2 gold pesos, a load of cacao at 10, and a pig at 20.[3] But on 29 May 1537, Pope Paul III Farnese published the bull *Sublima Deus*, excommunicating any Christian who enslaved an Indian (blacks, however, remained fair game). While this put an effective end to this practice, the institution of *encomienda* ensured that the *encomenderos* were getting what amounted to forced labor, in return for which they were to see that the Indians became Christians.

As the 16th century drew to a close, Soconusco and Guatemala were shipping large amounts of cacao via overland mule routes, to satisfy the burgeoning markets for this product in Oaxaca, Puebla, and Mexico City. Profiting from this commerce were not only the Spanish administrators, but also the clergy—the Council of Trent, 1543–63, had forbidden the clergy to engage in business, but no matter. It must have been exceedingly frustrating for them to see how the Indians who worked the cacao groves were dying off. Bernal Díaz del Castillo lamented thus:

> Let us turn to the province of Soconusco which lies between Guatemala and Oaxaca. I say that in the year 25 [1525] I was traveling through it for 8 or 10 days, and it used to be peopled by more than 15,000 inhabitants [i.e. heads of households], and they had their houses and very good orchards of cacao trees, and the whole province was a garden of Cacao trees and was very pleasant, and now in the year 578 [1578] it is so desolate and abandoned that there are no more than twelve hundred inhabitants in it.[4]

This sorry state of affairs was blamed by Díaz on pestilence, and on the natives being allowed no rest by the local mayors and by the priests.

The task of the governor and local officials was to collect the cacao tribute for the Royal Treasury: as late as 1820, three centuries after the Conquest, fine Soconusco cacao was still being sent to the Spanish king and his court. But with production down, the bureaucrats tried to offset the falling population in two ways: (1) by importing natives from the Maya highlands to work the plantations and (2) by imposing overseers to demand and control greater production. Both measures failed.

Yet for those Soconuscan Indians who survived, as the American ethnohistorian Janine Gasco has pointed out,[5] life was not entirely bad, since on those plantations under direct Indian control, the number of trees per capita actually increased, as did the overall wealth of those who owned them. In a report of 1549, it was claimed that because there were no *encomenderos* left in the district, the Indians had Negro servants and pieces of silver plate, and rode horseback[5] (something unknown elsewhere among the natives of New Spain, who were generally forbidden to own horses).[6]

The response of those living in Mexico and in the Guatemalan highlands was to obtain their cacao elsewhere; and obtain it they must, since chocolate was now a prime necessity. Nothing could keep the Guatemalans and Mexicans from having their daily chocolate (usually taken without vanilla, as this was generally held to be harmful to the health). During the Florentine businessman Francesco Carletti's around-the-world voyage of 1594–1606, he had stopped at a place called S. Jonat, apparently in the border area between Guatemala and El Salvador, a zone of very high cacao production. Carletti tells us that chocolate is used by both natives and Spaniards, "and any other nationality that goes there": "Once they start it they become so addicted that it is difficult for them not to drink it every morning, or late in the day when it is hot, or when on shipboard, because they carry it in boxes, mixed with spices, or made into tablets which dissolve quickly when put in water."[7]

An entertaining if not especially edifying story of chocolate addiction is related by Thomas Gage, whose 1648 book *The English-American, His Travail by Sea and Land, or a New Survey of the West Indies*[8] is our major source of the Maya area as it was in the 17th century. Born in 1600 into an English Catholic family, Gage was sent to France and then Spain for study with the Jesuits. Much to the disgust of his family, he subsequently broke with these mentors and entered a monastery of Dominicans. In 1625 he set off to the New World as a Dominican missionary. By 1637 he was back in Seville. But in 1640, when once again in England, he changed his religion to Anglicanism, to the even greater outrage of his relatives. Dedicated to Cromwell himself, *The English-American* was an anti-Catholic and anti-Spanish tract meant to reveal the weaknesses of the Spanish defenses in the Americas and thus to incite the English to an invasion. Gage was, in fact, present when the Cromwellian forces took Jamaica in 1655, dying there the next year.

Gage's particular story of chocolate addiction took place during his stay in Chiapa Real, now known as San Cristóbal de las Casas—a Colonial city surrounded by tens of thousands of highland Maya villagers, but until recently a city in which no Maya other than servants were allowed to spend the night. Not surprisingly, it was a target of the January 1994 uprising by the Zapatista Liberation Army. In any case, our tale has little to do with the Maya, but rather with the upper-class white ladies of the town. These claimed to suffer from such weak stomachs that they were unable to get through a prayer mass, let alone a High Mass with a sermon, without taking a *jícara* of very hot chocolate and some little bowls of conserves or syrup to fortify themselves. These were brought in by their Indian maids in the middle of the Mass or sermon, interrupting priests and preachers. The bishop at first tried verbal exhortation to put a stop to such practices, but they continued. Exasperated, the bishop had an order fixed to the door of the cathedral, excommunicating all who dared to eat or drink in the House of God during divine service. Greatly displeased but unrepentant, the ladies declared they would not go to Mass in the cathedral any more.

Thomas Gage and the local Dominican prior did their best to calm the waters, telling the bishop that the townspeople were muttering threats against his life, but the bishop was unmoved, replying that his life was worth nothing compared to the glory of God and the sanctity of His House. The ladies' Indian servants still carried chocolate into the churches, and there was turmoil as the clergy tried to take it away. The cathedral was by now deserted, as everyone went to Mass in the convents—thus bringing down another excommunication on those who refused to come to the cathedral.

The bishop then fell ill, after drinking chocolate (as we have seen, always a favorite vehicle for poison, in both hemispheres); he expired eight days later, after asking God to pardon the authors of the deed. As for the perpetrators, they were said to have been a female acquaintance of Gage's and one of the bishop's pages—with whom she was supposed to have been on intimate terms. The page administered the poison-laced chocolate in a *jícara*, giving rise to a ditty which made the rounds in 17th-century Mesoamerica: "Be careful with the chocolate of Chiapas."

A few pages further on, Gage gives a very detailed description of cacao and the making of chocolate, including the spices used to flavor it; he has read carefully in Colmenero de Ledesma about its supposed medical virtues and vices. It is here that he presents us with his putative etymology for the word *chocolate*—quite spurious, but quoted by food writers everywhere. The word derives, says Gage, from *atle*, meaning "water" in the Mexican [Nahuatl] language, which is more-or-less true; add to this the sound that the *molinillo* makes as it beats the chocolate—*choco, choco, choco*—and you have *chocolate*. Altogether, a "Just So" story, with little credibility.

In Colonial Mesoamerica as in the Catholic countries of Europe, there were ecclesiastical prohibitions to observe or flout, in particular the use of chocolate during fasts. The religious orders seem to have been unable to make up their minds whether or not chocolate should be altogether forbidden to those wearing the habit. The Society of Jesus in New Spain, for instance, published an act in June 1650 prohibiting the drink to Jesuits, but this was soon rescinded when it proved impossible to enforce, and when many of their students were leaving their school because of it.[9]

There are various pious anecdotes from Colonial Mesoamerica about members of the religious and secular clergy who were famed for their sanctity and abstinence from worldly pleasures: the substances from which they abstained often included chocolate. Here is one about Guatemala's closest approximation to a saint, the Venerable Pedro Betancourt, who died in 1667. According to a history of his order, the Belemites, this holy man customarily made his chocolate from crumbs of cheese and bread, chocolate scrapings, and bits of black sugar which he found in the pantry. The historian goes on to say:

> In the house of a religious man the Venerable Pedro was once offered a drink of chocolate, and the servant of God accepted the offering, on the condition that the person making it had to recite a Salve to the Queen of the Angels. A daughter of this benefactor went to make it, but she forgot to recite the Salve while she beat the chocolate. Having forgotten this, the girl took the *xícara* to the Venerable Pedro, who tried it and gave it back, saying, as one who identified the fault, "This chocolate does not taste of the Salve Regina."[10]

After his death, the poor woman got from the Venerable Pedro a little basket of bread, chocolate and sugar, and three pesos.

Guayaquil: The "Cacao of the Poor"

As the exportation of cacao to central Mexico from Guatemala and Soconusco fell in the 17th century to a half of what it had been in the previous century, the price of cacao shot up on the Mexican market, and other producers rushed in to supply the demand. Chief

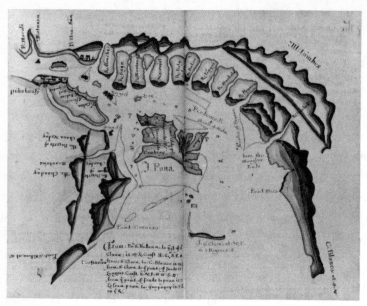

An 18th-century English chart of the Gulf of Guayaquil in Ecuador, a major source of cheap cacao throughout Colonial history.

among these were plantation owners on the Guayaquil coast of Ecuador, and the cacao planters of Venezuela.

Guayaquil seems to have been the first.[11] Lying only a few degrees south of the Equator, the lower reaches of the Guayas River and adjacent coast are thoroughly tropical, with heavy rainfall and lush vegetation, the result of being under the influence of the warm Mexican Current which bathes this coast before heading west into the reaches of the Pacific. When the Spaniards first settled here following the conquest of Peru, they came across extensive forests of wild cacao; this was the *forastero* variety of *Theobroma cacao*, native to tropical South America. Shortly after the beginning of the 17th century, these stands came under cultivation, merely by clearing the forest around the cacao trees. By 1635, there were cacao plantations throughout the Guayas basin; and merchants in Guayaquil, the provincial capital which had fully recovered from an invasion by Dutch pirates the year before, were shipping cacao in quantity to the Guatemalan and Mexican markets. So much, in fact, that local Guatemalan producers on several occasions induced the Colonial authorities to issue royal decrees forbidding the importation of Guayaquil cacao into Guatemala, or into Mexico through the port of Acapulco.[12] These had little effect, either in this or in the following century; and the free-trade policies of that most enlightened Bourbon king, Charles III (ruled Spain 1759–88), meant that trade in South American cacao finally had few if any restrictions. In the last decades of the Colonial period, between 1784 and 1821, 41 percent of all cacao coming into New Spain was from Guayaquil.

The bottom line was this: compared to the higher quality cacao of Mesoamerica, the *forastero* cacao of Ecuador was always abundant, and it was cheap. Never mind that it didn't taste very good—the beans were large, dry, and bitter—and that it was disdained by the Colonial elite of the Americas (who preferred Soconusco and Venezuelan cacao). It was generally known as *el cacao de los pobres*, "the cacao of the poor." And why was it so inexpensive? Firstly, because the *forastero* tree is simply more productive than the *criollo*, and secondly, because African slaves had been brought to this coast to work in the cacao groves in place of the Indians, who never took lightly to forced labor on white men's plantations. This meant that access to the chocolate drink was now within reach of all. Of course, because of its bitterness, large quantities of sugar had to be added to make the drink palatable, but sugar was not at all expensive since it, too, was produced by the "free" labor of slaves. We will touch on the unsavory subject of slavery and cacao later.

Venezuela

Venezuela was Ecuador's great rival for the lucrative Mexican market, and the chief cacao exporter to 17th and 18th-century

Europe.[13] Venezuelan cacao was grown along a narrow coastal plain on the north, or Caribbean, coast; narrow because it is hemmed in on the south by cloud-wreathed mountains which in places seem almost to tumble into the sea. Large swells often pound its shores, driven by the Northeast Trade Winds which blow for much of the year, and there are precious few natural harbors. Only the Gulf of Venezuela and Lake Maracaibo in the west would seem to offer much real protection for merchant fleets. Yet the harbor of La Guaira, now sheltered by artificial jetties, lying to the north of the inland capital of Caracas and cut off from it by a mountain chain, was the principal port for the shipment of cacao from the New World to the Old.

This cacao was a *criollo*, and was known as "Caracas" wherever it was imported. It was esteemed for its quality, not as highly as Soconusco, to be sure, but esteemed nevertheless. It must have grown wild in natural groves before the arrival of the Spaniards, for there are references to Venezuelan cacao in reports of the 1570s; eventually, inspired by the Mesoamericans' success with this tree, the colonists began growing it in plantations. Cacao flourished here, but where was the labor to come from? The Indians had unfortunately died off.

Until Paul III's papal bull, the Spaniards had no qualms about enslaving the native peoples of the Americas; in fact, that was an important part of Columbus's plan from the outset, and that is what happened to the unfortunate Arawak-speaking Indians of the Antilles. But the infamous "Middle Passage" from Africa across the Atlantic was something else, and apparently did not come under any papal prohibition. In this heinous enterprise, Spain's rivals France and Portugal, as well as the Protestant countries of England, Holland, and Denmark, all joined happily and profitably: the profits were huge on a cargo of surviving blacks from African slave ports such as Whydah. To expedite this commerce, all the countries concerned indulged in the "Three-way Trade" system: the slaving ships of a particular nation would carry manufactured goods like clothing, weapons, and metal tools to African slave depots; there, they would be used to barter for the human cargo, which was transported in pestilential holds to the sugar, cacao, indigo, and tobacco plantations of the New World colonies; the produce of those plantations would then be brought back and sold in the mother country.

Thus, the chocolate sipped by Europeans from Pepys in London to Cosimo III in Florence came largely from "Caracas" cacao groves worked by slaves. The traces of such trade can be seen in the population of the Venezuelan coast today, in which African genes have obviously freely mingled with those of Andalusia.

In theory, the cacao trade of Venezuela, like that of the rest of Latin America, was rigidly controlled by the Spanish Crown; but in practice, the merchants and planters of the coast were active contrabanders, and more and more of their commerce was going to the Dutch, and less and less through the port of Cádiz. Dutch pirates, as well as English, had been raiding this coast for a long time, but in the 1620s the Dutch seized islands strategically located off the coast to the northeast of the Gulf of Venezuela, and on one of them, Curaçao, they constructed a naval base. From there, as the English navigator and adventurer William Dampier reported in 1685,[14] the Dutch conducted a highly profitable if illegal trade with the ever-willing Venezuelans; he tells us that at any one time, three to four Dutch ships could be seen on the coast, bringing in all sorts of European commodities (especially linen), and making "vast returns," above all of cacao and silver; this cacao reached Amsterdam, from whence some of it almost surely wound up in Pepys' cup of "good Chocolatte." We know from other sources that the Dutch, who were adepts in the "Middle Passage," brought in many slaves from Curaçao: it has been estimated that in the period 1650 to 1750, 20,000 slaves arrived annually in Curaçao, and after 1750, sometimes up to 100,000 a year.[15]

It goes without saying that the Spanish Crown was losing a great deal through all this private enterprise. Monopoly had been

17th-century Dutch trading ships of the sort that plied the slave and cacao trade of the Caribbean and the coast of Venezuela.

the usual mode of trade for the state, and in 1728, Philip V granted privileges to the Real Compañía Guipuzcoana for all cacao production and commerce along this coast, together with the obligation to patrol its shores and suppress the contraband trade which had so damaged the Royal Treasury.[16] This was a Basque company, and the Basques were no strangers to the Atlantic, having come to northeastern North America as whalers, codfishermen, and traders, as early as the 16th century. They had the added advantage of speaking a difficult tongue unrelated to any other in the world, which must have been a help to them in keeping their plans secret from both the colonials and the Dutch (with whom they had many naval clashes).

Between 1730 and 1784, the Compañía Guipuzcoana exported more than 43,000 tons of cacao to Spain, so that in that respect it was a success. But it failed to stamp out the *contrabandistas* entirely, and it left a reputation for harshness and brutality that may have been a factor in the support that Venezuelans gave to the independence movement early in the next century.

At all events, the policy of trade liberalization imposed on the Spanish Empire by Charles III worked against monopolies, not for them. When he lifted the prohibition on trade between the viceroyalties of Peru and Mexico, this was an immense shot in the arm for the growers and merchants of Guayaquil, and they flooded the Mexican market once again with their *forastero* cacao, inferior to but always cheaper than "Caracas" cacao.

Brazil: The Jesuit Enterprise and Beyond

One cannot talk about the early cacao business in Brazil without talking about the Society of Jesus. As we said in the last chapter, the Order, founded in 1534, was the militant arm of the Church and a zealous defender of papal supremacy, with a tightly run, even secretive, worldwide organization. As such, it was perceived as a distinct threat by the temporal rulers of Catholic Europe, and to the Spanish and Portuguese settlers in those provinces to which Jesuit missions were sent. There were never many priests in the Order—at their height, in the mid-18th century, slightly over 22,000—yet they were often feared and disliked, by kings on down (Louis XIV was an exception, but he saw them as an effective force against his enemies the Protestants and Jansenists of France).

From a purely economic perspective, their most successful missionary effort in the New World was in Paraguay, but the way this enterprise was run made chills run down the spines of many people. There they controlled the lives of tens of thousands of Indians in 30 missions or "reductions," and had absolute control over their lives and labors—labors which produced, at great profit to the Jesuits, tobacco, hides, cotton, and so forth. So regimented were the natives that it is said that the Jesuit fathers rang a bell every night to tell the men it was time to perform their marital duties with their wives; we are not told whether these human "Pavlov's dogs" responded properly.

This particular Jesuit experiment, so reminiscent of the Chinese communes imposed by the late Chairman Mao, or even of Pol Pot's Cambodia, was not to be repeated elsewhere in the Americas; but the economic scenario which they had devised in Paraguay (and, concurrently, among their cacao-producing missions in the Mojos or Moxos region of northeastern Bolivia) was played out in more attenuated form in Brazil, along the banks of the mighty Amazon and its tributaries. There they had discovered extensive stands of wild, *forastero* cacao, as well as thousands of tropical forest Indians, most of them hunters, fishermen, and manioc farmers. These Indians, unfortunately, were the target of professional Portuguese and mestizo slave-hunters (a practice that continued well into the 20th century), and to their credit the Jesuits were the first to protest against this vile injustice.[17]

Organizing the natives, as they did in Paraguay, into *aldeas* where they could be controlled and isolated from the outside world, the Jesuits sent them on regular expeditions into the forest to collect the wild cacao. One of these early Jesuits, in a 1639 report, describes the important commodities produced along the Amazon, beginning with lumber:

> The second commodity is cacao, of which the banks are so full, that sometimes when wood was being cut for the lodging of the whole army, there was hardly anything but those trees which produce the fruit so esteemed in New Spain and everywhere else where they know what Chocolate is; which cultivated [i.e. cleared] is so profitable that every tree, yearly and free from all expenses, gives a profit of 8 silver reales; and one can easily see how little work it takes to cultivate these trees on this river, as without any application of art, nature fills them with abundant fruit.[18]

This was a "labor-extensive" operation in the fullest meaning of the term: collecting expeditions would go out in huge dugout canoes manned by 12 to 24 Indian paddlers. But careful, intensive preparation of the harvested seeds was lacking, and they often rotted and spoiled because of inadequate drying. Furthermore, this was *forastero* cacao, of low quality for chocolate. Nonetheless, since the authorities allowed the religious orders to ship without paying duty, cacao was a lucrative crop for the Jesuits, and continued to be the dominant export commodity of the Amazon until trade was interrupted by the smallpox and measles epidemics of the 1740s and 1750s, which decimated the Indian gatherers.

Quite naturally, these Jesuit commercial triumphs, as well as suspicions which non-Jesuits held about the Order, aroused a great deal of antipathy to them in both hemispheres. In his wonderfully chatty memoirs of the court of the pro-Jesuit Louis XIV, the duc de Saint-Simon relates with considerable relish an anecdote concerning the cacao operations of the Society of Jesus.[19] In the year 1701, the annual Spanish flotilla from the Indies arrived in Spain as usual. On unloading one vessel, there were discovered eight large crates marked "Chocolate for the Very Reverend Father General of the Company of Jesus." When the porters tried to lift them, they were bent double with their weight, but at last they got the crates into the proper warehouse in Cádiz. When the inspectors opened one of them, they found huge blocks of chocolate, one on top of the other, all extremely weighty: they proved to be bars of pure gold, each coated with a finger's thickness of chocolate. The Jesuits refused to acknowledge the shipment; Saint-Simon avers they would rather lose it than claim responsibility—after all, this was smuggling of the first degree, since all gold was royal property. The gold, as is proper, went to the king, and the chocolate "to those who had discovered the deception."

But the days of the Jesuits in Europe and the Americas were numbered. The immediate vehicle of their destruction was the Marquis Sebastião de Pombal, virtual dictator of Portugal during the reign of the weak José I (1750–77). In 1751, a new royal governor was installed in Brazil, Francisco Xavier de Mendonça Furtado, a brother to Pombal who shared with him his loathing of the

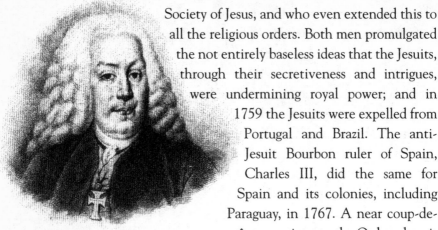

*Sebastião de Pombal (1699–1782),
who instigated the expulsion of the Jesuits from
Brazil, and encouraged the rise of slave-worked
cacao plantations there.*

Society of Jesus, and who even extended this to all the religious orders. Both men promulgated the not entirely baseless ideas that the Jesuits, through their secretiveness and intrigues, were undermining royal power; and in 1759 the Jesuits were expelled from Portugal and Brazil. The anti-Jesuit Bourbon ruler of Spain, Charles III, did the same for Spain and its colonies, including Paraguay, in 1767. A near coup-de-grâce was given to the Order when it was effectively abolished by Pope Clement XIV in 1773. But the Jesuits survived, ironically enough, in the non-Catholic countries of Prussia and Russia, where they were given protection by such unlikely figures as those "Greats," Frederick and Catherine.

For Brazil's Amazonian cacao lands, Pombal had other plans. Three years before he decisively got rid of the Jesuits, he had formed the General Company of Commerce of Great Pará and Maranhão—a state monopoly along the lines of Spain's Compañía Guipuzcoana, fully subsidized by the government.[20] Pombal made it a policy that the Indians were not to be enslaved, but the surviving natives refused to work on the cacao plantations. Pombal's solution was to accelerate imports of African slaves to replace them. When the Napoleonic Wars cut England off from Venezuelan cacao, Amazonia increased its exports; the chocolate drunk in English coffee-house may not have been of very high quality, but at least it was there. By the end of the 19th century, the Amazonian cacao plantations had disappeared, as slavery was finally abolished in Brazil, and as epidemics killed off what labor there was. Cacao survived as an industry in Brazil, but the commercial center of gravity had moved out of the Amazon, to the coastal region of Bahía, south of the great river's delta.

The Fortunate (and Not-So-Fortunate) Islands

The beautiful islands of the West Indies, winter playground of rich and not-so-rich North Americans and Europeans, have had a checkered and often deeply tragic history—or we should say "histories," since European powers struggled over them for centuries following their "discovery" by the Admiral of the Ocean Sea in 1492. The native inhabitants of the Antilles, the Arawaks and Caribs, were exterminated early on by disease and Spanish brutality. Fought over by pirates, settlers, and major European states, and the final destination of hundreds of thousands of unfortunate Africans brought across the "Middle Passage," the islands today are a kaleidoscope of races, tongues, cultures, and governments, not to mention political philosophies.

Spain had an extremely difficult time maintaining its hegemony over the West Indies, and for centuries the Spanish flotillas and ports were preyed upon by pirates of Dutch, English, and French nationality. By the mid-16th century, the Dutch freebooters knew the value of the cacao carried in the cargo holds of many of these ships, but the English pirates did not. Eventually, the English learned differently, and by 1684, John Esquemeling was able to state in his *Bucaniers of America*, regarding a foray on the Guayaquil coast: "But we had plundered some small quantity of good *Chocolate*, whereof the *Spaniards* make infinite use. So that now we had each morning a dish of that pleasant liquor, containing almost a pint."[21]

When the British took Jamaica in 1655, they came across many newly established cacao "walks" (as they called plantations). Jamaican cacao soon reached the London market, but was also enjoyed locally in the island. A few years ago we were shown the archaeological collections from the then capital of Port Royal, reputed to be the wickedest city of the Americas, and destroyed by the great earthquake of 1692. Among all the thousands of artifacts of largely English manufacture—glass, pewter, silver, and the like—

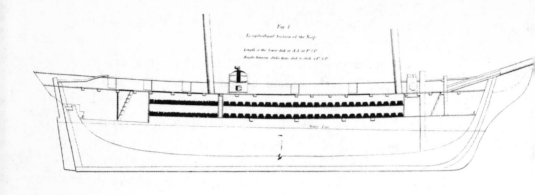

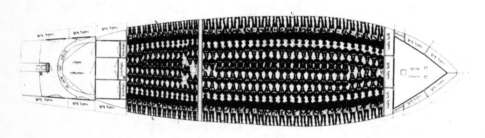

Lines and lower deck plan of the slaving bark Vigilante, *out of Nantes, France, 1822. Hundreds of thousands of Africans were shipped in such vessels to work the cacao plantations of the American tropics.*

were *metates* of Honduran manufacture which must have been used to grind cacao for the wealthy traders, smugglers, and pirates who had established themselves in the port. But calamities were a constant feature of these islands, and in the 1670s a so-called "blast"—probably a blight of some sort—wiped out Jamaica's cacao "walks."

Other islands of the Antilles were regularly disputed between the French and the English, but Martinique and Guadeloupe stayed in French hands, as did the western part of Hispaniola. Here there was no problem of labor, for French slaving ships poured their wretched human cargos into their West Indian possessions. Upon arrival, a trader would typically get up to five times for each slave over what he had paid for him (or her) on the African coast.

France's two main slave-trade ports, Nantes and Bordeaux, grew rich on the proceeds from the "Three-way Trade"; and the steady influx of tobacco, sugar, coffee, cacao, cotton, indigo, and other tropical commodities spawned sugar, textile, and chocolate mills in the mother country. Slavery was officially banned in 1817 in France, but Nantes was clandestinely trading in slaves for the next 20 years.[22]

According to the Jesuit priest Jean-Baptiste Labat,[23] the first person to plant cacao in Martinique was "a Jew named Benjamin Dacosta," some time around 1660, but he was deported in 1664, so the experiment was abortive. Serious cultivation, he says, only began about 1680, and proved to be extraordinarily successful, as it was on Dominica and Grenada, islands lying to the north and south respectively. Father Labat comments ironically on these planters:

> The use of chocolate is widely distributed in the islands. In fact, the inhabitants use it so commonly, along with brandy and tobacco, that these things seem to them as a clock and a measure; so that if you ask them at what time they left a place and when they arrived, they answer "I left at the stroke of brandy [*eau-de-vie*] and I arrived at chocolate," which is to say at 8 o'clock. And if one wants to know the distance between one place and another, they say "it is two smokes or three smokes," because it is their custom to smoke while walking.[24]

But in 1727 a tremendous earthquake hit Martinique (perhaps a harbinger of the terrible Mt. Pélée eruption that destroyed Saint-Pierre in the same region in 1902), and the cacao groves were gravely damaged. However, the industry survived, and cultivation of Martinique's good *criollo* cacao was extended to Guadeloupe. Through most of the 18th century, the production of these two islands was sufficient to supply the needs of the cacao market in Metropolitan France, supplanting "Caracas" cacao.[25]

Those *philosophes* of the Enlightenment may have been believers in human freedom, but the frothy West Indian chocolate they drank was produced by the sweat of slaves. But who are we to point out the hypocrisy? After all, the Declaration of Independence was written by a slave-owner.

Lying near the delta of Venezuela's great Orinoco River, the very large island of Trinidad has an important part to play in the history of chocolate. Discovered by Columbus, and then colonized by the Spaniards (who proceeded to exterminate its native Carib population), Trinidad was contended for over the centuries by the Dutch, French, and English, finally passing to Britain in 1802. Cacao trees, apparently *criollo*, were introduced by Aragonese and Catalan Capuchin friars, and became one of the principal resources of the island. Then, in 1727, a disaster of an undetermined nature struck the plantations, and the trees died.

Slaves being sold in Martinique in the 18th century. On the left food is being pounded in a mortar, an African technique.

Thirty years later, the Capuchin Fathers returned to re-establish their missions, this time carrying with them *Theobroma cacao* seedlings of the variety which they were the first to call *forastero* or "foreign"; these probably came from wild stands along the Middle Orinoco. Once in Trinidad, these began to hybridize with what was left of the local *criollo* trees, and the new variety *trinitario* was born.[26] *Trinitario* combined the taste qualities of *criollo* with the vigor, hardiness, and high yields of *forastero*, and this novelty— along with *forastero* itself—was to spread the cultivation of cacao around the world, sometimes even driving out *criollo*, as happened in Venezuela after *trinitario* had been introduced on its Caribbean coast.

New Horizons: Cacao Circumnavigates the Globe

It seems supremely ironic that West Africa, from which so many hundreds of thousands had been torn against their will to work as slaves in the white man's cacao plantations, should now be by far the world's leading producer of cacao.[27] How did this come about? This again was a European colonial enterprise. In 1824, the Portuguese transplanted *forastero* cuttings from Brazil to São Tomé, west of Gabon in the Gulf of Guinea, with the result that cacao became one of the islands's principal exports until the end of the 19th century. About 1850, some cacao cuttings were taken from São Tomé to Fernando Po (the island now known as Bioko, part of Equatorial Guinea), and that island also began exporting the ubiquitous *forastero*. From the colonies of Portuguese Africa, *Theobroma cacao* made the journey to the Gold Coast (Ghana), then to Nigeria, and by 1905 to the Ivory Coast. Towards the end of the 19th century, the Germans planted it in the Cameroons.

Heading east across the tropics of the Old World, the British carried it to Ceylon (Sri Lanka), and the Dutch to their colonies in the East Indies (Java and Sumatra). By the first part of the 20th century, the European imperial ascendancy had established cacao plantations in Oceania—in the New Hebrides and New Guinea, and even on Samoa. We have already seen in the last chapter that the Spaniards had brought *criollo* seedlings across the Pacific from Mexico to the Philippines; the new American masters of the islands established their own plantations after the defeat of Spain.

So, in a market report of 1991, Africa was now the source of 55 percent of the world's cacao, while Mexico (where not only chocolate was born, but the word *cacao* itself) accounted for only 1.5 percent. According to the Food and Agriculture Organization (FAO), the leading producers, in the order of importance, are: (1) the Ivory Coast; (2) Brazil; (3) Ghana; (4) Malaysia; (5) Indonesia; (6) Nigeria; (7) Cameroon;

(8) Ecuador; (9) Columbia; (10) Dominican Republic; (11) Mexico; (12) Papua New Guinea.[28] Even more *forastero* cacao is grown than ever, a consequence of the discovery of disease-resistant plants in the upper Amazon, so the *forastero* now accounts for 80 percent of world production; 10 to 15 percent is *trinitario*; and *criollo* comes in a poor third. In fact, *forastero* has been taken up by growers in Mexico and Guatemala, as well as in Costa Rica, the Antilles, and Sri Lanka.

Does this mean that *criollo*, still the best of the cultivated cacaos, the source of the chocolate drunk by the royal house of Spain, is finished? Gresham's Law states that bad money drives out good. But, happily for our story (as we shall find out in Chapter Eight), quality has not yet been completely driven out of the market by quantity, and there are still those who will pay the price for superior taste. There may not be any *criollo* cacao in the chocolate bars munched at European and American football games, but it lives on in luxury confections.

CHAPTER SEVEN

❧

Chocolate in the Age of Reason
(and Unreason)

W_e cannot think about the *anciens régimes* of 18th-century Europe without recalling what happened in 1789 to its then most populous country, France. Why did the convulsion of the Revolution strike this nation and not, say, England or Spain or Russia? Social and political historians since de Tocqueville and Carlyle have been looking for causes ever since, and no century has been more dissected and analyzed than the "Age of Reason." Whatever the root causes of the French Revolution—or the American one, for that matter—there can be little doubt that this was a century of rapid, worldwide change, worldwide because imperial and commercial networks now reached around the globe, with England, France, and Holland dominant on the high seas.

For reasons that are still not well understood, European and North American populations were growing at an unprecedented rate; and while many of these "new people" were poor, many of them were not, so that the century saw a rapid rise in consumerism, with ever-burgeoning numbers of small manufacturers turning out vast quantities of goods, especially textiles, for home consumption. Technological advances and a spirit of entrepreneurship led some countries, above all England, into the Industrial Revolution by the latter half of the century. All of this tended to make the rich grow richer, and the poor, poorer. We often view the 18th century in terms of drawing-room elegance, powdered wigs, and rarefied manners, but urban and rural riots—often food riots caused by lack of affordable grain—were the order of the day, and were usually savagely put down.

At the same time, there was a veritable information explosion, with presses turning out all sorts of material, some of it radical and even seditious; newspapers were to be found everywhere. If the Church often reacted by putting subversive, deistic, or even atheistic works on its Index, there was very little it could do to prevent this material from circulating clandestinely. Among the intellectuals of the most advanced countries (England, France, and the German and Italian states), philosophical schools took shape that proposed to examine the very basis of society, questioning the legitimacy of the Church, of the nobility, and of the monarchy itself, and championing the rights of men—that is, those with property—to a free and prosperous life. These were the leaders of the Enlightenment, and the fundamental questions they raised were to reverberate down the centuries. And yet such intellectual debates, at least in France, resounded more in the salons of the wealthy than among the pious and largely illiterate or semi-illiterate masses.

Food and drink, not surprisingly, reflected these economic, social, and religious cleavages. In his book *Tastes of Paradise*,[1] Wolfgang Schivelbusch characterizes chocolate as southern and Catholic and aristocratic, and coffee as northern and Protestant and middle-class. The average nobleman drank chocolate for a leisurely breakfast, while the bourgeois businessman was shaken awake by coffee; coffee, he says, gave to the mind what it took from the body, while chocolate was thought to do the reverse. We should remember that the staunchly Lutheran J.S. Bach wrote a Coffee Cantata, not songs in praise of chocolate. And the proletariat? They drank alcohol—inexpensive wine in the south, beer in the north (but, increasingly, cheap gin in the north, with the effects so memorably pictured by Hogarth in his print "Gin Lane"). Goethe, who made a cult of the chocolate drink, might seem an exception to the rule, but Schivelbusch explains this as the pretensions of a middle-class man making it into the aristocracy. And it was, he reminds us, those two arch-Protestant countries, Holland and Switzerland, that put an end to the Spanish (and ultimately Mesoamerican) chocolate-drink tradition in the next century.

Even among the *philosophes* of the French salons, coffee was the preferred drink, as opposed to the chocolate so closely associated with the Catholic clergy (above all, with the Jesuits), with the ultramontanists favoring papal supremacy, and with all those others who had been opposed to the Enlightenment.

The very essence of what the Protestant bourgeoisie of northern Europe thought about those 18th-century chocolate drinkers is to be found in the 1859 novel *A Tale of Two Cities* by that most determinedly middle-class writer, Charles Dickens, in the chapter entitled "Monseigneur in Town":

Monseigneur, one of the great lords in power at the Court, held his fortnightly reception in his grand hotel in Paris. Monseigneur was in his inner room, his sanctuary of sanctuaries, the Holiest of Holiests to the crowd of worshippers in the suite of rooms without. Monseigneur was about to take his chocolate. Monseigneur could swallow a great many things with ease, and was by some few sullen minds supposed to be rather rapidly swallowing France; but, his morning's chocolate could not so much as get into the throat of Monseigneur, without the aid of four strong men besides the Cook. Yes. It took four men, all four a-blaze with gorgeous decoration, and the Chief of them unable to exist with fewer than two gold watches in his pocket, emulative of the noble and chaste fashion set by Monseigneur, to conduct the happy chocolate to Monseigneur's lips. One lacquey carried the chocolate-pot into the sacred presence; a second, milled and frothed the chocolate with a little instrument he bore for that function; a third, presented the favoured napkin; a fourth (he of the two gold watches), poured the chocolate out. It was impossible for Monseigneur to dispense with one of these attendants on the chocolate and hold his high place under the admiring Heavens. Deep would have been the blot upon his escutcheon if his chocolate had been ignobly waited on by only three men; he must have died of two.

We have seen in the last chapter that throughout the Spanish and Portuguese possessions in the New World, chocolate-drinking was widespread among all classes, even though it may not have been of the best quality, but this was definitely not the case in Europe. There is an illuminating piece of social commentary in the first act of Mozart's *Così fan Tutte*, dating from 1790. The scene is the drawing-room in the house of those two flirts, Fiordiligi and Dorabella; their maid Despina enters, carrying a tray with cups and a chocolate-pot, and laments:

A young lady taking her chocolate, pastel by the Swiss artist
Jean-Etienne Liotard (1702–89).

What an abominable life a lady's maid leads! From morning till night, sweating, toiling, laboring, and then, after doing all this, we get nothing out of it ourselves. I've been beating the chocolate for half an hour, now it's ready, and is it my lot to stand and smell it with a dry mouth? Isn't my mouth just like yours? Oh gracious mistresses, why should you get the real thing and I only the smell of it? By Bacchus, I'm going to taste it. (*She does so*).
Oh, it's good![2]

There was very little difference between the chocolate quaffed in the 18th century, and that of the Baroque Age which preceded it: the method of preparation, the *batterie de cuisine*, the spices and flavorings were all more-or-less the same. What *was* different, however, was the amount of chocolate that was eaten: eaten in the form of bars and pastilles, as ices, and included in recipes for desserts, main dishes, and even pastas and soups. This was a foretaste of developments which would take place during the next two centuries.

The Medical Experts Testify

To adapt the famous opening line of *A Tale of Two Cities*, "it was the best of drinks, it was the worst of drinks." As usual, the medical opinions on chocolate—and on those two other hot drinks, tea and coffee—varied wildly, notwithstanding the fact that all were firmly rooted in the same tired old humoral medicine that had been passed down from Classical antiquity.

Many of these 18th-century authorities held that chocolate was on the whole beneficial, if not taken to excess. This was the opinion of Giovanni Maria Lancisi (1654–1720), physician to Pope Clement XI Albani, who on the pope's insistence conducted an investigation (which included post-mortem examinations) into a rash of sudden deaths which had taken place in Rome in 1705.[3]

The popular explanations for the calamity focused on bad snuff and overuse of chocolate; but in his 1707 report, Lancini absolved chocolate, and cited habitual users who had lived to a ripe old age.

Also positive about chocolate was the French food writer Louis Lémery; the 1704 London edition of his 1702 *Traité des Aliments* states: "It's strengthening, restorative, and apt to repair decayed Strength, and make People strong: It helps Digestion, allays the sharp Humours that fall upon the Lungs: It keeps down the Fumes of the Wine, promotes Venery, and resists the malignity of the Humours."[4]

Here we have yet once more the ageless "venery" myth about chocolate (according to Lémery and others, coffee had the opposite effect). A few decades later, one Dr. Giovanni Bianchi of Rimini, after listing a number of recipes to cure impotence, including such *materia medica* as stag's horn, ivory shavings, and sassafras root, admonishes the sufferer to "take chocolate often with a good dose of vanilla and aromatics."[5]

The French Huguenot physician Daniel Duncan (born in Montauban in 1649, died in London in 1735) wrote an extensive treatise on drinks, both alcoholic and non-alcoholic; first published in France in 1703, and subsequently in London in 1706, it was widely quoted as an authority throughout the century.[6] Taken moderately, coffee, chocolate, and tea were healthful, but not when abused, since in excess they made the blood too sharp, too "hot," and too thin. Coffee was the most dangerous of all, not only because it was the most common, but also because it was "hot and dry" and, if abused, would lead to jaundice. But one had to be careful of one's individual temperament: chocolate was bad for the sanguine (it makes the blood "over-inflammable") and for the choleric.

While there was general agreement that coffee was "hot and dry," there was little consistency of opinion about the humoral properties of chocolate. Some followed the Spaniards and held it to be "cold," others said it was "hot," while there were those who claimed it to be "temperate" if one avoided "hot" flavorings. The "temperate" school was generally more favorable towards chocolate than the others, and recommended the substance above all to old people to prolong their lives. An anonymous French author, writing in 1726, describes how a lady of Martinique, who had lost her lower jaw and was unable to take solid food, drank three bowls of chocolate a day, and lived a long and healthy life.[7]

This must have been very comforting to chocolate lovers—but then they could read exactly the opposite opinion in a 1728 treatise by Dr. Giovanni Batista Felici, physician to the Tuscan court. On its first page he has planted his bombshell: "Among the many disorders which the Intemperance of Mankind has introduced to shorten their lives, one of the greatest, in my opinion, is the use of Chocolate." Chocolate is not "cold" but "hot"—it is a mistake to think it "cold" and then proceed to add the "hottest drugs" like cinnamon, vanilla, pepper, clovers, ambergris, and achiote. "I know certain serious and taciturn persons, who by virtue of this Drink, become for a while the greatest chatterers, some lose sleep and get hot-headed, others become angry and shout. In children it awakens such an agitation that in no way can they be quiet or sit in one place."[8]

Italians could read with horror the list of bad effects alleged by Felici, which included palpitations, thickened blood, lack of appetite, and so on. Conceding that it might be all right for the treatment of some diseases like consumption (tuberculosis)—a widely held belief—Felici cautions that just because something cures sickness does not mean that it is good for one's health.

What Felici says about hyperactive children is interesting, for in Joseph Baretti's *An Account of the Manners and Customs of Italy*, 1768,[9] we are told that young people in that country were seldom or never permitted to drink anything hot in the morning, since it spoiled their teeth and enfeebled their constitutions; the morning cup of chocolate or coffee was for "all our polite people of an adult age." The era of chocolate for children was yet to come.

The life-enhancing virtues of chocolate were extolled by the last medical author whom we shall cite, Antonio Lavedán, a surgeon in the Spanish army, who published his tract on coffee, tea, and chocolate in 1796. Although—or perhaps because—chocolate was "hot and humid," it was especially valuable for the phlegmatic, for the old and decrepit, and for the consumptive. He approvingly quotes a panegyric by one Geronimo Piperni: "Chocolate is a divine, celestial drink, the sweat of the stars, the vital seed, divine nectar, the drink of the gods, panacea and universal medicine."[10]

Spain

Protestants, *philosophes*, bourgeois businessmen, and thus coffee were in short supply in 18th-century Spain, and chocolate made in the old style still reigned supreme. This was a nation of chocolate drinkers, and the Spanish attitude regarding it is revealed in these witty lines by Marco Antonio Orellana, a native of Valencia:

¡Oh, divino chocolate!	Oh, divine chocolate!
que arrodillado te muelan,	They grind thee kneeling,
manos plegadas te baten	Beat thee with hands praying.
y ojos al cielo te beben.	And drink thee with eyes to heaven.[11]

As usual, the Jesuits in Spain were great imbibers (and importers) of chocolate. The duc de Saint-Simon, when he was ambassador in 1721, visited a Jesuit establishment in Loyola, and was mightily impressed: ". . . in a word, one of the most superb buildings in Europe, the best planned and the most magnificently ornamented. We had there the best chocolate I ever tasted, and after some hours of curiosity and admiration we resumed our route . . ."[12]

Of course, such clerical luxury came to an abrupt end in 1767, when Charles III expelled the Company of Jesus from Spain and its overseas possessions. When this happened, the Conde de Aranda gave these magnanimous instructions to local judges: "There will be given to them for their personal use all the usual clothing and changes of clothes to which they are accustomed, without loss; their boxes, handkerchiefs, tobacco, chocolate and utensils of this kind . . ."[13] A Jesuit was not to be separated from his chocolate!

During the enlightened reign of Charles III, some 12 million pounds (about 5.4 million kg) of chocolate were consumed each year in the capital alone;[14] the Madrileños were famed for their love of the stuff. The best chocolate was supposed to be from the Mojos or Moxos region in the Amazonian drainage of Bolivia, valued for its fragrance and lack of bitterness; next best was the cacao of Soconusco and Tabasco, and Venezuelan cacao. At the bottom of the list were Guayaquil and Martinique because their bitterness had to be tempered with lots of sugar.

Chocolate was strictly for the upper and middle classes, who breakfasted on it after drinking a glass of cold water (the usual preliminary to chocolate-taking in Spain). After dinner, there was a siesta; then the taking of more chocolate, or iced drinks, and a man would go about his business again. By the latter half of the century, coffee-houses had sprung up in Madrid as in other European cities; in these and in the refreshment parlors one could get tea (always expensive), coffee, chocolate, French pastry, preserves, and liquors. These establishments were for men only: women stayed in their coaches and had cold drinks brought to them. According to the social historian Charles Kany, towards the end of the 18th century, a number of fashionable people deemed it proper to breakfast on coffee or tea, in order that Spain might occupy a dignified position among modern nations.[15] Since chocolate was identified with royal and/or papal absolutism, so inimical to the Enlightenment, tea— for a few radicals—came to symbolize civilization and liberty.

In 1772 there were nearly 150 chocolate grinders (*molenderos de chocolate*) in Madrid alone, and these formed a guild the next year; such guilds existed in many other Spanish cities. It required six years of apprenticeship to learn this trade. Chocolate grinders often went from house to house to serve customers who chose to have their chocolate ground at home. The guilds guarded against adulteration by unscrupulous grinders, who are said to have made their concoction with almonds, pine nuts, flour, acorns, coffee (!), bread and cake crumbs from confectionery shops and bakeries, pepper, and even orange peel that had been dried and ground.[16]

Travelers generally thought highly of Spanish chocolate. Writing in 1799 to his daughter from Ferrol, in Galicia, the American diplomat John Adams—later to become the second President of the United States—had this to say: "I have met with few Things more remarkable than the Chocolate which is the finest I ever saw. I will enquire whether it is the Superior Quality of the Cocoa Nut, or any other Ingredient which they intermix with it, or a better Art of making it, which renders it so much superiour to any other."[17] The only sour note we have been able to find was sounded by the French priest Barnabite De Livoy, who traveled in Spain in 1755; getting into an argument with the canon of the Saragossa cathedral about chocolate, he made this assertion: "I agreed with him that all Europe was obliged to the Spaniards for bringing it from so far away, but that all Europe was also indebted to the Italians, and particularly to the Milanese, for the better manner of preparing it."[18] The canon would have none of this.

From the pens of French and English travelers we have descriptions of the *tertulias* or *refrescos*, the social gatherings which the Spanish upper class found enchanting, but which foreigners found quite tedious and boring. A French visitor tells us that on arrival, the men stayed in one room and the women in another; when all had arrived, they were allowed to gather in the salon, where the hostess received her guests "as gravely as the Queen at a hand-kissing."[19] The English traveler William Dalrymple recounts that the company stood making "little societies of conversations" until about 11 p.m., when the *refrescos* ("refreshments") arrived. Then everyone's faces lit up. The servants came in with glasses of ice water, and sugar biscuits with which one was expected to sweeten

A drawing of the 1760s by Manuel Tramulles, showing the Spanish custom of taking chocolate at social gatherings. The mancerina *was designed to prevent spillages.*

the water. Next, the guests were treated to cups of chocolate, *confitures*, biscuits, marzipans, *dragées* (sugared almonds), and pralines. "One regaled oneself heartily, one filled one's pockets, handkerchief, hat; your servant carried it home with you."[20]

Italy

Across a country as varied in government and history as 18th-century Italy there was considerable variation in the preparation and use of chocolate and other stimulating hot drinks. Rome was still a papal city, and would remain that way until the unification of Italy in the next century; here we could expect a heavy use of chocolate, and in this we are not disappointed. The French traveler Pierre-Jacques Bergeret de Grancourt was in Rome on 26 January 1774, paying court to Cardinal Orsini. This was a Roman *conversazione* ("conversation"), not unlike the *tertulias* which we have described for Madrid:

One finds at this "conversation" all the most beautiful Roman princesses, and one is served a great deal of chocolate, very foamy, very well made and without vanilla, simply cacao with cinnamon. The Italians think themselves "burned" if they use vanilla. I didn't think I could get used to it, but I find it very good.[21]

Bergeret de Gramont tells us that the custom of the country (perhaps meaning by this the Papal States) was to take chocolate without vanilla in the morning, and lemonade and sometimes ices in the evening.

Let us now cross to the other side of the Tiber, to the Vatican itself and the Sistine Chapel, still the traditional *mise-en-scène* of the conclaves of cardinals who meet to elect the new pope on the death of the old. This was then, and is now, an arduous affair for these princes of the Church, and even more so when the deliberations are prolonged. The conclave of 1740 was the longest of modern times: it took six months to elect Benedict XIV. Francesco Valesio, whose diaries present a wonderful picture of daily life in 18th-century Rome, writes that at one point in this conclave, 30 lbs (13.6 kg) of chocolate were delivered to the Sistine Chapel for the refreshment of the cardinals;[22] and, in fact, throughout his journals, cardinals take their chocolate at frequent intervals. The accusation by radicals that this was the preferred drink of the Church hierarchy was well founded.

But chocolate has always had a far darker side: it was ideal for disguising the taste of poison. It will be remembered that Pope Clement XIV, although one of the weaker pontiffs of the century, had suppressed the Jesuits in 1773. During 1774—the year of his death—he was depressed and morbidly afraid of assassination. When he died, his. body rapidly decomposed, and his fingernails dropped off, leading to the widespread report that he had, in truth, been murdered; all fingers pointed to the Jesuits. In a letter of 8 October 1774 to his friend Horace Walpole, Sir Horace Mann expresses the general belief of Romans and foreigners alike:

. . . the murder of the Pope has been proved by the clearest evidence. A slow poison was given him by his own innocent *credenziere* [confectioner] in a dish of chocolate last Holy Thursday at the Vatican, where he assisted at the ceremonies of the day. It is surprising that he who from the beginning of his pontificate had taken every precaution to avoid what he always feared, should persist in drinking the chocolate, though from the first sip he told the servants that it had a bad taste. Nevertheless, they both continued to swallow their death. A few days after, they both fell ill, and during the whole interval till they expired the symptoms were the same, and the *credenziere* died a few days after his Holiness.[23]

In a letter written two days earlier to a friend, the Spaniard Fray Agustín Ferreu reported that even the surgeon who embalmed the Pope developed swollen hands and arms, and his fingernails dropped off just like the Pope's.[24]

Although J.N.D. Kelley, author of the *Oxford Dictionary of the Popes*, tells us that these allegations were disproved by the medical autopsy,[25] there is an Italian saying *si non è vero, è ben trovato* ("even if it's not true, it's a good one").

Just about at the other end of the "hierarchy-vs-Enlightenment" scale from papal Rome was Venice, the Italian city most open to intellectual, artistic, and commercial influences from the rest of Europe and the world, but now in deep economic decline. Here, a little dissent was acceptable as long as it did not challenge the authority and integrity of the Republic (which was to be wiped out anyway at the end of the century by the Venice-hating Napoleon). Protestant northerners and even Turks had been welcome in Venice for a long time. This was the Venice of the painters Canaletto and the Tiepolos, the playwright Goldoni, the composer Vivaldi, a vibrant and intensely beautiful city with numerous coffee-houses (such as the still-flourishing Florian's) where noble Venetians and equally noble Englishmen on the Grand Tour could sip their coffee and leaf through newspapers. A cup of coffee at these establishments was one third the price of a cup of chocolate, and so coffee was the most popular drink.[26]

Naples, on the other hand, where the Bourbons reigned, was under heavy Spanish influence, so that this was a kingdom of chocolate, not coffee. An anonymous English letter-writer of the period relates an incident that took place in Naples on 9 February 1771, after a vendor of lemonade and iced water had stabbed to death his 15-year-old younger brother: "Our hostess sent the mother of these sons a regale of maccaroni soup and a pot of chocolate, by way of consolation for her loss. . . . What a country is England, where neither maccaroni soup or chocolate would suffice to comfort a widowed mother for the loss of a son!"[27]

Chocolate in Cuisine: An Italian or Mexican Invention?

The idea of using chocolate as a flavoring in cooked food would have been horrifying to the Aztecs—just as Christians could not conceive of using communion wine to make, say, *coq au vin*. In all of the pages of Sahagún that deal with Aztec cuisine and with chocolate, there is not a hint that it ever entered into an Aztec dish. Yet today many food writers and gourmets consider one particular dish, the famous *pavo in mole poblano*, which contains chocolate, to represent the pinnacle of the Mexican cooking tradition.

The *pavo* in the dish's title is the Mexican-Spanish word for turkey, a Mesoamerican domesticate, to be sure: *mole* is a creolized version of the Nahuatl *molli*, (sauce); and *poblano* refers to the place of origin of the dish and its sauce, the Colonial Puebla de los Angeles; this beautiful city, unlike others in central Mexico, has no Aztec foundations—and neither does the dish, regardless of what food writers may say. Its true, creolized and hispanicized nature is given away by this list of ingredients from an authentic recipe:[28]

PAVO IN MOLE POBLANO

1 kg [2 lbs 3 oz] of mulato chillis

1¼ kg [2 lbs 12 oz] of ancho chillis

½ kg [1 lb] of tomatoes

1 tsp black pepper

1 tbsp cinnamon

3 maize tortillas

Salt to taste

500 g [1 lb 2 oz] lard

300 g [10 oz] sesame

1 turkey

¾ kg [1 lb 10 oz] pasilla chillis

¼ kg [9 oz] raisins

½ garlic bulb

1 tbsp anise seed

1 tsp cloves

1 golden-fried piece of bread

4 tablets chocolate

Sugar to taste

¼ kg [9 oz] peanuts

Ten of these 19 ingredients are Old World (by this time, the reader should be able to tell which!).

There are three rival but not entirely dissimilar tales about the invention of *mole poblano*,[29] but not one of them is backed up by contemporary documents; all three stories could well be 19th-century inventions. One would have it that the nuns of the Santa Rosa convent in Puebla were nervous over the impending visit of their bishop, Manuel Fernández de Santa Cruz y Sahagún (1637–99); Sor Andrea was in charge of making the sauce for the meal, but chocolate accidentally tumbled from a shelf into the basin in which the mixture was stewing. It was too late to make another sauce, and *mole poblano* was born. According to the second version,

Sor María del Perpetuo Socorro and other nuns deliberately put the chocolate in, in honor of the same bishop's visit. In the third version, which is that followed by the Mexican food writer Paco Ignacio Taibo I in his *Breviario del mole poblano*,[30] the famous sauce was deliberately created by Sor Andrea of the Convento de la Asunción (not far from the Santa Rosa convent), not in honor of the bishop, but of the 17th-century Viceroy of New Spain, don Tomás Antonio de la Cerda y Aragón, Conde de Paredes and Marqués de la Laguna; he and his wife were close friends of Sor Juana Inez de la Cruz, Mexico's great poetess and a lover of chocolate.

So, the middle and upper-class Creole population of Mexico *may* have been eating a dish prepared with chocolate as early as the late 17th century, but there is no proof whatsoever for this. In Italy, on the other hand, the first firmly dated recipes containing cacao (apart from recipes for the hot drink) appeared between 1680 and 1684, and were common in the next century. So widespread was this culinary experimentation with chocolate that in 1736 the poet Francesco Arisi, in his *Il Cioccolato*, listed his complaints against those who misused cacao. Among his targets were: (1) people stupid enough to blow the froth off the cup. (2) those who toast with it, (3) those who lace it with brandy, (4) he who "dirties his nose" by taking snuff with it, (5) those who drink it with broth, (6) those who mix it with coffee or tea, (7) those who put an egg yolk into it, (8) cooks who include it in their *pasticcie* (meat pasties) or "imprison" it in pastilles. His poetic diatribe continues:

Certo cuoco, a cui mancato	A certain cook, left without
Il formaggio era in cucina,	Cheese in his kitchen,
Sovra nobil polentina	On a noble polenta
Dispenso ben grattugiato	Grated well
Bolli due di cioccolato:	Two *bolli* of chocolate;
A tale novità fu così accetta,	And this novelty was so well received,
Che gli Apici ne voller la ricetta.	That the Apici asked for the recipe.

Desinando in un convito	Invited to a dinner,
L'assaggiai fatto in salsetta,	I tasted it made into a sauce,
Ma per dirvela alla schietta	But I tell you sincerely,
Non aguzza l'appetito,	It did not sharpen the appetite.
Nel torrone già s'e posto,	In nougat it has already found a place,
Nelle torte ha 'l primo loco:	And a first place in cakes;
Anzi un di spero che il cuoco	I even suspect that one day the cook
Colle quaglie il metta arrosto	Will put it to the roast with quails. [31]

Most of these imaginative cooks seem to have lived in the north of Italy, and explored the possibilities of chocolate not only in cakes and other pastries, but also in pastas and meat dishes. In the 1786 manuscript from Macerata there is mention of lasagna with a sauce of almonds, anchovies, walnuts, and chocolate[32]—a far cry from the tiresome, badly made stuff, drowned in tomato sauce, that is served in schools and airplanes today! A list of meals provided in the late 18th century for the city magistrates of Lucca[33] includes *papardelle* [ribbon macaroni] *di cioccolata*; chocolate, chocolate-and-coffee, and iced cakes; and a kind of *semifreddo* with chocolate. From Trento, in the foothills of the Alps, come several 18th-century cookbooks; one by the priest Felici Libera has a number of recipes with chocolate,[34] including:

- sliced liver dipped in chocolate, floured, dipped again, then fried
- black polenta (with chocolate breadcrumbs, butter, almonds, and cinnamon)
- chocolate pudding with veal, marrow, and candied fruit
- mocha custard
- *mosa di latte*, a chocolate pudding thickened with wheat flour, corn meal, and breadcrumbs
- two recipes for *crema di cioccolata* (pot-de-crème)
- almond cake, the dough to be dyed with chocolate, and green, red, and yellow coloring

"Chocolate soup" seems to have been popular in the Trento area; Libera's version calls for milk, sugar, cinnamon, and one egg yolk, this to be cooked and poured over toast. This sounds suspiciously like what was known as "health soup" in 18th-century Germany, and we hazard was of German origin.

Frozen desserts were a speciality of southern Italy, where they were probably invented in the 17th century—once the effect of large amounts of salt on snow or ice had been discovered. The long, detailed treatise by the Neapolitan F. Vincenzo Corrado, *La Manovra della Cioccolata e del Caffè*, 1794, contains precise instructions on how to make chocolate sorbet.[35] Corrado insists that only cacao from Caracas and Soconusco be used, since these are sufficiently fatty (that is, rich in cacao butter) to withstand the "nitres" from the salt which can enter the pores of the vase containing the liquid to be frozen; these nitres can otherwise absorb the sweetness, the butter, and the aromatic.

RECIPE FOR CHOCOLATE SORBET, NAPLES, 1794

2½ lb [1 kg] chocolate and 1½ lb [680 g] sugar are to be put to boil with 4 lb [3.2 pints or 1.5 l] water and ½ oz [14 g] powdered vanilla. When all has been dissolved, the liquid is passed through a fine sieve and returned to the fire to thicken (when sufficiently thick it will coat the spoon). Then it is ladled into a vase with the addition of a piece of cacao butter, and allowed to cool. Finally, the vase is buried in snow layered with salt, and frozen.

This was probably the culinary technology harnessed to create a Rococo dessert table of unbelievable extravagance at a festival given in Rome on 28 August 1714 by the Austrian ambassador, Giovanni Vinceslao Galasso.[36] The occasion was the birthday of Elisabetta Cristina of Austria, wife of Charles VI Habsburg, Holy Roman Emperor (this was a union which produced no son and heir, thus leading to decades of armed conflict in Europe over the succession). At the corners of the table were four Japanese porcelain

Table of ices, created for a festival in Rome on 28 August 1714.

shells filled with "iced fruits" (these were made of fruit conserves mixed with perfumed water, put in fruit-shaped molds, and frozen with snow and salt; when taken from the molds, stems and leaves were added). On the summit was a great alabaster vase adorned with carved ice, and in it was a tree with green leaves, bearing 150 of these "iced fruits" on its branches, and rising from roots of chocolate foam. On the side tables were whipped cream, more chocolate foam, biscuits, ice cream (*panna ghiacciata*), and chocolate sorbets in the shape of cheeses (*formaggi ghiacciati*). How did all this manage to survive the heat of an August evening in Rome, in the days before air conditioning? The participants must have had to attack the table's delights with lightning speed.

France Before the Deluge

The inclusion of Martinique and other Antillean islands in France's overseas empire gave the mother country a steady source of cacao not controlled by her old enemy, Spain. And the sybaritic way of life followed by the French planters of those parts had a definite influence on how chocolate was prepared, drunk, and eaten in France. The French West Indies are very much present in an important book published on the eve of

the Revolution by the physician and botanist Joseph Pierre Buc'hoz (1731–1807): the *Dissertation sur le tabac, le café, le cacao et le thé*.[37] In those islands, he says, to make the drink they take loaves of pure cacao, powder them, and add cinnamon, sugar, and orange-flower water, resulting in a beverage of great delicacy with an exquisite perfume. Alternatively, one may join this with a whole beaten egg, or substitute two drops of ambergris essence for the orange-flower water. Although vanilla was common in the islands, it was never used in chocolate (it was then believed to be harmful to the health throughout Europe).

On the evidence of Buc'hoz's treatise, the French were far more conservative than the Italians in their culinary use of chocolate: there is nothing here comparable to black polenta or chocolate *papardelle*. Rather, the great elaboration in France lies in desserts

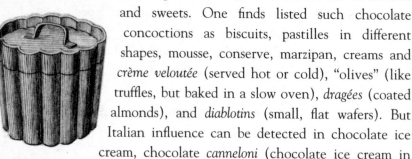

and sweets. One finds listed such chocolate concoctions as biscuits, pastilles in different shapes, mousse, conserve, marzipan, creams and *crème veloutée* (served hot or cold), "olives" (like truffles, but baked in a slow oven), *dragées* (coated almonds), and *diablotins* (small, flat wafers). But Italian influence can be detected in chocolate ice cream, chocolate *canneloni* (chocolate ice cream in molds), frozen chocolate "cheeses" (sorbets frozen in cheese molds). Later on we will meet—in his various prison cells—the greatest devotee of these chocolate delights, the marquis de Sade.

Marie Antoinette, the unfortunate queen decapitated by the Revolution, has been given by posterity the undeserved reputation of a sybarite, but she was far from it. When she was a small girl in the Habsburg court of Vienna, she may have been permitted to imbibe chocolate from time to time: there is a painting showing her as a five-year-old with her mother, the Empress Maria Theresa, and the rest of the family at breakfast—but by the chocolate-pot on the table are only two cups, so perhaps such small children were too young for so powerful a drink. We do know that as queen of France, she was notably abstemious, as we read in Mme. Campan's memoirs of the queen's private life: "Her sobriety was also remarkable. She breakfasted on coffee or chocolate, ate nothing at dinner but white meat, drank nothing but water, and supped on bouillon, a wing of fowl, and a glass of water in which she soaked some small biscuits."[38] Not a hint of that cake which she was falsely alleged to have recommended to the starving populace!

Denis Diderot (1718–84) was one of the *philosophes*, that remarkable group of French intellectuals whose goal was to prove

The Encyclopédie *of Diderot and d'Alembert illustrates the manufacture of chocolate in the 18th century (above); molds for chocolate 'cheeses', or sorbets, (opposite); a heated metate for grinding chocolate (overleaf).*

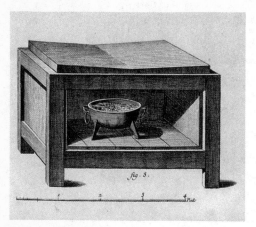

that reason and science could shape human values and human societies for the better, and release humans from the shackles of religious superstition and blind faith in customs handed down from the past. There is still controversy about the literary works and attitudes of a movement that contributed to one of the mightiest social cataclysms of all time, but of the lasting value and historical importance of one of its works—Diderot and Jean d'Alembert's great *Encyclopedia, or the classified dictionary of the sciences, arts, and trades*—there is no doubt. Funded by private subscription and issued in 28 volumes from 1751 to 1772, it was not intended as a mere reference work, but was designed "to change the general way of thinking." The science may now be outdated, but as a record of 18th-century technology, as engraved in its 11 volumes of illustrations, it is unsurpassed.[39]

The plate that deals with the preparation of cacao[40] is remarkable in its detail, but also remarkable for the obvious fact that cacao technology had hardly changed one iota from the time of the Olmecs, Maya, and Aztecs to that of the *confiseur* (confectioner) of Enlightenment France. Here the engraver shows a worker toasting cacao in a caldron; a worker winnowing the beans; another breaking them in a heated mortar; and another grinding them on a heated surface (*metate*). Motecuhzoma's chocolate specialists would have recognized all parts of this process. Diderot gives recipes for candied cacao beans, which we know from other sources was an innovation introduced from Martinique; for cacao butter, which was recommended as a skin pomade, as a cure for gout and all sorts of ulcers, as an antidote for corrosive poisons, and to keep weapons from rusting; and for the chocolate drink.

gentry might maintain town houses in London so as to be in contact with the sources of political power, they spent most of their time in the countryside among the very people upon whose rents they lived. This was a very different picture from Bourbon France, where the huge nobility was expected to dance attendance on the King at Versailles throughout the year.

Much of the political and cultural life of the nobility, gentry, and burgeoning middle class centered on the coffee and chocolate-houses of London, and eventually on the clubs that sprang from them. Such places from the moment of their founding were frequented by members of one or another parliamentary party, and often became their virtual headquarters. One of the oldest was the Cocoa-tree Chocolate-house in St. James's Street, a well-known meeting place for Jacobites (somewhat subversive upholders of the right of the Stuarts to the throne that had been abdicated by James II). In 1746, the year that the Stuart rebellion against the Hanovers was put down at the Battle of Culloden, it was converted into the Cocoa-tree Club, with a Tory membership; Jonathan Swift and Edward Gibbon were members. The Cocoa-tree, like other London clubs of the 18th century, became known for its high play: Horace Walpole, writing to Horace Mann in 1780, said that £180,000 had changed hands in only one night's gambling.

By far the best-known of the London clubs was White's, which has recently passed the three-hundred-year-mark. White's was born in 1693 as White's Chocolate House, at the bottom of St. James's. It was opened by the Italian Francis White (a name probably anglicized from Francesco Bianchi), and soon became known for its lively politics and high-stakes gambling.[46] In 1709, writing under the pen-name of "Isaac Bickerstaff," Richard Steele had this to say in the opening number of *The Tatler*:

All accounts of Gallantry, Pleasure, and Entertainment, shall be under the article of White's Chocolate-House; Poetry, under that of Will's Coffee-House; Learning, under the title of Grecian [this was frequented by scholars and Oxford dons]; Foreign and Domestic News, you will have from St. James's Coffee-house [a Whig stronghold]; and what else I have to offer on any other subject, shall be dated from My own apartment.[47]

In Alexander Pope's *Dunciad* of 1728, White's appears as the place where one may "Teach oaths to youngsters and to nobles wit." Jonathan Swift shook his fist at it every time he passed, for he had heard from a correspondent that at White's young noblemen were "fleeced and corrupted by fashionable gamblers and profligates,"[48] perhaps in the gaming-room called "Hell." By the middle of the 18th century, an inner club had developed, with access only for approved customers, and gaming was intensified. In this club, reported *The Connoisseur* in 1754, "There is nothing, however trivial or ridiculous, which is not capable of producing a bet." It is said that on one wet day, Lord Arlington bet £3000 on which of two raindrops would first reach the bottom of a window pane;[49] and

in 1750, Walpole related the newspaper report of a man who collapsed at the door of the club and, upon being carried up the steps, was immediately the object of bets as to whether he were dead or not.[50]

Apart from these diversions, White's, like other clubs, was a place for political decision-makers to meet and discuss; it started as Whig, but by the end of the 18th century had been steered into the Tory camp. It has counted in its membership every British prime minister from Sir Robert Walpole to Sir Robert

A chocolate pot and cups can be seen in this 1787 watercolor by Thomas Rowlandson.

Peel, three monarchs (George IV, William IV, Edward VII), the Duke of Wellington, Horace Walpole, Lord Chesterfield, and Beau Brummell. A few decades ago the writers Evelyn Waugh and Graham Greene could be seen looking out from its famous bow window. Among today's 1350 members are more than 30 earls, 11 marquesses, and a half dozen dukes.

But not all frequenters of 18th-century chocolate and coffee-houses were decision-makers or even gamblers, as Number 54 of *The Spectator* (1711) makes clear. In it, the editor claims to have received a communication from a correspondent at the University of Cambridge, identifying a "Sect of Philosophers" named *Lowngers*, who contrive to spend their days doing nothing. The editor assures his correspondent that he is going to inquire into such members of the Sect in London

> . . . as have arrived at the Dignity of being *Lowngers* by the Force of natural Parts, without ever [having] seen an University: and send my Correspondent, for the Embellishment of his Book, the Names and History of those who pass their Lives without any Incidents at all; and how they shift Coffee-houses and Chocolate-houses from House to House, to get over the insupportable labor of doing nothing.[51]

Curiously, the institution of the chocolate or coffee-house seems never to have crossed the Atlantic to England's North American colonies. Someone who could have transplanted the concept, but did not, was William Byrd II (1674–1744), Virginia planter, satirist, writer of diaries, owner of a vast plantation on the James River, and founder of the city of Richmond. While in England from 1713 to 1719 (part of the time as Colonial agent), Byrd recounts in his diary taking incessant "dishes" of chocolate at all hours, largely at establishments like Will's, St. James's, and Ozinda's—and once in a cockpit. But back in Virginia from January 1720 to May 1721, there is not one mention of either chocolate-houses or coffee-houses, although he drank a great deal of chocolate for breakfast and at friends' houses.[52] However, as we have all learned in school, parliamentary democracy did not extend to the colonies, and Americans were isolated from the give-and-take and political deals that were the daily fare of enfranchised Englishmen in establishments like Will's and White's. The colonial well-to-do took their chocolate, but at home.

Chocolate at the Dawn of the Industrial Revolution

A glance at the plate dealing with chocolate-making in Diderot's *Encyclopedia* will suffice to show how little the basic technology had changed since the days of the Aztecs. It is true that there were "factories" in several countries turning out chocolate on a large scale, primarily in wafer form for the drink, but this was all hand labor. In Germany, for instance, the Steinhund chocolate factory was founded in 1765; and even earlier, in 1728, Fry and Sons of Bristol was producing chocolate for the English market.

One of the earliest documented uses of power machinery in chocolate manufacture comes not from Europe but from the American colonies. By the mid-18th century, Massachusetts sea captains were bringing back cacao beans from the tropics as cargo, for there was already a chocolate-drinking public in New England (Boston apothecaries were advertising chocolate as early as 1712). In 1765, Dr. James Baker of Dorchester, Massachusetts, joined forces with John Hannon, a chocolate-maker newly arrived from Ireland. Baker put up the money to rent space in a grist mill in Milton Lower Falls, where Hannon ground the cacao beans with water power. In 1772 they started advertising their product as Hannon's Best Chocolate, in the form of cakes. When Hannon was lost at sea in 1799, the business became the Baker Company; in 1820, this was taken over by James Baker's grandson Walter, and it became the Walter Baker Company; it still flourishes under that name.[53]

Back in France, in 1776 (four years after the final volume of the *Encyclopedia* appeared), a certain M. Doret invented a hydraulic machine to grind chocolate and reduce it to paste. Once his invention had been approved by the Faculty of Medicine, Doret was authorized to give his factory the title of *Chocolatérie Royale*.[54] Other European countries began to follow suit, even though machinery based on Watt's steam engine was not to appear until early in the next century. Even in backward Spain, where chocolate grinders were still carrying their heavy stone *manos* and *metates* from house to house, the English traveler Joseph Townsend, on his journey of 1786 and 1787, noted that for the larger market, cacao beans were being ground on a machine.[55] This consisted of five rollers of polished steel, fitted into a frame like the spokes of a wheel, each turning on its own axis. These were placed between two millstones, whose motion was imparted by a cogwheel below stairs, turned by a mule.

Yet this could hardly be called an Industrial Revolution: that great technological and social innovation, which was to change the face of the earth more profoundly than the French Revolution ever did, was taking place largely in the manufacture of textiles. Its full effect on the story of cacao and chocolate will be seen in the next chapter.

The End of an Era: The "Divine Marquis" and Chocolate

On 2 July 1789, the working-class crowd thronging the streets of the St.-Antoine quarter of Paris was harangued by a strange man using a megaphone improvised from a urinal, high up in his cell in the Bastille, a medieval fortress which had been turned into a prison. This was none other than Donatien Alphonse François, marquis de Sade.[56] The gist of his tirade was that the Bastille guards had been given orders to kill all the prisoners (all seven of them!) by cutting their throats, and he urged the throng to tear down "this monument of horrors." Seized by the guards, Sade was removed to the madhouse at Charenton; but the Paris mob took his advice, and stormed and destroyed the Bastille on the 14th of July. The Bastille had no strategic importance whatsoever, but it served as a symbol and its destruction marked the beginning of the French Revolution.

Born in Paris in 1740, de Sade came from an ancient, aristocratic family. Shortly after his marriage to Renée de Montreuil, he was imprisoned for 15 days in the dungeon of Vincennes for "out-rageous libertinage." In all, de Sade passed 30 years of his tortured life in one prison or another; was officially condemned under Napoleon's Consulate; and died in 1814 in the lunatic asylum of Charenton. Through his fiction, which transcended all the moral bounds known to most societies in its treatment of sex

The marquis de Sade, a great lover of chocolate, in a moralistic French engraving of the mid-19th century.

and cruelty, Sade managed to outrage authorities of every political stripe, and suffered the consequences. His name has passed into the language as a synonym for the psychopathic infliction of pain. But biographers and literary critics are now generally agreed that the "Divine Marquis," as his modern admirers have called him, was more sinned against than sinning, and that the atrocities of which he was accused were mainly the work of his imaginative pen.

One of the most notorious episodes attributed to de Sade was said to have taken place in Marseilles in June 1772, and involved chocolate, for which the marquis had a true passion. In his *Secret Memoirs for the History of the Republic of Letters*, the writer Louis Petit de Bachaumont related the scandal thus:

> Friends write from Marseilles that M. le comte de Sade . . . gave a ball. . . . Into the dessert he slipped chocolate pastilles so good that a number of people devoured them. There were lots of them, and no one failed to eat some, but he had mixed in some Spanish fly. The virtue of the medication is well known. It proved to be so potent that those who ate the pastilles began to burn with unchaste ardor and to carry on as if in the grip of the most amorous frenzy. The ball degenerated into one of those licentious orgies for which the Romans were renowned. Even the most respectable of women were unable to resist the uterine rage that stirred within them. And so it was that M. de Sade enjoyed the favors of his sister-in-law, with whom he fled to avoid the punishment he deserves. Several persons died of their frightful priapic excesses, and others are still quite sick.[57]

It is now believed by de Sade scholars that much of this tale was invented or elaborated by his enemies: his guests appear to have been prostitutes, they were probably *not* administered cantharides, and the pastilles may have been anise *dragées* rather than chocolate confections.

Nevertheless, de Sade and his male servant (a Leporello type) were forced to flee to the estate of the king of Sardinia, who promptly had them arrested. They escaped from the fortress in which they were locked up, but the parlement at Aix sentenced them to death *in absentia*, and executed them in effigy.

As his biographer Maurice Lever informs us, "the marquis de Sade's palate was most keenly excited by pastry and sweets. He was capable of wolfing down frightening quantities. . . . Chocolate inspired an irresistible passion. He loved it in all its forms: in cream, in cakes, in ice cream, in bars."[58] In whatever prison he found himself, he was constantly writing to his loyal and long-suffering wife for books, clothes, and food to be sent to him. Included in his lists of demands are the following:[59]

Boxes of ground chocolate and of mocha coffee
Cacao butter suppositories [A Martinique remedy for his piles]
Crème au chocolat [a frequent demand]
Half-pound boxes of chocolate pastilles [lots of these]
Large chocolate biscuits
Vanilla pastilles *au chocolat* [perhaps chocolate-coated]
Chocolat en tablettes à l'ordinaire [chocolate bars]

There are frequent requests for chocolate cake; he writes in a letter of 9 May 1779 to Mme de Sade from his cell in Vincennes: "I asked . . . for a cake with icing, but I want it to be chocolate and black inside from chocolate as the devil's ass is black from smoke. And the icing is to be the same."[60] It is hardly to be wondered that the marquis became grossly obese in his long captivity. Yet, he continued to write his inflammatory, deeply subversive fiction, defiant to the last. Mme. de Sade passed her final days in a convent.

De Sade lived through the Revolution, and watched Unreason overwhelm the Age of Reason, as Robespierre's Reign of Terror obliterated the remaining *philosophes* and thousands of others in a bloodbath that was far worse than anything in his own writings. Ironically, de Sade almost lost his own head to the guillotine for his moderation (he was opposed to capital punishment, and persisted in believing British-style constitutional monarchy to be the best form of government). And he personally saved his hostile parents-in-law, who had been responsible for some of his own incarcerations, under the *ancien régime*, from decapitation by the Revolution's terrible blade. The "Divine Marquis," chocolate-lover *extraordinaire*, is a tragic but strangely sympathetic figure to close our account of the 18th century. Everything else to follow in this history belongs to the modern age.

CHAPTER EIGHT

&

Chocolate for the Masses

The last two miles of the hill were terrible and I said "Japhy there's one thing I would like right now more than anything in the world— more than anything I've ever wanted all my life." Cold dusk winds were blowing, we hurried bent with our packs on the endless trail.

"What?"

"A nice big Hershey bar or even a little one. For some reason or other, a Hershey bar would save my soul right now."

"There's your Buddhism, a Hershey bar. How about moonlight in an orange grove and a vanilla ice-cream cone?"

"Too cold. What I need, want, pray for, dying for, right now, is a Hershey bar . . . with nuts." We were very tired and kept trudging along home talking like two children. I kept repeating and repeating about my good old Hershey bar. I really meant it. I needed the energy anyway, I was a little woozy and needed sugar, but to think of chocolate and peanuts all melting in my mouth in that cold wind, it was too much.

Jack Kerouac, *The Dharma Bums*, 1958

For at least 28 centuries, chocolate had been a drink of the elite and the very rich. By the mid-20th century, when Kerouac, the spokesman for the Beat generation, was climbing his California mountain, chocolate had been transmuted into a solid food of the masses, available to all. The French Revolution, which (along with Napoleon) brought to an end the ascendancy of the Church and the aristocracy in Catholic Europe, and the Industrial Revolution, which changed chocolate from a costly drink to a cheap food, were the driving forces in this metamorphosis. Added to these factors was the challenge posed by tea and coffee; and tea prices had plummeted in the 19th century with the establishment of huge tea estates in those two jewels in Britain's imperial crown, India and Ceylon (Sri Lanka).

When the great transformation from liquid to solid took place, the technological breakthroughs that made it possible were pretty much confined to the Protestant and thoroughly capitalistic nations of northern and central Europe; the Catholic countries of the Mediterranean, which had played such a leading role in chocolate's history in preceding centuries, were now largely backwaters as far as such innovations went. In isolated pockets within southern Europe there were a few picturesque survivals of ancient ways of making chocolate. In the 1870s, confectioners and pharmacists in southern France still had their chocolate ground on *metates* "*à l'azteque*"; this was performed by specialists, mostly Spanish and Portuguese Jews who traveled from house to house with their stones.[1] In an article published in a French journal in 1920, the author describes the survival of the chocolate *metate* in Spain:

> I have seen Catalan chocolate makers—there are still four or five factories or ateliers of stone-ground chocolate in Barcelona—working kneeling on a little cushion, in sight of the public, in a little *entresol* where one cannot stand upright. This is so that the buyer can see that the chocolate he is buying is true stone-ground chocolate, made according to a procedure which, they think, makes it more difficult to add adulterants, as the work, hard as it is, would by that be made more difficult still.[2]

And as late as 1989 in Italy, the Romanengo chocolate and confectionery establishment of Genoa still had stones to grind the cacao.[3] Such artisans were (and perhaps are yet) the last upholders of the Mesoamerican tradition.

The typical French chocolatière can be seen in this painting by François Boucher, Le Déjeuner, 1739.

19th-century Italian signs advertising small-scale
chocolate-makers contrast with the increasing industrialization
of chocolate manufacture in the 19th and 20th centuries.
The hand-worker on the right continues to use the venerable
metate to grind his chocolate.

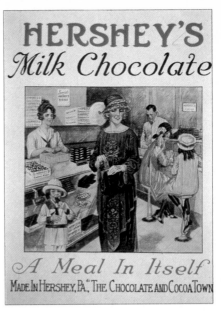

Posters claim that Cadbury's cocoa makes men stronger (left), and Hershey's milk chocolate is a meal in itself (above). Bird's eye view of Fry's chocolate factory in 19th-century Bristol (below).

The end of the 20th century has seen a revival of luxury high-quality chocolate with a high content of cocoa solids and cacao butter. These premier confections on display come from all over Europe.

Also to be taken into account is the replacement of the Galenic system of humors and temperaments by modern medicine during the course of the 19th century. By 1862, a French writer on cacao and chocolate was able to affirm that nobody believed in the therapeutic virtues attributed to chocolate any more.[4] The release of chocolate from such bonds meant that anyone, anywhere, was able to take chocolate whenever they chose, in any form they preferred (the worries about obesity, acne, tooth decay, and the like are phenomena of our own age). No longer did they have to fret over whether chocolate or its flavorings were "hot," "cold," or "temperate," "dry" or "moist."

Concurrent with these changes, the per capita consumption of chocolate, which had been fairly constant for centuries, shot up dramatically; this was coupled with an equally enormous upsurge in the intake of sugar, since the principal destiny of this new, solid chocolate was in the manufacture of confectionery and desserts. The daring Italian experiments in the use of chocolate in pastas and main course dishes undertaken in the two previous centuries had few 19th and 20th-century progeny. Candies reigned supreme, and gave rise to the great chocolate fortunes of Holland, England, Switzerland, and, eventually, the United States. The marquis de Sade's extravagant taste for such desserts and sweets—his chocolate pastilles, cakes, and ice creams—was an accurate harbinger of the future.

A Break with the Past: Van Houten's Inventions

1828 marks the beginning of the modern era in chocolate making and production. In that year, a Dutch chemist named Coenraad Johannes Van Houten took out a patent on a process for the manufacture of a new kind of powdered chocolate with a very low fat content. As early as 1815, in his own Amsterdam factory, he had been looking for a method better than mere boiling and skimming to remove most of the cacao butter from chocolate.[5]

Coenraad Van Houten, inventor of
defatting and alkalizing processes.

For this, he eventually developed a very efficient hydraulic press; untreated chocolate "liquor"—the end result of the grinding process—contains about 53 percent cacao butter, but Van Houten's machine managed to reduce this to 27 to 28 percent, leaving a "cake" that could be pulverized into a fine powder. This was what we know as "cocoa." To cause this product to mix well with water, Van Houten treated it with alkaline salts (potassium or sodium carbonates). While this "Dutching," as it came to be known, improved the powder's miscibility (*not*, as some believed, its solubility) in warm water, it made the chocolate darker in color and milder in flavor. Even today, many people prefer "Dutch" chocolate, thinking it to be stronger in taste, when it is ony the difference in color that makes it seem so.

At any rate, in the year 1828, the age-old, thick and foamy drink was dethroned by easily-prepared, more easily digestible cocoa. Van Houten's invention of the defatting and alkalizing processes made possible the large-scale manufacture of cheap chocolate for the masses, in both powdered and solid form.

Quaker Capitalists

Some of the most successful entrepreneurs of England's Industrial Revolution were members of the Society of Friends.[6] The story of Joseph Fry & Son is a case in point. In the mid-18th century, Dr. Joseph Fry, a member of an old Quaker family of Wiltshire, settled in Bristol and set up a large medical practice. He soon gave this up for commerce, and eventually founded the great Bristol firm of J.S.Fry & Sons, chocolate manufacturers. Following his death in 1787, the business was carried on by his widow and by his son Joseph Storrs Fry (1767–1835). It will be recalled that there had been sporadic attempts to mechanize chocolate manufacture in the last half of the 18th century, but it remained to the younger Fry to make the great leap forward into the industrial age by his purchase in 1789 of a Watt's steam engine to grind his cacao beans.

With Van Houten's breakthrough, the Fry enterprise—and the Fry dynasty—was ready to move into high gear, which it did under the leadership of the founder's grandson Francis Fry (1803–86) and great-grandson, another Joseph Storrs Fry (1826–1913). A milestone was passed in 1847, when the Fry firm found a way to mix a blend of cocoa powder and sugar with melted cacao butter (naturally, a by-product of the defatting process) instead of with warm water; this produced a thinner, less viscous paste which could be cast into a mold. The resulting chocolate bars, which they christened "Chocolat Délicieux à Manger" (French-sounding food had a considerable cachet by this time), were exhibited in Birmingham in 1849. Apart from the pastilles and bars of 18th-century France, which were brittle and dry, and impossible to mold, this was the world's first true *eating* chocolate. Thanks to a rapidly rising demand for the new confection, the price of cacao butter escalated, so that now it was cocoa powder which was within the reach of the masses, while solid chocolate—for a while—was mainly for the elite. But this would change, too, with mass production and cost-cutting methods on the horizon, particularly in the United States.

By the latter half of Victoria's century, J.S.Fry & Sons were the largest chocolate manufacturers in the world, in part because they had won the right to be sole supplier of chocolate and cocoa to the Royal Navy, gradually becoming weaned from its reliance on grog. But the firm always had to contend with its greatest rival Cadbury's, founded by another Quaker, John Cadbury (1801–89). In 1824, Cadbury opened a coffee-and-tea shop in Birmingham, where he

"Naval Manoeuvres"

Fry's MILK CHOCOLATE

Advertisement for Fry's Milk Chocolate; J. S. Fry & Sons were sole suppliers of chocolate to the Royal Navy.

sold the traditional chocolate drink. In time, the Cadbury family expanded the chocolate side of the business, and in 1853 scored a coup of their own when they obtained the royal privilege as purveyors of chocolate to Queen Victoria. Cadbury's greatest commercial triumph came in 1866. John Cadbury's son George (1839–1922) had traveled to Amsterdam, and returned with a model of Van Houten's machine for his factory; in that year, they presented to the public their own cocoa powder, labeled "Cadbury's Cocoa Essence," and it was an instant hit.[7] The Frys countered with their "Cocoa Extract." Two years later, Richard Cadbury introduced the first "chocolate box," containing chocolate candies and decorated with a painting of his young daughter Jessica holding a kitten in her arms (de Sade would surely have been disgusted by such Victorian sentimentality, but it boosted sales); he is also credited with the invention of the first Valentine's Day candy box[8]—a forerunner of the famous Perugina Baci ("kisses") boxes celebrating romantic love, first introduced in 1922 by the Buitoni family of Italy.

Chocolate confections had now become big business in Great Britain, on the continent, and in America (see below). Many candy manufacturers now began making their own chocolate, and using cocoa powder in liquid form to hand-coat sugar confections. Cocoa powder also reached wide use as a flavoring ingredient in many other sweet foods, such as cakes, ice-creams, and biscuits.

Of course, being Quakers, entrepreneurial families like the Frys, Cadburys, and Rowntree (another dynasty of chocolate-makers) had a social conscience in the midst of all this money-making, unlike many other Victorian captains of industry. In the Birmingham suburb of Bournville, where they had established their factory, the Cadburys created a model town with adequate housing for their workers, and even a dining room and reading room. Beer and stronger liquor were out: the Cadburys despised alcohol—and pubs are still notoriously absent in Bournville. Industrial paternalism still reigns in the Cadbury realm—employees who are about to be married still receive a Bible and a single carnation from the company.[9] Joseph Rowntree built a similar model factory town in a suburb of York. On the other hand, Fry & Sons chose to remain in the center of Bristol. The Fry family was deeply distressed by the wretched working conditions, approaching slavery, which then prevailed on the plantations of Portuguese West Africa, and they boycotted cacao from those parts until the situation improved.

The Fight for Pure Chocolate

One reads with horror the accounts of food adulteration which prevailed through much of the Victorian era—even of the bread which was the staple food of the urban poor, and of the tea which was their drink. Such abuses were equally prevalent on the continent and in North America, until the passage of pure food and drug laws made most of these practices illegal.

The rising demand for chocolate made it a target for unscrupulous producers and merchants in many countries. In France, for example after the restoration of the monarchy in 1815, chocolate was being adulterated with powdered dried peas, flour made from rice or lentils, and potato starch (a favorite with such cheaters). In a French treatise published in translation in Philadelphia in 1846, the author indignantly describes such starch-grain adulteration in chocolate, and methods of detecting it (using iodine is one), but then goes on to counsel the use of an even worse additive: Medical quackery was far from dead!

> The ferruginous chocolate, so beneficial to women who are out of order, or have the green sickness, is prepared by adding to the paste of chocolate iron in the state of filings, oxide or carbonate. The simplest method, and one pretty much in use, for having ferruginous chocolate in families, consists in dissolving good chocolate used in health in iron water, instead of making it in common water.[10]

In 1875, another French writer warns against two kinds of adulteration then prevalent in his country.[11] With the first, the expensive cacao butter is completely extracted (and sold elsewhere), then replaced with olive oil, sweet almond oil, egg yolks, or suet of veal or mutton; the resulting product goes rancid very quickly. With the second, foreign materials are added; the ubiquitous potato starch, wheat or barley flour, pulverized cacao shells, gum, dextrin, or even ground brick.

Across the Atlantic, "A Boston Lady" brought out her excellent *The Dessert Book* in 1872. The section on cacao and its history is very well informed, but her knowledge of chocolate is mainly restricted to its use as a drink—she gives very few confectionery recipes—and she has no mention of "Dutched" chocolate. But her section on "What Chocolate Should be" is worth repeating here:

> Many persons think that good chocolate thickens when prepared. This is a mistake; for this thickening only indicates the presence of farina. If, in breaking chocolate, it is gravelly; if it melt in the mouth without leaving a cool, refreshing taste; if it becomes thick and pasty on the addition of hot water, and forms a gelatinous mass on cooling—it is adulterated with starch and similar substances.[12]

Starch can also be detected by dissolving the chocolate in boiling water and, when cooled, adding a few drops of iodine solution—if starch is present, the mixture will turn blue. Other adulterants which she mentions are "earthy or other solid substances," red or yellow ocher, red lead, and vermilion (the latter two being outright poisons). If the chocolate has a cheesy taste, the cacao butter has been removed and animal fat added. Lastly, she admonishes, chocolate should be fresh—no more than three to four months old.

Governments finally moved to do something about this. In 1850, the British medical journal *The Lancet* announced the creation of a health commission for the analysis of foods.[13] Suspicions about chocolate proved to be well-founded: 39 out of 70 samples had been colored with red ocher from ground bricks. Most of the samples contained starch grains from potatoes, or from two tropical plants, *Canna giganta* and arrowroot. The examination of chocolate seized in France showed identical results. The investigation inspired the British Food and Drug Act of 1860, and the Adulteration of Food Act of 1872.

The scandal touched Cadbury's, and even George Cadbury admitted having adulterated their product with starch and flour. They then went on to the advertising offensive, claiming that their product was now the *only* pure one; Fry, put on the defensive, began to lose ground. And, in fact, it was Cadbury's which suggested that chocolate manufacturers state the exact percentage of the ingredients on the wrappings.[14] "Absolutely Pure, Therefore Best" became their fighting slogan. By the time of Victoria's Diamond Jubilee in 1897, they had surpassed Fry & Sons in total sales, and the latter never recovered.

So, even though tea had become the national drink, Britons had also become great consumers of cocoa, a thin, tame product (70 percent of it is sugar) compared to the thick, bitter stuff Pepys had once sipped. So thin, in fact, that in 1914 G.K. Chesterton had these jaundiced words to say about the immensely popular cocoa drink:

> Tea, although an Oriental,
> Is a gentleman at least:
> Cocoa is a cad and coward,
> Cocoa is a vulgar beast,
> Cocoa is a dull, disloyal,
> Lying, crawling cad and clown,
> And may very well be grateful
> To the fool that takes him down.[15]

Switzerland: Land of Cows and Chocolate

For most of us, the words "Swiss" and "chocolate" are inseparable. Since the end of the last century, Switzerland has dominated the world of chocolate, and today its citizens are the number one consumers of the substance (in 1990–91 the annual per capita intake was an astonishing 5.09 kg, or 11 lb, compared with the puny 2.24 kg, or 5 lb, eaten by the individual American).[16]

Switzerland is a picture-postcard country of lovely alpine meadows dotted with contented cows, and it is those picturesque bovines that are the secret of the amazing success of the Swiss—relative latecomers to the business—in the manufacture and marketing of chocolate.

The story of Swiss chocolate begins with François Louis Cailler (1796–1852), who learned the art of chocolate-making with the Caffarel firm of Turin, in Italy. In 1819, Cailler opened the first Swiss chocolate factory, in Corsier, near Vevey on Lake Geneva, using machinery of his own invention.[17] Next is Philippe Suchard (1797–1874). At age 12, Suchard was sent to an apothecary in Neuchâtel to collect a pound of chocolate for his sick mother; the realization that it cost six francs, the equivalent of three days' wages for a workman, stimulated him eventually to try his hand at producing it. By 1826, Suchard (still a major name in the industry) began making chocolate, again with machinery that he had invented, which included the world's first *mélangeur* or mixing machine.

For the next revolution which took place in the history of chocolate, let us return to those peacefully grazing cows. As far as we know, the first person to combine milk with chocolate was the Englishman Nicholas Sanders;[18] in 1727, he produced a drink with these ingredients for Sir Hans Sloane, then first surgeon to George II, but better known as the founder of the British Museum and for the London street and square named after him. This was not really "milk chocolate" as we know it, but a drink made of chocolate liquor and hot milk.

Milk chocolate, advertised here in the 1930s, was a Swiss invention of 1879. Swiss chocolate manufacture began with F.L. Cailler in 1819.

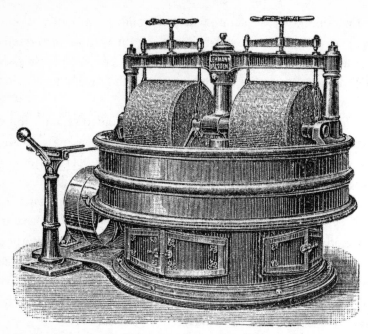

A turn-of-the-century mélangeur *manufactured by Lehmann of Dresden. In this machine, heated by steam or water, granite runners revolve on a stone bed to mix the cacao paste, dry sugar, and flavoring matters into semi-liquid crude chocolate.*

The invention of true milk chocolate was a collaboration between two men. The first was Henri Nestlé (1814–90), a Swiss chemist who in 1867 discovered a process to make powdered milk by evaporation; when mixed with water, this could be fed to infants and small children. A very lucrative discovery this proved to be, since his firm has grown into what is currently the world's largest food corporation. The second man was Daniel Peter (1836–1919), a Swiss chocolate manufacturer of Alsatian origin; he came up with the brilliant idea of using Nestlé's powder in the fabrication of a new kind of chocolate, and, in 1879, the first milk chocolate bar was produced. The basic part of their process was simple: they dried out the moisture in the mix and replaced it with cacao butter, so that it could be poured into a mold.

1879 was a star year for the Swiss, for during it, Rudolphe Lindt (1855–1909) invented "conching," which vastly improved the quality of chocolate confectionery. The name of Lindt's machine, *conche*, is supposedly derived from the Latin word for its shell-like shape.[19] The traditional conche is formed by a flat, granite bed with curved ends, upon which heavy granite rollers attached to robust steel arms move backwards and forwards; the rollers slap against the curved ends, causing the chocolate liquor to splash back over the rollers into the main body of the mechanism. Since the action of the process causes friction and therefore heat to build up in the chocolate dough or paste, the preliminary roasting of the cacao beans may sometimes be omitted. After 72 or more hours of such rock-and-roll treatment, the chocolate mass reaches the desired flavor, as well as attaining a high degree of smoothness, due to a reduction in the size of particles. Before Lindt, eating chocolate was usually coarse and gritty; now it had achieved such a degree of suavity and mellowness that Lindt was justified in calling it "fondant," after the smooth sugar creams of that name. The public on both sides of the Atlantic developed a taste for fondant chocolate, and the use of the conche for solid chocolate became universal in the business.

These inventions put the Swiss at the technological—and financial—peak of the chocolate confectionery business. But there were other refinements as well. For example, in 1899 Jean Tobler began marketing his famous "Toblerone," a still-popular candy bar, triangular in cross-section, in a chocolate shell filled with almond-and-honey nougat; his company merged with Suchard in 1970. Eventually, it was found that the cacao butter in the chocolate liquid which was used in coating higher-quality confections could crystallize out and cause their surfaces to become blotchy and granular, with a poor color. The invention of *tempering* solved this: in it, the temperature of the mass is raised, then carefully lowered so that the crystal structure of the fat may be destroyed. Tempering remains a vital step in the manufacture of the finest quality chocolate, which is high in cacao butter (as we shall see at the end of this chapter).

Milton S. Hershey (1857–1945) was the 'Henry Ford' of the American chocolate industry. His model factory town of Hershey, Pennsylvania, was on a scale undreamt-of by George Cadbury.

Milton Hershey and the "Good Old Hershey bar"

It is a long way from the cantons of Switzerland to the rolling hills of southeastern Pennsylvania. But in that traditionally "Pennsylvania Dutch" country there rose a chocolate operation that would be a formidable rival to its European competitors, whether Swiss Calvinists or English Quakers. Here, among these wooded hills, lies the town of Hershey (population c.12,000), the main thoroughfares of which are called Chocolate and Cocoa, and with sidestreets named from the ports from which Hershey's cacao beans came: Caracas, Granada, Aruba, Trinidad, Java, Para, and Ceylon.

Milton Snavely Hershey (1857–1945) has been aptly characterized as "the Henry Ford of Chocolate Makers"; a compatriot and almost exact contemporary of that pioneer automobile magnate, he brought the same inspired version of mass production to the venerable chocolate industry as Ford had done to his business—with the difference that Hershey had a social conscience, and Ford did not.[20] Born into a family of pious Pennsylvania Mennonites, Hershey was apprenticed at age 15 in a Lancaster confectionery store. With his Aunt Mattie's help, by the time he was 19, he had established his own candy business in Philadelphia, which he eventually moved back to Lancaster, producing mainly caramel confections. For Hershey, the light on the road to Damascus came in 1893, when he visited the World's Columbian Exposition in Chicago, and saw in operation chocolate machinery which had been brought to this great fair by Lehmann and Company of Dresden (the same

Street signs of the town of Hershey, Pennsylvania.

Hershey kisses being manufactured, 1937.

firm that had helped Van Houten perfect his defatting press many decades earlier). When the exhibition closed, Hershey bought this machinery, and began turning out chocolate coatings for his caramels. But after a trip to the chocolate centers of Europe, he sold the caramel business for one million dollars (a huge sum in those days), bought a farm in Derry Township, Pennsylvania, and built his chocolate factory on it.

This became the nucleus of "Hershey, the Chocolate Town," a model development on a scale beyond the wildest dreams of Cadbury and Rowntree. The town of Hershey was dominated by Milton Hershey's imposing private mansion, a gigantic version of George Washington's porticoed Mount Vernon. From there the great man would sally forth each day to survey the vast domain which he had built: the milk chocolate and cocoa factory (described in pious company literature as the "heart-beat" of the community), the industrial school for orphan boys (the Hersheys were childless), the Hershey Department Store, the Hershey Bank, men's and women's clubs, five churches, the free library, the Volunteer Fire Department, two schools, Hershey Park with its fine gardens, zoo, and rollercoaster, the Hershey Hotel, and a golf course which once had Ben Hogan as its pro. It would appear that Hershey's several thousand employees had everything one would want in life, yet this triumph of paternalistic capitalism was a town in name only: it had no mayor nor any form of elected municipal government—it existed only at the whim of its benevolent dictator, Milton S. Hershey.

Hershey's mass-produced milk chocolate demanded vast amounts of milk and sugar. The first was supplied from 8000 acres of dairy farms in the surrounding countryside, all, of course, Hershey-owned. According to a 1926 company pamphlet,[21] every morning 60,000 gallons of "fresh, creamy milk from grass-fed Holsteins" were delivered to the factory, where they were pumped into condensers before combining with powdered sugar.

This was not the only Hershey on the map. The inspiration for Hershey, Cuba, the chocolate magnate's sugar-mill operation and tropical-style model town, came during a trip that he made in 1915 to the beautiful and fertile north coast of that island nation. The complex was built at Santa Cruz del Norte, some 100 km (60 miles) due east of Havana. Hershey's Cuban operation might not have had all the amenities available to his Pennsylvania employees, but it did boast a baseball diamond (baseball is the Cuban national sport) and a race track. To transport the refined sugar so that it could be shipped by sea to his chocolate and cocoa factory, Hershey built modern electric railroads, one to the port of Matanzas, the other to Havana; both had passenger service. Along with other American enterprises in Cuba, Hershey's sugar town was ended when Fidel Castro and his bearded revolutionaries toppled the Batista government in 1959. But, incredibly, Hershey's 70-year-old electric railroad still has regular passenger runs between Havana and Santa Cruz, and is lovingly maintained by aging former Hershey employees with replacement parts that they themselves have made and installed.[22]

There is no doubt that Hershey was a marketing genius. Enlisting nutritionists to boost the healthful qualities of his products, which he turned out in hygienically spotless conditions, Hershey and his chocolate bars and cocoa soon commanded the American market. Everything was mechanized, with machines and conveyor belts organized into a true assembly-line operation. Hershey's best-selling bar contained almonds imported from southern Europe, dropped by machines into the waiting molds. And by the late 1920s, some 50,000 pounds (23,000 kg) of Hershey's Cocoa was being produced each day by the factory. But even more popular than these were "Hershey's Kisses," little, bite-sized, flat-bottomed drops of milk chocolate, individually wrapped by machine; these found immediate favor with the public, and by the 1980s no less than 25 million Kisses daily dropped off Hershey's conveyor belts into their waiting boxes. Small wonder that the streetlights of "The Chocolate Town" are the shape of Kisses.

Milton Hershey died peacefully at the age of 85, in his own hospital. His paternalistic empire lives on: as the Hershey Foods Corporation, it now has annual sales of over two billion dollars, and, together with its arch-rival the M&M/Mars Company, controls about 70 percent of the American candy market.[23] So many tourists flock to the wonders of Hershey, Pennsylvania, that the company no longer offers tours of its chocolate factory. Instead, visitors are whisked along on automated carts through "Chocolate World," where they can see how their favorite chocolate bars and Kisses are produced.[24]

Yet the great multinationals are not to be outdone by a mere American in pushing their chocolate products through Disney-like theme parks. Here is a journalistic glimpse of just two tableaux in "Cadbury World," a tourist attraction in the Cadbury model village of Bournville which draws in 400,000 paying visitors a year:

> In a Yucatan jungle clearing, a knife-wielding Indian priest prepares to sacrifice a small brown dog with the misfortune to bear markings resembling a cocoa bean. A small boy peers at the scene while pensively munching a Twirl chocolate bar. His family call to him, their voices raised against the thunderclaps echoing through the forest fronds, and he skips across to see Hernando Cortés entering the court of Montezuma.[25]

How They Make Chocolate

Our readers are by now probably aware that almost all aspects of the processes involved in modern chocolate manufacture were already in place by the turn of the 19th into the 20th century, if not earlier. Essentially, there are three processes, to result in three different products: (1) cocoa powder; (2) dark chocolate; (3) milk chocolate.[26] We have already seen that cocoa powder is manufactured by removing most of the cocoa butter by hydraulic presses, but this may also be done by solvents; the resulting cake is then pulverized, after which sugar is added through a cooking procedure. Alkalization can be applied to the cacao nibs, to the liquor, or to the cake. To make "instant cocoa," especially for a cold cocoa drink, there is a problem: low-fat cocoa powder by itself does not

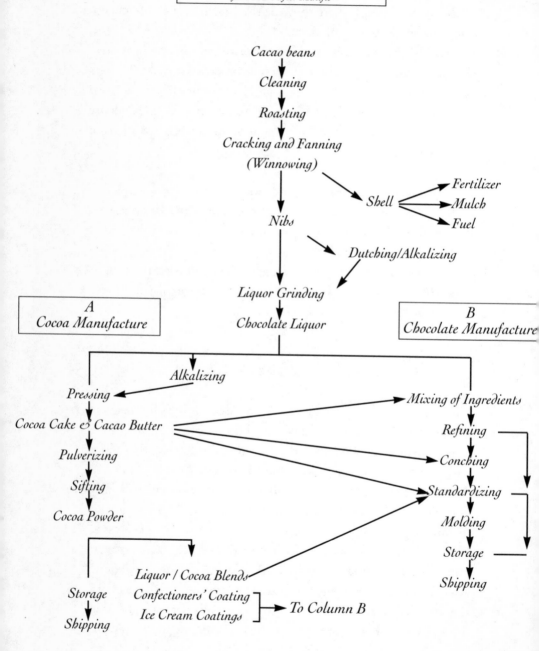

Chocolate Manufacture
~flow chart after Minifie~

Cacao beans

Cleaning

Roasting

Cracking and Fanning
(Winnowing)

Shell → Fertilizer
Shell → Mulch
Shell → Fuel

Nibs

Dutching/Alkalizing

Liquor Grinding

Chocolate Liquor

A
Cocoa Manufacture

B
Chocolate Manufacture

Alkalizing

Pressing

Mixing of Ingredients

Cocoa Cake & Cacao Butter

Refining

Pulverizing

Conching

Sifting

Standardizing

Cocoa Powder

Molding

Storage

Liquor / Cocoa Blends

Shipping

Confectioners' Coating
Ice Cream Coatings → To Column B

Storage

Shipping

mix readily with water or milk. Thus, a wetting agent is called for, and this is usually lecithin, a vegetable fat described as "nature's supreme emulsifier and surface action agent." Lecithin can be obtained from egg yolks, but this is quite expensive, so the usual source is soya beans. To mass producers of chocolate, lecithin is additionally attractive, as it can be used as a cheap substitute for valuable cacao butter, which they would rather sell elsewhere than add to their product.

Cocoa powder is the basis for most confectionery coatings, since "pure" chocolate is high in cacao butter and thus will set too hard and flake off when applied (as children, we remember this happening to chocolate-coated ice cream bars on hot summer days, to our distress). This problem is again solved by lecithin, a vegetable fat which results in less viscous coatings.

To fabricate dark chocolate, the roasted cocoa nibs are ground into liquor, and the sugar pulverized; these two are then brought together in a *mélangeur* or mixer, which is a rotating pan, generally with a granite bed on which granite rollers rotate; heat is applied by steam or hot water, essentially making this an up-to-date version of the old heated *metate* with *mano*. Next, the mixed mass is worked by multiple-roller refiners to ensure smoothness. Conching is the last step, imparting the final flavor to the chocolate mass; in good-quality dark chocolate, this might take from 72 to 96 hours.

For milk chocolate, the basic steps are much the same as for dark chocolate, with the addition of milk from which most of the water has been removed. In Hershey's factory, his Cuban sugar was ground into a snow-white powder, and the milk from his farms was reduced to a creamy paste; these were then put together with chocolate liquor into the *mélangeurs* for mixing. The mass was then conveyed to the refiners, where it was ground between water-cooled steel rollers, then passed to the conches; it finally ended up in the molding department, where it was cast into such items as Kisses and chocolate bars.

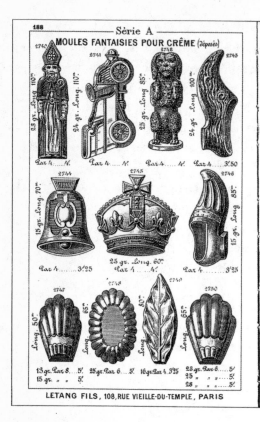

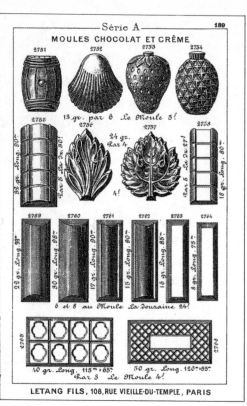

Molds for chocolate creams (above), and for hollow Easter eggs and chocolate hens (below), from a catalogue of equipment for professional chocolate-makers, published in Paris in 1907.

It is in molding, and in the enrobing (mechanical coating) of confectionery centers, that most of the high elaboration of eaten chocolate comes. Hollow molded shells, for example, can be left hollow—as in Easter bunnies and eggs—or filled with fondants, fudge, soft caramels, or even exotic liqueurs; wrapping, packaging, and huckstering all play their roles in the saleability of these items.

Quality vs. Quantity: The Search for Better Chocolate

With the near-disappearance of the connoisseurship that had typified the aristocratic and clerical chocolate-drinkers of a bygone era, mass-produced chocolates seem to have conquered all. But not everyone was content with this state of affairs. In spite of Jack Kerouac's enthusiasm, there was something missing in his "good old Hershey bar." True, there were no longer unscrupulous manufacturers willing to foist brick dust, potato starch, and cacao shells on an unsuspecting public; the law made sure of that. But in the interests of economy and of achieving a chocolate that could be easier to use in "enrobings" and moldings, the mass producers began skimping on, or even cutting out altogether, the substance that gives the quality to superior chocolates: cacao butter. As we have said before, most of them sell this at a very tidy profit to the pharmaceutical industry, where it has many uses. But where cacao butter would have a natural place, such as in milk chocolates, instead of adding it during the conching or earlier steps in the process, large-scale manufacturers prefer to substitute cheap vegetable fats such as lecithin and palm oil. This is the usual practice with "summer" coatings—confectionery coatings used in budget or medium-priced boxed chocolates; such coatings are easier to work with because of their low viscosity, and they do not have to be tempered, but they have an inferior, watered-down flavor.[27]

Until relatively recently, the *chocolatiers* of the European continent, especially in France and Belgium, had been far more concerned with the taste quality of their products than their colleagues in Great Britain or the United States. Most famous of the firms that produce luxury, superior-quality chocolate confections for an elite market is Godiva Chocolatier of Brussels, founded after World War II; their expensive, attractively packaged candies are marketed around the world, even in Saudi Arabia (we have already dealt with the Middle Eastern resistance to chocolate).

Even more prestigious among chocolate connoisseurs is the French firm of Valrhona,[28] founded in 1925, with headquarters at Tain-l'Hérmitage, about one hour south of the great culinary

As this wrapping indicates, premium high-quality chocolate always includes more than 50 percent "cocoa" solids (chocolate liquor), along with a generous amount of cacao butter.

capital of Lyon. With only 150 employees (compared to Hershey's thousands), Valrhona has working for it a full-time jury of ten who do nothing but sit and eat chocolate all day, testing new products. At one time, Valrhona produced chocolate only for professionals, who melted it down, molded it, and packaged the chocolates as their own. In 1986, they decided to do this themselves. Like the 17th and 18th-century *amateurs* of the chocolate drink, these small, up-market manufacturers have realized that the amount of chocolate liquor, and the source and variety of the beans from which it is ground, make a large difference in the product's quality. As reported by journalist Christopher Petkanas,[29] Valrhona's marketing director Alphonse Daudet holds that one can forget about any chocolate that is less than 50 percent "cocoa solids" (read "chocolate liquor")—to him, this is not even chocolate. In the United States, most of the chocolate sold and eaten is less than 43 percent. Why? Because sugar is a lot cheaper than cacao!

During the 1980s, "the brightest jewel in Valrhona's crown" was "Guanaja 1502" (named for the place and year of Columbus's encounter with the canoe-borne Maya traders and their cacao), produced from beans from ten different places (but dominated by the *trinitario* variety); this has 70 percent "cocoa solids," a world record—but only one tenth the calories of the typical, mass-produced chocolate.

Valrhona's latest discovery is Manjari (meaning "bouquet" in Sanskrit).[30] This is made from 100 percent *criollo* beans, from a single plantation in the Indian Ocean, the location of which is a house secret. Manjari is said by chocolate epicures to be a dark, intense, yet not bitter, chocolate, with a slight flavor of raspberries. Only 20 metric tons of Manjari are available worldwide, and are mainly purchased by "exclusive" restaurants for their own desserts and pastries. In spite of *criollo*'s decline to only 2 percent of the world crop of cacao, the *premiers chocolatiers* have definitely returned to the variety which was once held in the highest esteem in the Spanish court.

In pace with the rise of *grand cru* chocolate-making in Europe (and in the United States, as shall be seen), interest groups devoted to chocolate have sprung up, like England's "The Chocolate Society" which is headed by Chantal Coady, owner of Rococo Chocolates in London: the primary task of this particular coterie of connoisseurs is to assess the relative merits of chocolates with over 50 percent "cocoa solids," and the varieties of beans from which they are made. In a 1991 interview,[31] Ms Coady states that her group is *not* for so-called "chocoholics"—these, in her view, are not addicted to chocolate but to sugar, and thus suffer from an eating disorder. According to her, the only necessary ingredients for good chocolate are pure, unadulterated "cocoa solids" (the higher the proportion the better), blended with a little cacao butter and a small amount of sugar. As for commercial "chocolate" (her inverted commas), its principal ingredients are sugar, solid vegetable fat, and powdered milk. "These dietary villains," she holds, "are responsible for chocolate's undeserved reputation as a fattening, tooth-rotting, addictive indulgence."

Aloha to a New Chocolate

We shall end our 3000-year history of chocolate in the Hawaiian Islands, a place neither known nor dreamed of by the ancient Mesoamericans who created this sublime substance. We are talking here of Hawaiian Vintage Chocolate, produced from cacao grown in the "Big Island," the Island of Hawaii—actually, from the very first cacao ever grown commercially in the United States.[32] This chocolate is manufactured by Jim Walsh, a former advertising and travel executive from Chicago. In 1984, acting on an idea that came to him as he was recovering from a near-fatal head injury suffered during a rafting trip in Chile, he decided to move to Hawaii with his family and begin raising cacao, something that had never been tried in the islands. Walsh spent the next two years traveling around the world's tropics, learning how cacao was grown, and gathering 130 samples to determine which strain would do best. He settled on *criollo*, and in December 1986 planted his first 18,000 trees. Today, Walsh has several plantations in different parts of the island; chocolate produced from beans harvested in Kona (in the dry western part of the island) has a fruity taste quality, while beans from Keaau (near Hilo, on the rain-soaked east side of the island) tend to have an earthy flavor. While the six-day fermenting period and the drying are carried out on the island, the beans are then sent to a plant in northern California for the roasting, grinding, mixing, conching, and tempering parts of the process.

In Walsh's view, the advantage of Hawaii is that these islands have high populations of midges (which, as we have seen in Chapter One, are cacao's main pollinators). "There are five kinds of midges and we have them all," he says. Where one can count at the most five mature pods on a tree in other places, in Hawaii they get 25; and in Hawaii, 1350 trees can be planted per acre, compared with only 200 to 600 elsewhere. The yields are thus fantastic. But this is not unthinking mass production—Walsh carefully regulates the amount of water each tree gets, to create just enough stress, resulting in the right concentration of flavor.

The final product consists of round, flat "pistoles," each the size of an American quarter, sold to the pastry chefs of the finest restaurants of the United States. To ensure that he was creating chocolate of the highest quality, Walsh engaged the services of Philippe Padovani, then executive chef of the Ritz-Carlton Mauna Lani on Hawaii; Padovani tested all the best chocolates from around the world, and developed an extremely smooth chocolate that had a high concentration of cacao butter and chocolate liquor. So good it proved to be that by 1994 Hawaiian Vintage Chocolate was selling at a price that was nearly two dollars per pound higher than Valrhona.

And all this was achieved at a time when the mass producers (and producers for the masses) were boasting of such successes with their products as:

- a method for stamping chocolates with hologram pictures
- the invention of a chocolate which could withstand the 120–140°F (50–60°C) temperatures of Operation Desert Storm
- a "personal weight loss program for chocolate lovers," which included a substance called "Cherry Chocolate Peanut Butter"

Jim Walsh's emphasis on quality and on *real* chocolate would surely please the spirits of such true devotees of fine chocolate as the *Huei Tlatoani* Motecuhzoma, Cosimo III de' Medici, Cardinal Alphonse Richelieu, and Samuel Pepys. Perhaps some day the world of premier chocolate-making will return to the rich, frothy, delicious concoction that gave so much pleasure to their lives.

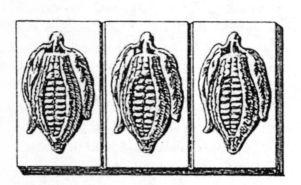

TABLETTES NOIX DE CACAO
Par 3.... Le Moule 5.

ﾞﾞ

Full Circle

Early in 1994 a new chocolate bar appeared on the shelves of supermarkets across the United Kingdom. Named "Maya Gold," it came with the endorsement of the Fairtrade Foundation, an organization established by Oxfam and other groups to ensure that Third World producers (in this case the Kekchi Maya of Belize) were given a better trading deal for their raw products.

Forget that the "gold" in this confection's name was known to the ancient Maya only in the very latest period of their history. Ignore the fact that none of the Mesoamerican art themes printed on its colorful wrapper are Maya at all (they are Teotihuacan and Mixtec). Overlook the astringent after-taste of this chocolate (it has 70 percent "cocoa solids" but no cacao butter). And never mind that its flavors include essence of orange (citrus fruits were unknown in the pre-Conquest New World). What *is* important is that "Maya Gold" is made from cacao beans grown by the Maya— and that these same Maya have a considerable share in the profits.

"Maya Gold" is the brainchild of Josephine Fairley, a long-time supporter of "green" causes. The story of its creation begins in southern Belize during the mid-1980s, when an American corporation persuaded local Kekchi Maya farmers to substitute high-yield, hybrid cacao trees for the semi-wild trees that they had traditionally harvested on their small plots. Even though the introduced disease-susceptible variety required large amounts of costly herbicides and pesticides, many farmers were lured into this enterprise by a promised price of a dollar per pound for the beans when they matured, and they borrowed heavily from the banks to cover their expenditures.

A few years later, just as the new cacao trees were ready for harvesting, the bottom dropped out of the world cacao market. When the American buyers returned, they offered only 27 cents per pound, not enough to cover the cost of harvesting and marketing; the pods were allowed to fall to the ground and rot. After two millennia or more, Maya cacao commerce was a thing of the past.

In stepped Jo Fairley. Her newly founded Green & Black's company had already been marketing chocolate bars made from pesticide-free African cacao. Now she contracted with the local co-operative of Maya cacao-farmers to pay 48 pence (75 cents) a pound—if they would give up the fertilizers and pesticides; so back went the Maya to their three-acre plots. They could now afford to send their children to secondary schools and their sick to distant hospitals. In a Green & Black's brochure, Justino Peck (chairman of the Maya cacao-growers association) writes: "We are grateful for the good luck that we still live on the land that has been carefully farmed by our ancestors for thousands of years.... Maya Gold, with your help, will help us preserve our environment and create a better world for all our children."

This is something altogether new in the world of chocolate. The English, continental European, and American chocolate manufacturers may have been benevolent towards their own factory workers, but they have seldom displayed concern for the welfare of the producers in the tropical countries where cacao is grown, where heavy use of chemicals—regardless of the medical consequences—is usually the norm on cacao plantations. Green & Black's has gambled that an increasingly aware chocolate-loving public will be willing to pay extra for a more "ethically-correct" product.

This brings chocolate full circle, back to the Maya who were largely reponsible for the development of one of the world's culinary delights. It is also fitting that this latest episode in chocolate's history concerns the Kekchi Maya, for it seems to have been they who introduced chocolate to Europe when they presented their foam-topped beverage to Prince Philip of Spain in 1544.

Notes

Chapter 1 The Tree of the Food of the Gods (pp. 16–34)

1. For an accurate and up-to-date account of the biology of cacao and its cultivation, see Young 1994. Another useful introduction to these subjects is Urquhart 1961.
2. Thoroughly described in Young 1994.
3. Admirably clear descriptions of all steps involved in the processing of cacao and the manufacture of chocolate can be found in Cook 1963 and Minifie 1980.
4. Cuatrecasas 1964.
5. In a recent article, Cruz et al. (1995) report research on DNA in modern cacao samples which raises substantial questions about the previously postulated Mesoamerican origin of *criollo*. It appears that the molecular markers of their *criollo* samples, including some from Tabasco, Mexico, are far closer to the wild and domestic (*forastero* and *trinitario*) varieties of South America than they are to possibly wild samples collected in Yucatán. From this, they conclude that *criollo* originated in South America. The yet-unanswered questions are: (1) did *criollo* reach Mesoamerica before or after the Conquest? (2) if *criollo* was *not* in Mesoamerica before the Spaniards, then what variety was cultivated there? Unless actual cacao beans are found in an early archaeological context, which seems unlikely given adverse conditions of preservation, these problems may never be resolved.
6. For headaches resulting from caffeine withdrawal, see Rosenthal 1992.

Chapter 2 The Birth of Cacao (pp. 35–66)

1. A detailed study of nixtamalization is by Katz, Hediger, and Valleroy 1974. See also S. Coe 1994: 14–15.
2. Justeson et al. 1985; Kelley 1986.
3. Personal communication from John Justeson.
4. This English from the *Popol Vuh* is in Tedlock 1985: 163.
5. Fuentes y Guzmán 1932–33 (2): 330.
6. See M. Coe 1992: 145–66 for an account of these discoveries.
7. Discussed in Thompson 1956.
8. For the study of Classic Maya ceramic

texts and their decipherment, see M. Coe 1973 and Reents-Budet 1994, as well as the many articles and books cited by the latter. This is currently one of the most active areas of Maya epigraphy and iconography.
9. MacLeod n.d.
10. Stuart 1988.
11. Stephen Houston, personal communication.
12. ibid.
13. The Balberta find is described in Bove 1991: 135–39. If these clay effigies accurately represent the original beans, then *criollo*—or something like it—was being grown on the Pacific coastal plain long before the Conquest. Unfortunately, none of the *criollo* samples analyzed for DNA markers by Cruz et al. (1995) came from this area, or from Soconusco further to the northwest (Richard Whitkus, personal communication).
14. Nicholas Hellmuth, personal communication.
15. See Thompson 1970 for a thorough discussion of the Putún Maya.
16. No satisfactory monographs have yet appeared on Cacaxtla, nor are there adequate reproductions of all the murals. In various reports, the Mexican archaeologists in charge of the project have chosen to ignore the obvious connections with the Maya lowlands.
17. Quoted in Scholes and Roys 1938: 118. Our translation.
18. Gómez-Pompa et al. 1990.
19. Cárdenas Valencia 1937: 124.
20. Quoted in Tozzer 1941: 95, note 417.
21. Tozzer 1941: 90.
22. ibid.
23. Tozzer 1941: 92.
24. Tozzer 1941: 164.
25. Dennis Tedlock, personal communication.
26. Thompson 1938: 602.
27. Vocabularies from this and all other Colonial Yucatec dictionaries can be found in Barrera Vásquez 1980.
28. Baer and Merrifield 1971: 209–10.
29. Popenoe 1919.
30. Fuentes y Guzmán 1932–33 (2): 97. Our translation.

Chapter 3 The Aztecs (pp. 67–103)

1. Sahagún 1950–59.
2. Durán 1964, 1967, 1971.
3. Townsend 1992 is a succinct, up-to-date account of Aztec history and culture. For a general article on the Aztec use of cacao, see Paradis 1979.
4. For the gods of Mexico, see Miller and Taube 1992.
5. León-Portilla 1963.
6. Sahagún 1950–59 (9).
7. Sahagún 1950–59 (6): 71.
8. Torquemada 1943 (1): 117.
9. Durán 1964: 134–38.
10. Durán 1964: 136.
11. Durán 1964: 137.
12. Durán 1964: 138.
13. Hernández 1959.
14. The fullest study of the *pochteca* is in Zantwijk 1985.
15. Cited in Cooper-Clark 1938: 58.
16. How many cups or drinking-bowls (*xicaltin*) of chocolate drink might this have represented? Figures of this sort are extremely hard to come by. A Spanish recipe given by Colmenero de Ledesma (1644) calls for 100 cacao beans, along with water and flavorings, to produce one pot of chocolate—perhaps equivalent to two Aztec *xicaltin*. If so, then the daily consumption of the Texcocan establishment may have been about 640 cups.
17. Torquemada 1969 (1): 167.
18. Cervantes de Salazar 1936 (2): 107.
19. Durand-Forest 1967.
20. This story is recounted in Cervantes de Salazar 1936 (2): 107–8.
21. ibid. Our translation.
22. Anonymous Conqueror 1556: 306a. Our translation.
23. Sahagún 1950–59 (10): 93.
24. Steck 1951: 275.
25. Clavigero 1780: 219–20.
26. Further details on this subject can be found in S.Coe 1992.
27. Sahagún 1950–59 (8): 37–40.
28. Sahagún 1950–59 (8): 40.
29. Hernández 1959 (2): 246, 305. The folkloristic notion that chocolate has aphrodisiac properties has been revived in every generation. In our own time, this has centered on one of chocolate's many

chemical compounds, phenylethylamine, a mood-altering chemical said to be released into the brain when one is in love; although it has never been proved to stimulate sexual desire and performance, let us hope that this will be the case, and thus lower the demand for rhinoceros horn and the like!
30. M.Martínez 1959.
31. Popenoe 1919: 405.
32. Sahagún 1950–59 (11): 201.
33. Ximénez 1886:45–46; Sahagún 1950–59 (11): 202.
34. Díaz del Castillo 1982: 185. SDC translation.
35. Las Casas 1909: 552. Our translation.
36. Sahagún 1950–59 (9): 35.
37. Durán 1967: 358.
38. Quoted in Thompson 1956: 95.
39. Anderson et al. 1976: 213.
40. Sahagún 1950–59 (10): 65.
41. Sahagún 1950–59 (6): 256.
42. Durán 1971: 132.
43. Torquemada 1969: 177.
44. León-Portilla 1992: 92.

Chapter 4 Encounter and Transformation (pp. 104–24)
1. Colón 1867, 1959; Morison 1963: 327.
2. For the dimensions of Venetian galleys, see Rubin de Cervin 1985: 39–40.
3. Cited in Tozzer 1941: 7.
4. Morison 1963: 327. We have slightly emended his translation of this famous passage.
5. Benzoni 1962: 103–4. SDC translation.
6. Fernández de Oviedo 1959 (1): 272.
7. Díaz del Castillo 1982: 607–11.
8. Acosta 1590: 251. Our translation.
9. In the discussion which follows below, we have greatly benefited by León-Portilla 1981: 230–35.
10. Hernández 1959 (2): 305.
11. Dávila Garibí 1939.
12. León-Portilla 1981: 235.
13. Ortiz de Montellano 1990.
14. Ortiz de Montellano 1990: 31.
15. Cárdenas 1913.

Chapter 5 Chocolate Conquers Europe (pp. 125–78)
1. Sewall 1973: 380.
2. Piso 1658: 197–202.
3. López de Gomara 1964: 390; J.L.Martínez 1990: 492.
4. Estrada Monroy 1979: 195.
5. Veryard 1701: 273.

6. Colmenero de Ledesma 1644: 21.
7. Marradón's dialogue was reprinted in Dufour 1693: 383–87.
8. Mota 1992: 175–76.
9. Sánchez Rivero n.d.:1890–90.
10. Olmo 1680.
11. Villars 1868: 132. Our translation.
12. Aulnoy 1926: 347. Our translation.
13. Aulnoy 1926: 344. Our translation.
14. Aulnoy 1926: 469.
15. See Casati and Ortona 1990 for some of these theories.
16. Redi 1742 (3): 52–54.
17. Zacchia 1644: 326. Our translation.
18. Hibbert 1980: 289.
19. Villari 1911: 39.
20. Acton 1932: 119.
21. Acton 1932: 151.
22. Hibbert 1980: 296–97.
23. Villari 1911: 39.
24. There are several early editions of this work. The one which we have consulted is Redi 1742(3).
25. Hunt 1825: 11.
26. Croce 1931: 237. Our translation.
27. Hunt 1825: 122–23. Leigh Hunt translation.
28. See Chase 1992: 59 for a discussion of these exotic substances, and their culinary use in past times.
29. Redi 1811: 315.
30. Given in Redi 1811: 345–46, note 1.
31. Malaspina 1741.
32. Malaspina 1741: 21–22. Our translation.
33. Quoted in Bourgaux (1) 935: 107.
34. Cárdenas 1913: 108–13.
35. Suárez de Peralta 1878:344, note 34.
36. Solorzano y Pereyra 1972.
37. León Pinelo 1636. According to Nikita Harwich (1992: 95), León Pinelo was a Peruvian Creole who had moved to Spain.
38. Hurtado 1645.
39. Brancatius 1664.
40. Gudenfridi 1680: 73–74. Our translation.
41. These are reviewed by Bourgaux (1935).
42. Argonne 1713: 8–9. Our translation.
43. Franklin 1893: 162–63. Our translation.
44. ibid. Our translation.
45. Le Grand d'Aussy 1815: 120.
46. Sévigné 1860: 165. Our translation.
47. Sévigné 1860: 228–29. Our translation.
48. Sévigné 1860: 383. Our translation
49. ibid. Our translation.
50. Le Grand d'Aussy 1815: 123.
51. Visconti 1992: 50.
52. Franklin 1893: 171.
53. Deitz 1989.

54. The entire tale of the Siamese embassy and their gifts is told in Smithies 1986: 71–80 and Franklin 1893: 170.
55. See Deitz 1989.
56. Published as a 'Supplement' to Dufour 1693.
57. Blegny 1687: 232.
58. Pan American Union 1937. This episode is also related by Thomas Gage (see Thompson 1958: 158).
59. Acosta 1590: 251.
60. Gerard 1633: 1551.
61. Huxley 1956.
62. Gualtieri 1586: 10.
63. Mangetus 1687: 392–94, 491.
64. Pepys 1970–83 (1): 253.
65. Hewett 1873: 8–9.
66. Pepys 1970–83 (1): 178.
67. Pepys 1970–83 (4): 5.
68. Pepys 1970–83 (5): 64.
69. Pepys 1970–83 (5): 139. "Slabbering my band" means that he has dribbled on his neck-band.
70. Pepys 1970–83 (5): 329.
71. Magalotti 1972: 135. Our translation.
72. Dunn 1979: 192–95.
73. Huxley 1956: 78.
74. Hughes 1672.
75. Dufour 1685: 107. The French version of Dufour's treatise appeared in Paris in 1693.
76. ibid: 109.
77. Lister 1967: 170.
78. Stubbes 1682. An earlier version appeared in 1662, under the title *The Indian Nectar*.
79. Stubbes 1682: 18.
80. Gemelli Carreri 1727 (1): 240. An earlier Italian edition, not available to us, was published in Venice in 1719.
81. "Tempering" is the process of heating, then cooling, the chocolate to be used to coat confections, so as to maintain a high content of cacao butter.
82. Anonymous report in *The Economist*, 7 August 1993, p. 7.
83. Gemelli Carreri 1727 (5): 180.

Chapter 6 The Source (pp. 179–202)
1. Squier 1858: 377–78.
2. Arcila Fárias 1950: 41. Our translation.
3. Bonaccorsi 1990.
4. Díaz del Castillo 1916 (5): 329–30.
5. Gasco n.d.
6. Pineda 1925.
7. Carletti 1701: 91.
8. Gage 1648. For a biography of Gage, see
9. Thompson 1958.
10. Alegre 1959: 377.
11. García de la Concepción 1956: 276.

For historical and economic data on the cultivation of Guayaquil cacao, see Stevenson 1825 (2): 227; Guerrero 1980; and Chiriboya 1980.

12. García Pelaez 1971 (2): 37.
13. Information on early Venezuelan cacao production and trade can be found in Córdova Bello n.d.: 719ff and Arcila Fárias 1950: 40ff.
14. Dampier 1906 (2): 93.
15. Córdova Bello n.d.: 719.
16. Details on the Company's operations can be found in Córdova Bello n.d.: 719; Arcila Fárias 1950: 41; and Constant 1988: 34.
17. See Hemming 1987: 43. There are extensive treatments of the Amazonian cacao industry in Alden 1976 and Nunes Dias 1961.
18. Acuña 1986: 57. Our translation.
19. Saint-Simon 1977: 172–74.
20. Hemming 1987: 211.
21. Esquemeling 1684 (pt.4): 99.
22. Simons 1993.
23. Harwich 1992: 60–62.
24. Labat 1979: 259–60. Our translation.
25. Harwich 1992: 60–62.
26. Harwich 1992: 61–62.
27. For the worldwide travels of cacao, see Constant 1988: 48–52.
28. Reyes Vayssade 1992: 140.

Chapter 7 Chocolate in the Age of Reason (pp. 203–34)

1. Schivelbusch 1992.
2. Da Ponte 1985: 107. Translated by Diana Reed. We have changed the translation's "by Jove" to the original's "by Bacchus."
3. Lancisi 1971: xiv.
4. Lémery 1704: 213. This book is an English translation of his *Traité des Aliments*, published in Paris in 1702.
5. Quoted in Rimondini 1992: 21.
6. Duncan 1706.
7. Anonymous 1720: 46.
8. Felici 1728: 8. Our translation.
9. Baretti 1768: 192.
10. Lavedán 1991: 233–34. Our translation.
11. Martínez Llopis n.d.: 355. Our translation.
12. Saint-Simon 1974: 247.
13. Martínez Llopis n.d.: 355.
14. Kany 1932: 151.
15. ibid.
16. Kany 1932: 152.

17. Butterfield et al. 1975: 246.
18. Livoy 1772(1): 106–8.
19. Desdevises du Dezert 1925: 571.
20. Dalrymple 1777: 15.
21. Bergeret de Grancourt 1895: 208. Our translation.
22. Valesio 1979: 311.
23. Lewis 1971: 49.
24. Quoted in Pacheco y de Leyva 1915: 63.
25. Kelley 1986: 300–1.
26. Plebiani 1991.
27. Anonymous 1776: 246.
28. Mota 1992: 377.
29. Recounted in Mota 1992: 196–98.
30. Taibo 1981.
31. Translation by Count Ernesto Vitetti. The Arisi poem is given in Montorfano 1991: 167–68. "The Apici" were a society of gourmets named after Apicius, the cookbook writer of ancient Rome.
32. Morelli 1992: 59.
33. Giovannini 1987: 87–88.
34. Libera 1986.
35. Corrado 1794. Readers interested in the early history of Neapolitan iced sorbets and ice creams should consult David 1994: 141–80; according to her, Corrado was a Benedictine monk, and was born near Lecce in Apulia.
36. Salvini 1992: 55.
37. Buc'hoz 1785.
38. Campan 1823: 297.
39. Woloch 1982: 231, 241.
40. Diderot 1763, Pl.V.
41. Diderot 1778: 785.
42. Diderot 1778: 285.
43. Diderot 1778: 785.
44. Besterman 1968.
45. Woloch 1982: 83–86.
46. Historical data on White's and other early London chocolate-houses and clubs can be found in Weinred and Hibbert 1987: 961; Timbs 1866; Graves 1963; and Anonymous 1993.
47. Steele 1803 (1): 10.
48. Weinred and Hibbert 1987: 961.
49. Anonymous 1993a.
50. Weinreb and Hibbert 1987: 961.
51. Addison and Steele 1711: 210–12.
52. Byrd 1958.
53. Morton 1986: 33–34.
54. Franklin 1893: 181.
55. Townsend 1791: 140–41.
56. We have largely based our biographical

account of the marquis de Sade on Lever 1993.
57. Translation from Lever 1993: 208.
58. Lever 1993: 311.
59. Sade 1980: 147.
60. Lever 1993: 311.

Chapter 8 Chocolate for the Masses (pp. 235–66)

1. Blanchard 1909.
2. Aranzadi 1920: 169–73.
3. Lingua 1989.
4. Mangin 1862.
5. Harwich 1992: 130–31.
6. For these Quaker families and their manufacturing companies, see Harwich 1992: 162ff. For Joseph Fry and his descendants, see Anonymous 1910.
7. Freeman 1989: 90.
8. Fuller 1994: 147.
9. Hirst 1993: 29.
10. Saint-Arroman 1846: 83–87.
11. Riant 1875: 90–91.
12. Anonymous 1872: 113–14.
13. Harwich 1992: 164–67.
14. Crespi 1890.
15. Chesterton 1914: 224.
16. Reyes Vayssade 1992: 136.
17. Casati and Ortona 1990. For historical data on the history of the Swiss chocolate industry, see Rubin 1993: 17–20; Cook 1963: 117–19; Reyes Vayssade 1992: 82–88; and Harwich 1992: 137–38, 172ff.
18. Cook 1963: 117.
19. A good description of the conche and its action is in Minifie 1980: 117–28.
20. Snavely 1957 contains many details of Hershey's life and business career. The author was both employee and relative. See also Young 1984: 681.
21. Anonymous 1926.
22. Medero 1995.
23. Fuller 1994: 33.
24. Young 1984: 681.
25. Hirst 1993: 26.
26. These are described in detail in Cook 1963 and Minifie 1980.
27. Anonymous 1993b.
28. Petkanas 1987: 24–28.
29. ibid.
30. Blythman 1991.
31. ibid.
32. Our account of Hawaiian Vintage Chocolate is based on Fabricant 1994.

Bibliography

Acosta, José de 1590 *Historia natural y moral de las Indias*. Seville.

Acton, Harold 1932 *The Last Medici*. London: Faber and Faber.

Acuña, Cristobal de 1986 "Nuevo descubrimiento del Gran Río del Amazonas en el año 1639." In *Informes de Jesuitas en el Amazonas*, by Francisco de Figueroa et al. Iquitos, Peru: Monumenta Amazonica.

Addison, Joseph, and Richard Steele (eds.) 1711 *The Spectator 54*. London.

Alden, Daniel 1976 The significance of cacao production in the Amazon during the late Colonial period: an essay in comparative economic history. *Proceedings of the American Philosophical Society* 120, 2. Philadelphia.

Alegre, Francisco Javier 1959 *Historia de la Provincia de la Compañia de Jesus de Nueva España* 3, bks.7–8 (1640–75). Rome: Institutum Historicum S.J.

Anderson, Arthur J.O., Francis Berdan, and James Lockhart 1976 *Beyond the Codices: The Nahua View of Colonial Mexico*. Berkeley and Los Angeles: University of California Press.

Anonymous 1720 Review of *Histoire naturelle du cacao et du sucre* by de Caylus, in *Journal des Savants*, January 1720. Paris.

Anonymous 1776 *Letters from Italy*, vol. 2. London: Edward and Charles Dilly.

Anonymous ["A Boston Lady"] 1872 *The Dessert Book*. Boston: J.E. Tilton and Co.

Anonymous 1910 "Fry." *Encyclopedia Britannica*, 11th edn, 11: 270. New York.

Anonymous 1926 *The Story of Chocolate and Cocoa*. Hershey, Penna: Hershey Chocolate Corporation.

Anonymous 1993a "White's Club: toffs' museum." *The Economist*, 10 July 1993: 55.

Anonymous 1993b *The Chocolate Report (The Cookbook Review)*. Cambridge, Mass.

Anonymous Conqueror 1556 *Relatione di Alcune Cose della Nuova Spagna, e della gran città di Temestitan Messico*. Venice: Ramusio Giunti.

Aranzadi, T. de 1920 "La pierre à chocolat en Espagne." *Revue d'Ethnographie et des traditions Populaires* 1: 169–73. Paris.

Arcila Farías, Eduardo 1950 *Comercio entre Venezuela y México en los Siglos XVI y XVII*. Mexico City: El Colegio de México.

Argonne, Bonaventure d' 1713 *Mélanges d'histoire et de littérature*. Paris: Claude Prudhomme.

Aulnoy, Mme D' 1926 *Relation du voyage d'Espagne*. Paris: C. Klincksieck.

Baer, Phillip, and William R. Merrifield 1971 *Two Studies on the Lacandones of Mexico*. Norman: University of Oklahoma Press.

Baretti, Joseph 1768 *An Account of the Manners and Customs of Italy*. London: T. Davies.

Barrera Vásquez, Alfredo 1980 *Diccionario Maya Cordemex*. Mexico City: Ediciones Cordemex.

Benzoni, Girolamo 1962 *Storia del Mondo Nuovo*. Facsimile of 1575 edition. Graz: Akademische Druck- u. Verlagsanstalt.

Bergeret de Grancourt, Pierre-Jacques-Onésyme 1895 *Journal inédit d'un voyage en Italie 1773–1774*. Paris: Société des antiquaires de l'Ouest.

Besterman, Theodore (ed.) 1968 *Voltaire's Household Accounts, 1760–1778*. Geneva: Institut et Musée Voltaire.

Blanchard, R. 1909 "Survivances ethnographiques au Mexique." *Journal de la Société des Américanistes*, n.s., 6. Paris.

Blegny, Nicolas de 1687 *Le Bon Usage du Thé, du Caffé et du Chocolat*. Paris: Estienne Michallet.

Blythman, Joanna 1991 "Older than the Aztecs, as complex as claret." *Independent*, 14 September 1991: 33. London.

Bonaccorsi, Nélida 1990 *El trabajo obligatorio indígena en Chiapas, siglo XVI*. Mexico City: UNAM.

Bourgaux, Albert 1935 *Quatres Siècles d'histoire du cacao et du chocolat*. Brussels: Office International du Cacao et du Chocolat.

Bove, Frederick J. 1991 "The Teotihuacan-Kaminaljuyú-Tikal connection: a view from the South Coast of Guatemala." In *Sixth Palenque Round Table 1986*, ed. Virginia M.Fields, 135–42. Norman: University of Oklahoma Press.

Brancatius [Brancaccio] 1664 *De chocolatis potu diatribe*. Rome.

Buc'hoz, Joseph Pierre 1785 *Dissertation sur le tabac, le café, le cacao et le thé*. Paris.

Butterfield, L.H., M.Friedlander, and M.J.Kline 1975 *The Book of Abigail and John*. Cambridge: Harvard University Press.

Byrd, William 1958 *The London Diary (1717–1721) and Other Writings*. New York: Oxford University Press.

Campan, Mme 1823 *Mémoire sur la vie privée de Marie Antoinette*. London: Henri Colburn and Co.

Cárdenas, Juan de 1913 *Primera parte de los problemas y secretos maravillosos de las Indias*. Mexico City: Museo Nacional de Arqueología, Historia y Etnología.

Cárdenas Valencia, Francisco de 1937 *Relación historial eclesiástica*. Mexico City: Antigua Librería Robredo.

Carletti, Francesco 1701 *Ragionamenti di Francesco Carletti Fiorentino sopra le cose da lui veduta ne' suoi viaggi*. Florence: Giuseppe Manni.

Casati, E., and G.Ortona 1990 *Il Cioccolato*. Bologna: Calderini.

Cervantes de Salazar, Francisco 1936 *Crónica de Nueva España*. 2 vols. Mexico City: Museo Nacional de Arqueología, Historia y Etnografía.

Chase, Holly 1992 "Scents and sensibility." In *Spicing Up the Palate: Studies of Flavourings—Ancient and Modern (Proceedings of the Oxford Symposium on Food and Cookery 1992)* 52–62. London: Prospect Books.

Chesterton, G.K. 1914 *The Flying Inn*. New York: John Lane.

Chiriboya, Manuel 1980 *Jornaleros y gran proprietarios en 135 años de explotación cacaotera (1790–1925)*. Quito: Consejo Provincial de Pichincha.

Clavigero, Francesco Saverio 1780 *Storia Antica del Messico*. 2 vols. Cesena.

Coe, Michael D. 1973 *The Maya Scribe and His World*. New York: Grolier Club.

Coe, Michael D.   1992   *Breaking the Maya Code*. London and New York: Thames and Hudson.

Coe, Sophie D.   1992   "Chocolate: not the flavor but the flavored." In *Spicing Up the Palate: Studies of Flavourings—Ancient and Modern (Proceedings of the Oxford Symposium on Food and Cookery 1992)* 63–66. London: Prospect Books.

—— 1994   *America's First Cuisines*. Austin: University of Texas Press.

Colmenero de Ledesma, Antonio 1644   *Chocolata Inda Opusculum*. Nuremberg: Wolfgang Enderi.

Colón, Ferdinando [Fernando]   1867   *Vita di Cristoforo Colombo*. London: Dulan and Co.

—— 1959   *The Life of Admiral Christopher Columbus by His Son Ferdinand*. New Brunswick: Rutgers University Press.

Constant, Christian   1988   *Le Goût de la vie: le chocolat*. Paris: Nathan.

Cook, L. Russell   1963   *Chocolate Production and Use*. New York: Magazines for Industry, Inc.

Cooper-Clark, James 1938   *Codex Mendoza*. 3 vols. London: Waterlow and Sons Ltd.

Córdova Bello, Eleazar   n.d.   *Historia de Venezuela: Época Colonial*, primera parte. Caracas: Ediciones Edima.

Corrado, F. Vincenzo   1794   *La Manovra della Cioccolata e del Caffè*. 2nd edn. Naples: Nicola Russo.

Crespi, Alfred J. H.   1890   "Cocoa and chocolate." *The Gentleman's Magazine*, October 1890: 371–80.

Croce, Benedetto 1931   *Nuovi Saggi sulla letteratura italiana del Seicento*. Bari.

Cruz, Marlene de la, Richard Whitkus, Arturo Gómez-Pompa, and Luis Mota-Bravo   1995   "Origins of cacao cultivation." *Nature* 375 (6532): 542–43.

Cuatrecasas, José   1964   "Cacao and its allies. A taxonomic revision of the genus *Theobroma*." *Contributions from the United States National Herbarium* 35, part 6. Washington, D.C.

Dalrymple, William   1777   *Travels through Spain and Portugal in 1774*. London: J. Almon.

Dampier, William   1906   *Dampier's Voyages*, ed. John Masefield. London: E. Grant Richards.

Da Ponte, Lorenzo   1985   *Così fan tutte*. Libretto with CD album, translated by Diana Reed, 107. London: Decca (Éditions l'Oiseau-Lyre).

David, Elizabeth   1994   *Harvest of the Cold Months: The Social History of Ice and Ices*. London: Michael Joseph.

Dávila Garibí, Ignacio   1939   *Nuevo y más amplio estudio etimológico del vocablo chocolate y de otros que con él se relacionan*. Mexico City: Emilio Pardo y Hijos.

Deitz, Paula   1989   "Chocolate pots brewed ingenuity." *New York Times*, 19 February 1989: 38.

Desdevises du Dezert, G.   1925   "La société espagnole au XVIIIᵉ Siècle." *Revue Hispanique* 64. Paris.

Díaz del Castillo, Bernal   1916   *The True History of the Conquest of New Spain*, trans. and ed. Alfred P. Maudslay. 5 vols. London: Hakluyt Society.

—— 1982   *Historia verdadera de la conquista de la Nueva España*. Madrid: Instituto Gonzalo Fernández de Oviedo.

Diderot, Denis (ed.)   1763   *Recueil de planches, sur les sciences, les arts libéraux, et les arts méchaniques, avec leur explication* 3. Paris.

Diderot, Denis, (ed.)   1778   *Encyclopédie, ou Dictionnaire raisonné des sciences, des arts et des métiers*. Geneva: Jean-Léonard Pellet.

Dufour, Philippe Sylvestre   1685   *The Manner of Making Coffee, Tea, and Chocolate As It Is Used by Most Parts of Europe, Asia, Africa and America, With Their Virtues*. London: William Crook.

—— 1693   *Traitez nouveaux et curieux du café, du thé et du chocolat*, The Hague: Adrian Moetjens.

Duncan, Daniel   1706   *Wholesome Advice Against the Abuse of Hot Liquors, Particularly of Coffee, Chocolate, Tea, Brandy, and Strong-Waters*. London: M.Rhodes and A.Bell.

Dunn, Richard S.   1979   *The Age of Religious Wars, 1559–1715*. 2nd edn. New York and London: W. W. Norton.

Durán, Fray Diego   1964   *The Aztecs*, translated by Fernando Horcasitas and Doris Heyden. New York: Orion Press.

—— 1967   *Historia de las Indias de Nueva España e Islas de la Tierra Firme*. 2 vols. Mexico City: Porrúa.

—— 1971   *Book of the Gods and Rites and the Ancient Calendar*. Norman: University of Oklahoma Press.

Durand-Forest, Jacqueline de   1967   "El cacao entre los aztecas." *Estudios de Cultura Náhuatl* 7:155–81. Mexico City.

Esquemeling, John   1684   *Bucaniers of America*. London: William Crook.

Estrada Monroy, Agustín   1979   *El mundo k'ekchi' de la Vera-Paz*. Guatemala City: Editorial del Ejército.

Fabricant, Florence   1994   "It's time to say Aloha to a new chocolate." *New York Times*, 11 May 1994, Section C: 1, 6.

Felici, Giovanni Batista   1728   *Parere Intorno all'uso della Cioccolata*. Florence: Giuseppe Manni.

Fernández de Oviedo, Gonzalo   1959   *Historia natural y general de las Indias*. (Biblioteca de Autores Españoles, vols. 117–21). Madrid: Atlas.

Franklin, Alfred   1893   *La Vie privée d'autrefois: le café, le thé et le chocolat*. Paris: Plon.

Freeman, Sarah   1989   *Mutton and Oysters*. London: Victor Gollancz.

Fuentes y Guzmán, Antonio   1932–33   *Recordación Florida*. 2 vols. Guatemala City: Biblioteca "Goathemala."

Fuller, Linda K.   1994   *Chocolate Fads, Folklore, and Fantasies*. New York and London: Harrington Park Press.

Gage, Thomas   1648   *The English-American, His Travail by Land and Sea, or a New Survey of the West Indies*. London.

Garciá de la Concepción, Joseph   1956   *Historia Belemítica*. Guatemala City: Biblioteca "Goathemala."

García Pelaez, Francisco de Paula   1971   *Memorias para la historia del Antiguo Reino de Guatemala*. 2 vols. Guatemala City: Sociedad de Geografia e Historia.

Gasco, Janine   n.d.   "The social and economic history of cacao cultivation." Paper presented at "Chocolate, Food of the Gods" conference, Hofstra University, December 1988.

Gemelli Carreri, Giovanni Francesco   1727   *Voyage du tour du monde*. 8 vols. Paris: Etienne Ganeau.

Gerard, John   1633   *The Herball or Generall Historie of Plantes*. London.

Giovannini, Francesco   1987   *La Tavola degli Anziani: I Pranzi di Palazzo nella Lucca del '700*. Lucca: Maria Pacini Fazzi Editore.

Gómez-Pompa, Arturo, José Salvador Flores, and Mario Aliphat Fernández   1990   "The sacred cacao groves of the Maya." *Latin American Antiquity* 1 (3): 247–57.

Graves, Charles 1963 *Leather Armchairs. The Chivas Regal Book of London Clubs*. London: Cassell and Company Ltd.

Gualteri, Guido 1586 *Relationi della venuta degli ambasciatori giaponesi*. Rome: Francesco Zannetti.

Gudenfridi, Giovanni Batista 1680 *Differenza tra' il cibo e il cioccolate*. Florence: Condotta.

Guerrero, Andrés 1980 *Los oligarcas del cacao*. Quito: El Conejo.

Harwich, Nikita 1992 *Histoire du chocolat*. Paris: Editions Desjonquères.

Hemming, John 1987 *Amazon Frontier*. Cambridge, Mass.: Harvard University Press.

Hernández, Francisco 1959 *Obras completas*. 5 vols. Mexico City: UNAM.

Hewett, Charles 1873 *Cocoa: Its Growth and Culture, Manufacture, and Modes of Preparation for the Table*. London: Spon.

Hibbert, Christopher 1980 *The House of the Medici: Its Rise and Fall*. New York: Morrow Quill Paperbacks.

Hirst, Christopher 1993 "Choc Treatment." *The Independent Magazine*, 10 April 1993: 26–29. London.

Hughes, William 1672 *The American Physician*. London: William Crook.

Hunt, Leigh 1825 *Bacchus in Tuscany: A Dithyrambic Poem form the Italian of Francesco Redi, with Notes Original and Select*. London: John and H. L. Hunt.

Hurtado, Tomás 1645 *Chocolate y tabaco. Ayuno eclesiástico y natural*. Madrid: Francisco García, Impresor del Reyno.

Huxley, Gervas 1956 *Talking of Tea*. Ivyland, Penna: John Wagner and Sons.

Justeson, John S., William M. Norman, Lyle Campbell, and Terrence Kaufman 1985 *The Foreign Impact on Lowland Mayan Language and Script*. New Orleans: Tulane University, Middle American Research Institute (publication 53).

Kany, Charles E. 1932 *Life and Manners in Madrid 1750–1800*. Berkeley: University of California Press.

Katz, S.H., M.L.Hediger, and L.A.Valleroy 1974 "Traditional maize processing techniques in the New World." *Science* 184: 765–73.

Kelley, David H. 1987 "Culture history and linguistics in Mesoamerica." *The Quarterly Review of Archaeology* 7 (3–4): 12–13.

Kelley, J.N.D. 1986 *The Oxford Dictionary of the Popes*. Oxford: Oxford University Press.

Kerouac, Jack 1950 *The Dharma Bums*. London: Andre Deutsch. 1958 New York: The Viking Press.

Labat, Jean-Baptiste 1979 *Voyage aux Îles de l'Amérique*. Paris: Seghers.

Lancisi, Giovanni Maria 1971 *De subitaneis mortibus (On Sudden Deaths)*. New York: St John's University Press.

Las Casas, Fray Bartolomé de 1909 *Apologética historia de las Indias*. Madrid: Nueva Biblioteca de Autores Españoles.

Lavedán, Antonio 1991 *Tratado de los usos, abusos, propriedades y virtudes del tabaco, café, té y chocolate*. Almarabe.

Le Grand d'Aussy, Pierre Jean-Baptiste 1815 *Histoire de la vie privée des Français*. Paris: Laurent-Beaupré.

Lémery, Louis 1704 *A Treatise of Foods*. London: John Taylor.

León Pinelo, Antonio de 1636 *Questión moral si la bebida del chocolate quebranta el ayuno eclesiástico*. Madrid: Viuda de Juan González.

León-Portilla, Miguel 1963 *Aztec Thought and Culture*. Norman: University of Oklahoma Press.

—— 1981 "Otro testimonio de aculturación hispano-indígena." *Revista Española de Antropología Americana* 11: 220–43. Madrid.

—— 1992 *Fifteen Poets of the Aztec World*. Norman and London: University of Oklahoma Press.

Lever, Maurice 1993 *Sade: A Biography*. New York: Farrar, Strauss and Giroux.

Lewis, Wilmarth S. (ed.) 1971 *Horace Walpole's Correspondence with Sir Horace Mann and Sir Horace Mann the Younger*, vol. 9. New Haven: Yale University Press.

Libera, Felici 1986 *L'Arte della Cucina*. Bologna: Arnaldo Forni.

Lingua, Paolo 1989 *La Cucina degli Genovesi*. Padua: Franco Muzzio Editore.

Lister, Martin 1967 *A Journey to Paris in the Year 1698*. Urbana: University of Illinois Press.

Livoy, P. Barnabite De 1772 *Voyage D'Espagne Fait en L'Année 1755*. 2 vols. Paris: Costard.

López de Gomara, Francisco 1964 *Cortés. The Life of the Conqueror by His Secretary*, trans. and ed. by Lesley Bird Simpson. Berkeley and Los Angeles: University of California Press.

MacLeod, Barbara n.d. *Deciphering the Primary Standard Sequence*. Ph.D. thesis, 1990, University of Texas at Austin.

Magalotti, Lorenzo 1972 *Relazioni D'Inghilterra 1668 e 1688*. Florence: Leo S. Olachki Editore.

Malaspina, Marcello 1741 *Saggi di Poesie Diverse*. Florence: Bernardo Paperini.

Mangetus, John 1687 *Pharmacopoeia Schrödero-Hoffmanniana*. Cologne: Philip Andreae.

Mangin, Arthur 1862 *Le Cacao et le Chocolat*. Paris: Guillaumin et Cie.

Martínez, José Luis 1990 *Hernán Cortés*. Mexico City: Fondo de Cultura Económica.

Martínez, Maximino 1959 *Plantas útiles de la flora mexicana*. Mexico City: Ediciones Botas.

Martínez Llopis, Manuel n.d. *Historia de la gastronomía española*. Madrid: Editora Nacional.

Medero, Enrique 1995 "Reliquias eléctricas." *Sol y Son* 1: 35–39. Havana.

Miller, Mary E., and Karl Taube 1992 *The Gods and Symbols of Ancient Mexico and the Maya: An Illustrated Dictionary of Mesoamerican Religion*. London and New York: Thames and Hudson.

Minifie, Bernard, W. 1980 *Chocolate, Cocoa and Confectionary*. Westport, Conn.: AVI Publishing Company.

Molina, Alonso 1571 *Vocabulario en lengua castellana y mexicana*. Mexico City: Antonio de Spinola.

Montorfano, Emilio 1991 *L'uovo di Colombo*. Milan: Terziaria.

Morelli, Roberto 1982 "Antonio Nebbia un singolare cuoco settecentesco." *Appunti di Gastronomia* 8. Milan.

Morison, Samuel E. 1963 *Journals and Other Documents on the Life and Voyages of Christopher Columbus*. New York: Heritage Press.

Morton, Marcia and Frederic 1986 *Chocolate: An Illustrated History*. New York: Crown Publishers.

Mota, Ignacio H. de la 1992 *El libro del chocolate*. Madrid: Ediciones Piramide.

Nunes Dias, Manuel 1961 *O cacau luso-brasileno na economia mundial—subsidios para a sua historia*. Lisbon: Studia.

Olmo, Joseph del 1680 *Relación histórica del Auto General de Fé, que se celebró en Madrid este Año del 1680*. Madrid: Roque Rico de Mirando.

Ortiz de Montellano, Bernard R. 1990 *Aztec Medicine, Health, and Nutrition*. New Brunswick: Rutgers University Press.

Pacheco y de Leyva, Enrique 1915 *El cónclave de 1774 a 1775*. Madrid: Imprenta Clásica Española.

Pan-American Union 1937 "Cocoa." *Commodities of Commerce Series* 18. Washington D.C.

Paradis, Louise I. 1979 "Le cacao précolombien: monnaie d'échange et breuvage des dieux." *Journal d'agriculture traditionelle et de botanique* 26 (3–4): 181–99. Paris.

Pepys, Samuel 1970–83 *The Diary of Samuel Pepys*, ed. Robert Latham and William Matthews. 11 vols. Berkeley: University of California Press. London: Bell and Hyman.

Petkanas, Christopher 1987 "Very serious about chocolate." M, July 1987: 24–28: New York.

Pineda, Juan de 1925 Descripción de la Provincia de Guatemala. *Anales de la Sociedad de Geografía e Historia* 1(4). Guatemala City.

Piso, G. 1658 *De Indiae utriusque re naturali et medica*. Amsterdam: Elzevir.

Plebiani, Tiziana 1991 *Cioccolata: La Bevanda degli Dei Forastieri*. Venice: Centro Internazionale della Grafica di Venezia.

Popenoe, Wilson 1919 Batido and other Guatemalan beverages prepared from cacao. *American Anthropologist* n.s., 21: 403–409.

Redi, Francesco 1742 *Opere di Francesco Redi*. 5 vols. Venice: Eredi Hertz.

—— 1811 *Opere*. Milan: Clasici Italiani.

Reents-Budet, Dorie 1994 *Painting the Maya Universe*. Durham and London: Duke University Press.

Reyes Vayssade, Martin (ed.) 1992 *Cacao: historia, economía e cultura*. Mexico City: Comunicación y Ediciones Tlacuilo.

Riant, A. 1875 *Le Café, le Chocolat, le Thé*. Paris: Librairie Hachette et Cie.

Rimondini, Giovanni 1992 "Cucina per l'impotente." *La Gola*, October 1992, Anno XI, no. 93.

Robert, Hervé 1990 *Les Vertus thérapeutiques du chocolat*. Paris: Editions Artulen.

Rosenthal, Elizabeth 1992 "Headache? You skipped your coffee." *New York Times*, 15 October 1992, section A:18.

Rubin, Cynthia Elyce (ed.) 1993 *Bread and Chocolate: Culinary Traditions of Switzerland*. New York: published by author.

Rubin de Cervin, G.B. 1985 *La flotta di Venezia*. Milan: Automobilia.

Sade, Donatien Alphonse François, marquis de 1980 *Lettres et mélanges littéraires*. Paris: Éditions Broderie.

Sahagún, Fray Bernardino de 1950–59 *General History of the Things of New Spain*. Trans. from the Nahuatl by Arthur J.O. Anderson and Charles E. Dibble. 12 vols. Santa Fe: School of American Research and University of Utah.

Saint-Arroman, A. 1846 *Coffee, Tea and Chocolate: Their Influence upon the Health, the Intellect, and the Moral Nature of Man*. Philadelphia: Townsend Ward.

Saint-Simon, Louis de Rouvray, duc de 1974 *Mémoires 1692–1694*. Paris: Éditions Ramsay.

Saint-Simon, Louis de Rouvray, duc de 1977 *Mémoires 1695–1699*. Vol. 2. Paris: Editions Ramsay.

Salvini, Riccardo 1992 *Feste Romane. Appunti di gastronomia* 9.

Sánchez Rivero, Angel (ed.) n.d. *Viaje de Cosme de Médicis por España y Portugal (1668–1669)*. Madrid: Sucesores de Rivadeneyra.

Schivelbusch, Wolfgang 1992 *Tastes of Paradise*. New York: Pantheon.

Scholes, France V., Rubio Mañé, and Eleanor B.Adams 1938 *Documentos para la Historia de Yucatán, Vol. 2: La Iglesia en Yucatán, 1560–1610*. Mérida: Carnegie Institution of Washington and Diario de Yucatán.

Sévigné, Mme. de 1860 *Lettres*. 2 vols. Paris: Firmin Didot Frères, Fils et Cie.

Sewall, Samuel 1973 *The Diary of Samuel Sewall*. New York: Farrar Straus and Giroux.

Simons, Marline 1993 "Nantes journal. Unhappily, port confronts its past: slave trader." *New York Times*, International edn, 17 December 1993.

Smithies, Michael (ed.) 1986 *The Discourses at Versailles of the First Siamese Ambassadors to France 1686–7*. Bangkok: The Siam Society.

Snavely, Joseph Richard 1957 *An Intimate Story of Milton S. Hershey*. Hershey, Penna: Hershey Chocolate Corporation.

Solorzano y Pereyra, Juan de 1972 *Política indiana*. Biblioteca de Autores Españoles, 252. Madrid: Atlas.

Squier, Ephraim G. 1858 *The States of Central America*. New York: Harper and Bros.

Steck, Francis Borgia 1951 *Motolinía's History of the Indians of New Spain*. Washington: Academy of American Franciscan History.

Steele, Richard ["Isaac Bickerstaff"] 1803 *The Tatler* 1. Philadelphia, Penna.

Stevenson, William B. 1825 *A Historical and Descriptive Narrative of Tweny Years' Residence in South America*. 2 vols. London: Hurst, Robinson and Co.

Stuart, David 1988 "The Río Azul cacao pot: epigraphic observations on the function of a Maya ceramic vessel." *Antiquity* 62: 153–57.

Stubbes, Henry 1682 *The Natural History of Coffee, Thee, Chocolate, and Tobacco*. London: Christopher Wilkinson.

Suárez de Peralta, Juan 1878 *Noticias históricas de la Nueva España*. Madrid: Manuel G. Hernández.

Taibo, Paco Ignacio I 1981 *Breviario del Mole Poblano*. Mexico City: Editorial Terra Nova.

Tedlock, Dennis (transl. and ed.) 1985 *Popol Vuh*. New York: Simon and Schuster.

Thompson, J. Eric S. 1938 "Sixteenth and seventeenth century reports on the Chol Mayas." *American Anthropologist* n.s., 40: 584–604.

—— 1956 Notes on the use of cacao in Middle America. *Notes on Middle American Archaeology and Ethnology* 128: 95–116. Cambridge, Mass.: Carnegie Institution of Washington.

—— 1958 *Thomas Gage's Travels in the New World*. Norman: University of Oklahoma Press.

—— 1970 *Maya History and Religion*. Norman: University of Oklahoma Press.

Timbs, John 1866 *Club Life in London*. London: Richard Bentley.

Torquemada, Juan de 1943 *Monarquía indiana*. Mexico City: Salvador Chávez Hayhoe.

—— 1969 *Monarquía indiana*. 2 vols. Mexico City: Porrúa.

Townsend, Joseph 1791 *A Journey through Spain in the Years 1786 and 1787*. London: C.Dilly.

Townsend, Richard F. 1992 *The Aztecs*. London and New York: Thames and Hudson.

Tozzer, Alfred M. 1941 Landa's Relación de las Cosas de Yucatán. *Papers of the Peabody Museum of Archaeology and Ethnology, Harvard University*, 18. Cambridge, Mass.

Urquhart, D.H. 1961 *Cocoa*. London: Longmans, Green and Co.

Valesio, Francesco 1979 *Diario di Roma* 6. Milan: Longonesi.

Veryard, E. 1701 *An Account of Divers Choice Remarks Taken in a Journey through the Low-Countries, France, Italy, and Part of Spain*. London: S. Smith and B. Walford.

Villari, Luigi 1911 "Medici." *Encyclopedia Britannica*, 11th edn, 18: 31–41. New York.

Villars, Marie de 186 *Lettres de Madame de Villars à Madame de Coulanges*. Paris: Henri Plon.

Visconti, Primi 1992 *Memorie di un avventuriero alla Corte di Luigi XIV*. Palermo: Sellerio.

Weinreb, Ben, and Christopher Hibbert (eds.) 1987 *The London Encyclopedia*. London: MacMillan.

Woloch, Isser 1982 *Eighteenth-century Europe: Tradition and Progress, 1715–1789*. New York: W. W. Norton and Co.

Ximénez, Francisco 1888 *Cuatro libros de la naturaleza*. Mexico City: Secretaría de Fomento.

Young, Allen M. 1994 *The Chocolate Tree: A Natural History of Cacao*. Washington: Smithsonian Institution Press.

Young, Gordon 1984 "Chocolate, food of the gods." *National Geographic* 166 (5): 664–87. Washington.

Zacchia, Paolo 1644 *De' Mali Hipochondriaci*. Rome: Vitale Mascardi.

Zantwijk, Rudolf A. van 1985 *The Aztec Arrangement*. Norman: University of Oklahoma Press.

Sources of Illustrations

The illustrations are identified by their page numbers in **bold**

10 From Cardinal Brancaccio, *De Chocolatis potu diatribe*, Rome, 1664. **16** From J.B. Labat, *Nouveau Voyage aux Isles de l'Amérique*, Paris, 1722. **18** After a painting by Hoffman, courtesy of the Linnaean Society. **20** From F. Hernández, *Rerum medicarum Novae Hispaniae thesaurus*, Madrid, 1649. **22** Photo Nicholas Hellmuth. **23** Photo Nicholas Hellmuth. **24** Courtesy Société des Produits Nestlé S.A., Vevey, Switzerland. **27** From "Historicus", *Cocoa: All About It*, London, 1896. **37** Michael D. Coe. **41** Drawing by Karl Taube from Mary Miller and Karl Taube, *Gods and Symbols of Ancient Mexico*, London, 1993. **44** From Dresden Codex, Sächsische Landesbibliothek, Dresden. **45 above** From Madrid Codex, Museo de América, Madrid. **45 below** Michael D. Coe. **46** Photo © Justin Kerr. **47 above** Drawing by Diane Griffiths Peck. **47 below** Michael D. Coe. **49** Courtesy George Stuart. Photo by George Molloy. **50** Drawing by Diane Griffiths Peck. **54** From S. Linné. **57** Drawing by Tracy Wellman. **69** After Codex Boturini, from E. Matos Moctezuma, *The Great Temple of the Aztecs*, London, 1988. **74** From Codex Borbonicus, Bibliothèque de l'Assemblée Nationale, Paris. **76** From Sahagún, *Historia de Las Cosas de Nueva España*, Biblioteca Medicea-Laurenziana, Florence. **82** From Codex Mendoza. Bodleian Library, University of Oxford. **85** Drawing by Annick Petersen, after *Primeros Memoriales*, from Richard F. Townsend, *The Aztecs*, London, 1992. **88** From Codex Tudela, Museo de América, Madrid. **95** From Codex Nuttall. Copyright British Museum. **100** From Codex Féjérváry-Mayer. Board of Trustees of the National Museums & Galleries on Merseyside. **104** From C. Colombus, *Regnü Hyspanie*, Basel, 1493. **108–9** From G. Benzoni, *La Historia del Mondo Nuovo*, Venice, 1565. **111** From J. Ogilby, *America*, London, 1671. **116–17** From N. de Blegny, *Le Bon Usage du Thé, du Café, et du Chocolat*, Paris, 1687. **120** From "Historicus", *Cocoa: All About It*, London, 1896. **127** From L. Thurneysser, *Quinta Essentia*, Leipzig, 1574. **129** Staatliche Museen Berlin, © bpk, Berlin. **144** By courtesy of the Board of Trustees of the Victoria & Albert Museum, London.

153 From Antonio de León Pinelo, *Questión moral si la bebida del chocolate quebranta el ayuno eclesiástico*, Madrid, 1636. **156** Engraving by Claude Mellon. Bibliothèque Royal Albert Ier, Brussels. **160** Courtesy S.J. Phillips Ltd., London. **161** By courtesy of the Board of Trustees of the Victoria & Albert Museum, London. **164** From "Historicus" *Cocoa: All About It*, London, 1896. **166** From N. de Blegny, *Le Bon Usage du Thé, du Café, et du Chocolat*, Paris, 1687. **167** From S. Dufour, *Traitez nouveaux et curieux du Thé, du Café et du Chocolat*, Lyon, 1685. **171** Copyright British Museum. **188** By permission of the British Library, London. **206** Courtauld Institute of Art, University of London. **213** Artephot, Paris. **222–24** From D. Diderot et J. d'Alembert, *Encyclopédie*, Paris, 1777. **226** Sterling and Francine Clark Art Institute, Williamstown, Massachusetts. **228** The Museum of London. **242** Courtesy Netherlands Cocoa Association, Amsterdam. **244** Courtesy Cadbury Ltd, Bournville. **249** Courtesy Société des Produits Nestlé S.A., Vevey, Switzerland. **250** From P. Zipperer, *Die Schokoladen Fabrikation*, Berlin, 1901. **252–53** Courtesy Hershey Food Corporation, PA. **254** Range/Bettmann/UPI. **260** From the catalogue of Maison Letang père et fils, Paris, 1907. Courtesy Chantal Coady of Rococo Chocolates, London. **262** Courtesy Chantal Coady of Rococo Chocolates, London. **266** From the catalogue of Maison Letang père et fils, Paris, 1907. Courtesy Chantal Coady of Rococo Chocolates, London.

COLOUR PLATES
113 Photo Nicholas Hellmuth. **114 above** Photo Nicholas Hellmuth. **114 below** Photo © Justin Kerr. **131** The Hermitage, Leningrad. Photo: Scala. **132** Museu de Ceràmica, Barcelona. **237** Musée du Louvre, Paris. Photo © RMN. **238** Photo Scala. **239 above right**, Courtesy Cadbury Ltd., Bournville; **239 above left**, courtesy Hershey Food Corporation, PA. **239 below** Courtesy Cadbury Ltd., Bournville. **240** Photo Joël Laiter, courtesy Flammarion, Paris.

Index

Numerals in *italics* refer to the page numbers of text illustrations, numerals in **bold** to the page numbers of colour plates